W9-AGE-365

DANCING WITH FEAR

Overcoming Anxiety in a World of Stress and Uncertainty

Paul Foxman, Ph.D.

Jason Aronson Inc.
Northvale, New Jersey
London

Director of Editorial Production: Robert D. Hack

This book was set in 11 on 13 point Caslon by FASTpages of Nanuet, New York and printed and bound by Book-mart Press of North Bergen, New Jersey.

10 9 8 7 6 5 4 3 2 1

Library of Congress Cataloging-in-Publication Data

Foxman, Paul.
Dancing with fear: overcoming anxiety in a world of stress and uncertainty / Paul Foxman.
p. cm.
Includes bibliographical references and index.
ISBN 1-56821-549-5
1. Anxiety. 2. Fear 3. Stress (Psychology)
4. Stress management. I. Title.
BF575.A6F68 1996
152.4´6—dc20 96-567

Manufactured in the United States of America. Jason Aronson Inc. offers books and cassettes. For information and catalog write to Jason Aronson Inc., 230 Livingston Street, Northvale, New Jersey 07647.

For Sheryl, my wife and soulmate, whose love is the gift I receive for facing my fears. And for my children, Kali and Leah, who brought home to me and me to home.

Contents

Acknowledgments

Many people deserve recognition for their time and support during the creation of this book. Let me begin by thanking those who reviewed chapters of the book-in-progress: Lynn Murray, Jeanne Albertson, R.D., Sue Nyhagen-Adams, R.D., Katie Lessor, Leslie Purple, Ron McConnell, Gail Shaw, Debra Lopez, M.D., and Rabbi James Glazier.

Special thanks to Barry Weiss, for his unwavering support throughout the years and for the inspiring dialogues we had while skiing at Stowe, Vermont. There are not enough lifetimes to write the many books we have already outlined on the way up the mountain.

Many thanks to John Pullen, Ph.D., National Director of CHAANGE, who reviewed most of the chapters while they were still warm from my laser printer, and who encouraged me to share with others the good news about the CHAANGE program for anxiety recovery.

Thanks also to Ann Seagrave, co-founder of the CHAANGE program, who felt at the outset that my work was important to share with others, and who assures me that her enthusiasm for the book has nothing to do with her association with CHAANGE. Ann also encouraged me to include my own recovery story.

I am grateful to Saul Neidorf, M.D., whose trusted ears were the first to hear about my painful childhood and anxiety condition. As therapist, teacher, and mentor par excellence, Saul demonstrated that therapy heals by shared heart, and he had a significant influence on my therapeutic style.

I also wish to thank the many patients who offer living proof that anxiety recovery is attainable. Some of these courageous people, whose names and identities have been changed to protect their confidentiality, appear in the following pages as examples of successful anxiety treatment. I respect my patients, and I rejoice in their growth and freedom from fear.

Thanks to Jason Aronson Inc., for taking a chance on a first book by an unknown writer. May this be the beginning of a long and fruitful collaboration.

I can only begin to express my appreciation to Sheryl Anne Foxman, my soulmate and wife, whose faith in me—and willingness to do the parenting and household chores when I was writing—made this book possible.

And finally, thanks to the One whose patient presence reminds me that every experience has a higher purpose, and that whatever happens, everything will be all right. Thank you for the opportunity to serve through words.

alternatives, most are based on a medication approach to anxiety, and only one other book deals with the CHAANGE program. This anxiety recovery option has already helped over 14,000 people overcome their fears, and the latest results are now available. In addition, the chapter on children's anxiety, which examines how anxiety begins and what can be done to prevent it, fills a void left by other books on anxiety.

I also want to reach the vast number of anxiety sufferers who have not sought help and who are suffering unnecessarily. Seventy-five percent of anxiety sufferers receive no help at all.

There is a growing need and desire for more information about anxiety and effective treatment options. One example is the incredible response to a Panic Disorder Education Program established in 1994 by the National Institute of Mental Health (NIMH). The main goal of the program was to increase the number of people with panic disorder who are properly diagnosed and treated. The NIMH indicates that when properly treated, there is a 70 to 90 percent partial or complete recovery rate for panic disorder sufferers. This U.S. government organization reports that after installing a toll-free telephone number (1-800-64-PANIC), they received *30,000* calls in the first three months of operation! When the telephone number was mentioned on ABC television's "Good Morning America" show (August 20, 1994), 12,000 calls were received, 3,000 of which were placed within five minutes after the broadcast, causing a temporary circuit jam. Another 2,900 calls were generated by a CNN broadcast, "Sonja Live," which featured the personal stories of panic disorder patients in New York and Los Angeles.

about learning how to "go with the flow," relax, enjoy work, have peace of mind, and appreciate the gift of life.

Strange as it may seem, many of my patients have remarked that they are fortunate to have had an anxiety condition because in coming for help, they re-examined their lives and made profound changes. It is not unusual for people to learn that their anxiety was a signal, a message that their lives were out of balance and that change was needed. Anxiety serves a productive purpose in many cases, leading to greater understanding about oneself, new skills for living, less stress, a more positive attitude, and a higher quality of life. Chapter 20, "Spirituality and Anxiety," explores the idea that anxiety recovery and spiritual development overlap to a great extent.

There are many other books about anxiety. Some are self-help manuals, while others offer insight and understanding about the condition. So why add another book on anxiety? Anxiety disorders are the most prevalent emotional conditions, outranking depression and possibly alcohol/drug abuse.[4] However, only 25 percent of the millions of people who suffer from anxiety seek help, and most receive inappropriate or ineffective care. Many people who seek help for anxiety are treated with tranquilizers for up to fifteen years, often with no significant improvement. Other alternatives need to be made available, particularly the idea that anxiety is a learned condition that can be unlearned with proper help, and without drugs. While available books do offer some psychological treatment

---

4. Based on a five-year study conducted by the National Institute of Mental Health. Reported in American Psychological Association *Monitor* (March, 1990).

a condition that is continually being re-created. This book is intended to help change such thinking and behavior.

This book points to several ingredients in the development of severe anxiety: biological sensitivity, a specific personality type, and stress. Severe anxiety develops from the combination of these ingredients, and usually signals an overload of stress in sensitive people. We will discuss this view of anxiety and focus on those factors that can be changed, such as how we think and behave, and how we deal with stress.

A word about the book title, *Dancing With Fear: dancing* is used to capture the ritualized ways in which we often cope with fear and anxiety. For example, we may habitually avoid certain situations or places in which we anticipate feeling anxious. We may develop a passive communication style because we fear rejection or conflict. We may develop compulsive behavior patterns and busywork to distract ourselves from anxiety. Or, we may repeatedly engage in "what-if" thinking in an effort to prepare for what may happen: "What if something bad happens, how will I handle it? What if I have a panic attack while driving to work?" and so on. We want to feel in control and we develop a kind of dance (and waste a lot of energy) to ward off anxiety and fear. We can't sit still when we are anxious. We dance around anxiety when we are afraid of it, and when we do not know how to deal with it.

However, dancing has another, more positive meaning. Dancing is usually associated with freedom of movement, having fun, enjoying music, letting go, and celebrating. This book is about overcoming anxiety and increasing your ability to dance without fear. Living without anxiety is

This book is not a substitute for the CHAANGE or LifeSkills programs, or for professional help. No book on anxiety can replace the healing relationship with a trained therapist, someone who knows the territory of anxiety and how to guide you out of it.

On the other hand, understanding your anxiety condition, knowing you are not alone, and having concrete skills to practice will make a difference. In fact, just having a proper diagnosis of an anxiety disorder is usually a relief for people who are afraid of what is happening when they are anxious. People with severe anxiety see an average of ten doctors before a correct diagnosis is made, a process that can take years. The fear of having a heart attack, of going "crazy," of having a fatal illness or dying, or fear of losing control, all begin to subside when people understand what is happening and why. One purpose in writing this book, therefore, is to offer the information with which people can understand their anxiety and why it developed. Most anxiety sufferers can diagnose themselves if given the proper information because they can identify their physical symptoms and associated fears. This book is intended to help with that process. In addition, the book describes the path out of anxiety and what it is like to live without it.

Anxiety recovery usually requires knowledge and regular practice of the appropriate skills, with help from an experienced guide. In addition, recovery involves changing those aspects of thinking and behaving that continually produce anxiety. Anxiety sufferers typically have nonproductive thought habits and behavior patterns that create and reinforce the anxiety, such as worrying, trying to predict the future, negative thinking, and the need to always be in control. It would not be realistic to seek recovery from

Coordinator for CHAANGE, with responsibility for training therapists in this approach to anxiety recovery.[2] The CHAANGE program is described in Chapter 7, and at other points throughout this book. Anyone interested in the CHAANGE program, including psychotherapists who wish to join the national network, may contact the national headquarters for a free information kit.[3]

This book describes the recovery skills required to overcome anxiety, drawing from the CHAANGE program and other sources. All have been personally tested and used to enhance and maintain my own recovery.

In addition, there is a chapter devoted to children. While it is common knowledge that children and adolescents suffer from irrational fears and anxiety, there are few treatment programs offered specifically for these age groups. Furthermore, there are few books on the subject of children's anxiety recovery. In my opinion, the seeds of most adult anxiety disorders are sown in childhood. Therefore, several chapters ("My Anxiety Story," "Understanding Anxiety," "Family Background," and "Anxiety's Personality") deal with how anxiety develops beginning in childhood. The chapter on children's anxiety includes a description of the LifeSkills program, a treatment process available for children.

---

2. At the time of writing I am responsible for training therapists in New York, New Jersey, Connecticut, Massachusetts, Rhode Island, Pennsylvania, Maryland, Washington, DC, New Hampshire, Maine, Vermont, North Carolina, Delaware, Virginia, West Virginia, Illinois, Wisconsin, Iowa, Minnesota, and Canada.

3. Contact: CHAANGE, 128 Country Club Drive, Chula Vista, CA, telephone (800) 276-7800.

anxiety-ridden life, and my discovery of life without fear, is included. It took me more than thirty years of experimenting to achieve my recovery. This book was undertaken to drastically shorten the recovery time for others whose lives, like mine, have been limited by anxiety.

My personal recovery led me as a clinical psychologist to specialize in severe anxiety treatment. I work directly with anxiety sufferers and train other therapists in anxiety treatment. This is gratifying work because people can and do recover, usually in a relatively short period of time. As I share in the joy of each client's new freedom, I am continually reminded that anxiety can be "unlearned." You will meet some of these individuals in the book and hopefully appreciate their triumph over fear. Their successful recovery stories are told in Chapter 21. If you see yourself reflected in any of these stories there is a high likelihood that you, too, can recover completely from anxiety.

In the course of developing my anxiety treatment skills I discovered the Center for Help for Anxiety/Agoraphobia through New Growth Experiences (CHAANGE). The CHAANGE program for severe anxiety recovery was developed by two anxiety sufferers and their therapist. Ann Seagrave and Faison Covington, who suffered for years from panic anxiety with agoraphobia—the pattern of avoidant behavior that emerges as people attempt to cope with their anxiety—were able to recover completely with help from their therapist, Lou Owensby. The CHAANGE program consists of the same skills I learned over a period of many years, organized in a structured, step-by-step process. I met Ann and Faison in 1982 at the CHAANGE national office in Charlotte, North Carolina, and decided to join the network of CHAANGE affiliated therapists. I am now Regional

I recently had an experience which indicates the need for more information and more effective programs for anxiety recovery, and therefore a place for this book. I was interviewed on a Vermont Public Radio program, "Switchboard," accompanied by two former patients who recovered from anxiety through the CHAANGE program. After the interview, the public was invited to call in with questions or comments. Calls flooded in from Vermont, New Hampshire, Canada, and New York. Beginning the next day, my office received over 150 phone calls from people seeking more information on the CHAANGE program. Listeners also requested that information be sent to friends and relatives as far away from Vermont as Alaska, South Carolina, and North Dakota. In addition, the radio station received a record number of calls for taped copies of the program. I sent an information packet to all callers and spoke with many individuals. In some cases, the individuals had never received help or a diagnosis of their anxiety condition. In many cases, however, people had received help but were still suffering. What amazed me most was how many people were willing to travel considerable distances, in spite of their fears of driving, travel, and new situations, to get specialized help.

I know of many other instances of widespread public responses to media coverage of severe anxiety and the CHAANGE approach to treatment. One example occurred during the first year of the "Oprah" show. On October 2, 1986, the founders of the CHAANGE program were interviewed by Oprah Winfrey. After informing viewers about this approach to anxiety treatment and how to get further information about CHAANGE, over 3,500 people contacted the national office. Larry King also interviewed the two recovered anxiety sufferers, with similar results.

Another example was the response to National Anxiety Disorders Screening Day, sponsored by several grassroots organizations on May 3, 1995. Some 35,000 people visited more than 1,200 anxiety screening sites in all 50 states for information and guidance about coping with anxiety disorders. In a more modest example, 50 calls came in one day after a CHAANGE-affiliated therapist was interviewed by a newspaper in Portsmouth, New Hampshire (population 26,000). Eight callers signed up immediately for the CHAANGE anxiety recovery program.

In addition, there is a growing number of organizations devoted to public information about anxiety disorders. They include the Anxiety Disorders Association of American (ADAA), Free From Fear (FFF), The Obsessive-Compulsive Foundation (OCF), The Center for Help for Anxiety/Agoraphobia through New Growth Experiences (CHAANGE), the National Anxiety Foundation, and the Council on Anxiety Disorders. More information on these organizations is found in Appendix B.

More women than men seek help for anxiety. The ratio is four to one, in spite of the fact that there are more men than women in the general population. There are two possible explanations for this discrepancy. One explanation—an unlikely possibility—is that more women than men develop anxiety disorders. The more likely explanation is that both men and women are equally susceptible to anxiety, but men are less inclined to reveal their fears or ask for help. There may be a greater barrier to seeking help for men, who are conditioned to hide their feelings and not show weakness or fear. Hopefully, a book written by a man who is willing to reveal his own anxiety story will open the door for other men. I would like to increase the numbers of both men and women who find effective help and learn how to dance without fear.

The need is apparent, so let us begin. . . .

1

My Anxiety Story

I realize that it requires a tremendous leap of faith to imagine that your childhood—punctuated with pain, loss, and hurt—may, in fact, be a gift.

Wayne Muller, *Legacy of the Heart*

Fear haunted me since childhood, and as I grew up I sensed that I was more sensitive and fearful than other people. This is an overview of how I developed an anxiety disorder and how I overcame it.

A number of conditions and traumatic experiences were responsible for my fears. One strong influence was exposure to violence in the volatile community in which I was raised. It was the 1950s on the West Side of New York City, in a neighborhood known as Hell's Kitchen. The Broadway play *West Side Story* portrays the tension and violence I experienced in this primarily Puerto Rican and black community.

Some sharp images and memories stand out about this aspect of my childhood. Racial tension was high and, as a white boy, I was an accessible target for racial hostility. When I dated a Puerto Rican girl, for example, I was threatened and physically harassed by a group of Puerto Rican boys who would say, "We don't want you messing around with our women." In high school, a black member of the track team (I was the team's only white athlete) punched me in the face in the locker room, while mouthing a racial unkindness.

Many other forms of violence surrounded me in Hell's Kitchen. I recall a hunting knife being thrown into the lobby of my apartment building, entering blade first into a wall near me. While bicycling in Central Park, my brother, Marc, was mugged and had his bicycle stolen. An aggressive boy pushed another from a pier to his death in the Hudson River. A friend of mine, whom I can still vividly picture, was beaten regularly by a brutal father; he finally ran away from home, and I never saw him again. Although I never witnessed it, there were stories of violent gangs from uptown with names like the Viceroys and Marlboros, who would fight with pipes and chains.

I was myself a victim of violent abuse. On the way to school at the age of 12, I was raped in an abandoned building by a man who threatened to "smash" my head with the brick he held over me if I did not do what he said or if I ever told anyone. I was so frightened that I not only complied but was unable to tell anyone about the humiliating and painful trauma for over ten years. I was always on the lookout for that man and, unbelievably, I did see him on one occasion roaming the neighborhood. There must have been other victims.

There were more subtle incidents that also contributed to my anxiety. I recall, for example, my father telling me that he had joined the army to fight against Hitler. I learned at a young age that, because of their beliefs, millions of Jews were systematically exterminated in gas chambers and ovens. Since my father was Jewish, the Holocaust struck even closer to home. As I matured, I learned that racism, war, economic exploitation, and political oppression have occurred throughout history, and that the world was indeed unstable and often dangerous.

One aspect of anxiety discussed later in this book is that there are several ingredients in the development of an anxiety disorder. One of them is a sensitive disposition—a tendency to react strongly to many things, including stress, our own body reactions, and even thoughts. This was certainly true in my case. While I was not a sickly child, I had severe symptoms when I caught a cold or flu and when I contracted the usual childhood illnesses such as mumps and measles.

Indeed, a near-death experience when I was 7 years old added to my anxiety. I had a cold, which developed into croup. During the night, I was awakened by a phlegm obstruction in my windpipe, which had blocked off my breathing. I tried to scream for help but could make no sound and, due to oxygen deprivation, I fell unconscious. Waking up the next day, after an emergency tracheotomy operation, I found myself strapped to a hospital bed, breathing through an opening in my throat. I was unable to speak, and my parents were told I might never speak again due to surgical damage to my vocal chords. The only pleasant part of the following two weeks in the hospital was a caring nurse named Peggy, towards whom I felt my first feelings of falling in love. The life-threatening episode was a frightening brush with death, leaving me with a sense of vulnerability and life's fragility.

Another source of anxiety was the separation and divorce of my parents when I was 10 years old. From this trauma I learned that relationships can be tense, unstable, and hostile. Avoiding commitment and intimacy became a pattern by which I protected myself in relationships for many years to follow.

Due to family and childhood background, the personality style of people who become anxious seems to form a recognizable profile. We are hard-working, perfectionistic people who try hard to please others. We are sensitive to criticism and fearful of rejection. We are uncomfortable with conflict and tend to avoid it whenever possible, often by passive behavior and saying "yes" even when we feel "no." We have a strong need to feel in control, and therefore we tend to control or deny our feelings. In order to feel in control, we may also try to control others or try to anticipate the future. Our thinking pattern includes worrying, thinking negatively, judging others, and having many "shoulds" and rules. Although we would like to be more relaxed, we have difficulty letting go and relaxing. All these traits are characteristic of anxious people, and they need to be addressed as part of the anxiety recovery process.

How did the traumas of my childhood show up in my personality and my problem with anxiety? First of all, I was ashamed of my fear. In Hell's Kitchen a boy was "chicken" and "sissy" if he was afraid. I believed it was weak to be afraid, so I disguised it from friends and family. My feelings of insecurity, fear, and self-doubt became hidden behind my visible accomplishments, a pattern I later discovered to be common in people with anxiety. I developed a drive for achievement and success. I became a varsity athlete and captain of my high school track team, medaling frequently and earning the dubious distinction of "fastest white boy" in New York City. I became editor of the high school yearbook. I received a scholarship to Yale University, where I became a ranking scholar (top 10 percent of the class) and repeatedly made dean's list. At Yale, I had a research project published in a prestigious psychology journal. I went on to earn a Ph.D. in clinical psychology in less than the average length of time.

In my relationships, I was hesitant to make commitments, but I was afraid to be alone. Hiding my fear led to difficulty expressing other feelings. My external accomplishments seemed possible only if there was someone to cheer, admire, and approve. I felt dependent, and I worked hard to please others. I was unusually sensitive to criticism and rejection, and I avoided conflict whenever possible. I had intense separation anxiety and fears of abandonment. These are common traits in people who tend to develop anxiety disorders.

I had difficulty relaxing. I was restless, impatient, and tense, continually burying myself in activity. I was certainly not enjoying life, except for a sense of gratification in my accomplishments. My stress level was high, due to my perfectionism and my need to achieve and prove myself.

Those aspects of my personality controlled me, but I was unaware of the problem. It was just normal survival to me and I was unconscious of my behavior patterns. However, my whole approach to life was exhausting and slowly wearing me down. I realized there was a problem when I began to feel depressed.

Depression, as we will see later in the book, often arises as a secondary response to anxiety. In my case, fear of being alone was at the heart of the depression that would occur when I was without a companion. At one point, I found myself between relationships, and both my anxiety and depression intensified. I began to have panic attacks, with fears of losing control. The worst period consisted of daily panic attacks for several weeks, during which I feared I was going to die, go crazy, or disintegrate.

For a period of approximately ten years, I experienced some relief with drugs. The drugs consisted of frequent use of marijuana and periodic use of psychedelics, such as mescaline, peyote, and LSD. This was both a defense against anxiety and depression and a source of pleasure. Marijuana helped me relax and slow down. I was able to let go and begin to experience an inner peace previously unknown to me. Ironically, the use of these drugs marked the beginning of my anxiety recovery. However, I paid the price: my social life suffered, my efficiency dropped, and I had some "bad trips" that reinforced my anxiety. Fortunately, I later discovered healthier methods for relaxing and experiencing inner peace.

My anxiety recovery was an eclectic, trial-and-error process. I experimented with many techniques and methods, concentrating on those I found useful. I will share them with you in later chapters.

I discovered, for example, that I could relax and find inner peace not only through drugs but also through meditation. I studied meditation with a Sufi group in San Francisco, where I began to understand the role of mind in fear. I received teachings and training in meditation from Ram Dass, Pir Vilayat Khan, Stephen Gaskin, Swami

Satchitananda, and other gurus. Through regular sitting practice, which I describe in Chapter 8, I was able to face and let go of my fear-producing thoughts. I emptied my mind and experienced my true nature. I frequently enjoyed a state of inner peace, with quiet mind and open heart.

At first, my mind resisted vigorously because it had served for so long as a sentinel against danger. It was necessary to learn other methods, such as yoga and breathing techniques. As I released my body's tension, I could go deeper into trust, peace, and security. I also resumed regular exercise, and I gradually adopted a vegetarian diet, which enhanced my peacefulness. In addition, I entered psychotherapy, where I could talk openly and safely about my fear and other feelings.

Spiritual studies also became part of my recovery from fear and anxiety. I explored many wisdom traditions, including Buddhism, Hinduism, Christianity, Judaism, and Native American sources. In addition, I studied many aspects of health and the healing arts, such as massage, herbology, reflexology, and various forms of body work.

Equipped with these tools for relaxing my body, controlling my mind, understanding myself, and tapping into spiritual power, I was able to desensitize myself to fear and recover from anxiety. At one point, I faced my biggest fear by taking a year off and traveling by myself, with no itinerary, plans, or audience. During this psychological pilgrimage, I spent considerable time with myself, facing my fears and letting go of the past. At another point, I relocated by myself from San Francisco, California, to Nashville, Tennessee, where I knew no one, to further my professional training. Taking such risks and testing my skills and faith, I experienced a quantum leap forward in my recovery.

Unfortunately, the CHAANGE program and other recent developments in anxiety treatment were not available when my need for help was acute. Now, however, there are specialists in anxiety treatment and programs that can speed anxiety recovery and lead to freedom for those who are willing to seek help and do the work. The most effective program I have encountered is CHAANGE, a 16-week process that provides all the information and skills necessary for overcoming an anxiety disorder. Much of what I discovered on my own to be helpful in anxiety recovery is contained in this one structured program. I use it frequently in my work as a psychologist and emphasize it throughout this book.

What is the reward for working at recovery from anxiety, apart from sheer relief? Anxiety recovery boosted my self-confidence, energy level, and general enjoyment of life. In the recovery process, I learned how to express my feelings more openly and how to deal with conflict. I learned how to love, forgive, and let go of negativity. Anxiety recovery prepared me for a healthy intimate relationship and the joys of marriage and raising children. Through recovery methods such as meditation and relaxation, I now control my mind rather than my mind controlling me. I do not fear aging, or even dying, although I am in no rush to pass on. While I may plan for the future, I live much more in the present. My hope is that more anxiety sufferers will, through their successful recovery, experience these rewards and blessings. I also hope that *Dancing with Fear* will help.

2

Understanding Anxiety

Anxiety is the fear of fear.
Paul Foxman

Anxiety is a normal part of life for everyone. Taking an exam, meeting with a boss or authority figure, having a near accident, starting a new job, or traveling by airplane may all evoke anxiety. Anxiety can even be helpful in preparing for a challenge or change. However, persistent or intense anxiety is abnormal, interfering with daily life and becoming an anxiety disorder that requires professional help to overcome.

Anxiety disorders are surprisingly common, and their prevalence appears to be rising due to increasing stress and uncertainty in the world. Approximately 25 million American adults and 3 million children now suffer from anxiety severe enough to warrant professional help. It is estimated that one out of every four adults will have an anxiety disorder at some point in their lifetime. Anxiety is the most common emotional disorder, outranking all others, even depression. According to some sources, severe anxiety is a bigger problem than drug and alcohol abuse. Indeed, it is estimated that up to 60 percent of substance abusers have a severe anxiety disorder that they are attempting to control through drugs and alcohol. In a review of studies on the relationship between alcoholism and anxiety, Barlow (1988) concludes that severe anxiety precedes the onset of drinking in most cases.

What is anxiety and why is it so prevalent today? To begin with, anxiety is related to the survival instinct. Normally, when we are confronted with danger or a life-threatening situation, our bodies react quickly with an automatic survival mechanism—the fight/flight response. Under threat or danger, the brain's survival center, the *locus ceruleus*, triggers the survival alarm, setting in motion an instantaneous set of body reactions to cope with the situation. The adrenal glands release adrenaline and the sympathetic nervous system is activated. All systems are mobilized. Muscles tense to prepare for fight or flight, heart rate increases to supply extra oxygen, vision and hearing become acute and focused, breathing intensifies to assist in oxygen supply, and posture assumes a defensive mode. Instantly, the body becomes charged and energized to protect itself, and all this takes place instinctively, without thinking.

To appreciate how the fight/flight survival reaction works, imagine for a moment that you are an animal—a rabbit living in the wilderness. In a natural environment, there is a clearly established system of predators and prey. As a rabbit you are prey to other animals such as hawks and foxes. On a typical day you would spend your time foraging for food—eating and storing berries, leaves, and roots. However, when you are even remotely approached by a predator, you sense danger. Your survival instinct is so attuned that your body begins to react without your knowing the specific threat. The sensitivity of your survival instinct recognizes the early warning signals of danger and activates your body to take refuge immediately. As a rabbit, you run for cover until the danger signal subsides. When the danger passes, your body relaxes and you resume foraging for food.

Survival's fight/flight reaction is the original "dance with fear." The survival mechanism described above is a conservative instinct, taking no chances and giving you little time to think or evaluate the situation. The survival center makes no distinction between *possible* and *actual* threat, because if you take the time to evaluate the situation before responding it could easily be too late.

The situation is far more complex with human beings for whom danger is often imagined or ambiguous. When the survival reaction occurs in response to a life-threatening situation such as an assault, fire, riot, or tornado, the fight/flight reaction is normal and natural. One reason anxiety is so common is that the amount of global stress and number of perceived threats are increasing, and the media make these external conditions vivid and immediate. However, there are many situations that trigger the fight/flight reaction despite the fact that they are not life-threatening. This is exactly what happens in most cases of severe anxiety: the person's body reacts as if there is a life-threatening situation when in reality no danger exists. Indeed, most people who have an anxiety problem recognize that their fear is irrational, but they are unable to control it.

The body is quickly aroused by activating hormones upon receiving the danger signal. There are a number of chemicals produced by the body for this purpose, such as adrenaline, norepinephrine, adrenocorticotropic hormone (ACTH), and serotonin. Once these chemical messengers are released into the bloodstream, the fight/flight response is launched and cannot readily be stopped. Unlike insulin, the chemical that counteracts high blood sugar, your body produces no chemicals to neutralize the activating hormones. This means a person will need some time to calm down after a fight/flight reaction, as the activating hormones are metabolized, even when there is no longer any danger. This is important for the anxiety sufferer to understand in order to stop being fearful if and when the body remains activated for no apparent reason.

It is normal to go into the fight/flight reaction under threat or danger. However, there are several other situations that can trigger the fight/flight reaction. Let's look at these to see how anxiety begins to develop when the body is activated. To begin with, a *perception* of danger has the same effect as actual danger. As mentioned earlier, the survival mechanism is a conservative instinct that does not take any chances, and makes no distinction between actual and possible danger. Recalling the rabbit in the wilderness, if we take the time to think and evaluate the danger level in a potentially threatening situation before responding, it could easily be too late. Therefore, if you *perceive* danger, or just *think* danger may exist, a danger signal is sent to the survival center and the fight/flight reaction is triggered. For example, if you have a traumatic experience in a particular situation—say a panic attack while driving a car or a nervous feeling while giving a presentation in front of other people—you may begin to perceive the situation as dangerous. Thereafter, just thinking about entering the situation—driving the car or giving a presentation—will set the fight/flight survival reaction into motion. In reaction to the perception of danger, your body will go into the fight/flight reaction. Certain situations or places become linked to a negative emotional experience—and the associated body reactions—and then they are perceived as threatening. Some typical phobic situations are traveling away from home, flying, being alone, shopping in crowded stores or malls, business meetings, and social gatherings. In those situations, the body reaction itself is normal, but it is triggered by a false alarm.

Stress is another situation leading to the fight/flight reaction. Stress can be any situation that involves many demands, adjustments, or changes, and it can be both positive and negative. One measure of stress is the Life Change Scale (Holmes and Masuda 1967), which lists 43 life events that are considered stressful, ranked according to the degree of stress and the likelihood of producing body reactions. At the top of the list are events such as the death of a loved one, divorce, separation, and serious illness in a family. Lower on the list are events such as increased responsibilities at work, financial problems, and family relocation. At the bottom of the list are events such as a minor traffic violation, holiday stress, and even planning and taking a vacation. I always ask new clients to tell me about any stress that might be affecting them, and it surprises me how many are unaware of the amount of stress in their lives. One example was a youthful-looking 59-year-old woman who sought help for her uncontrollable fear of having panic attacks. When I interviewed Cynthia and took her history, I learned that she had experienced seven deaths of relatives in the last four years, as well as numerous relocations due to her husband's military job. In addition, a son was going through a divorce, and she was experiencing some medical problems. In spite of all this, Cynthia never thought she was under stress and felt that she should be able to handle her life with no problem.

In my opinion, one of the most common sources of stress is the recurring demands of daily life that we assume are normal and that fill our schedules with increasing speed and intensity. Working for a living, raising children, maintaining a home, doing the laundry, food shopping, cooking and kitchen cleanup, recreation, and even socializing may all combine to yield an overload of stress. While any one or two of our commitments and responsibilities are manageable, the overall combination can result in stress overload. Stress can also be cumulative; the harmful effect of stress can build on itself if there is insufficient stress recovery. Even our efforts to recover from stress through recreational activities, exercise, and vacations are often approached with the same rush and time pressure as the rest of our daily life. Recognizing this, Selye (1956), a biologist who wrote the now-classic book on stress, spoke about "the stress of life." He asserted that stress is an inherent and inevitable part of life.

Stress itself is not really the problem, as far as body activation is concerned. First of all, body activation is an adaptive response to any situation that involves demands, adjustments, or change. The activation of body systems and resources helps to meet the challenge of stress. Second, our bodies are designed to handle stress. The problem is not stress; the problem is lack of stress recovery. We can handle stress without negative impact if we restore ourselves at regular intervals, preferably daily. If we do this, our stress recovery pattern becomes balanced, our energy reserves are replenished, and we can deal effectively with more stress. However, when our recovery practices do not keep pace with stress demands, we gradually deplete our energy reserves and wear down our resistance. We then go out of balance and develop early warning signals of stress overload in the form of mild symptoms. Headaches, backaches, difficulty relaxing, muscle twitches, and low energy, for example, can all be early warning signals of stress overload. When the early warning signals are ignored, they intensify until we are forced to notice. Unfortunately, this often occurs as anxiety symptoms, such as panic attacks or phobias. Why some people develop an anxiety disorder while others develop a different kind of health crisis is determined by family background and personality type, as we will discuss later.

In coping with stress, the body activates itself in much the same way as the fight/flight response. This is normal and helpful in handling stress. However, due to their particular personality type, most anxiety sufferers do not recognize their stress, and they do not take the necessary steps to either reduce it or practice stress recovery on a regular basis. The characteristics of the "anxiety personality" are discussed in Chapter 4.

Strong emotions can also trigger the fight/flight mechanism. Actually, it would be more accurate to say that emotional arousal and the fight/flight response involve the same body reactions. Anger, for example, involves arousal in the form of muscle tension, increased heart rate, increased blood pressure, and intensification of breathing.

Excitement is another recognizable example. But other emotions, such as guilt, grief, and shame, can also involve body reactions similar to the fight/flight response. In addition, the distinction between danger and strong emotions can be confusing, especially for the sensitive, anxiety-prone person, who tends to fear strong body reactions. As we will see later in the book, many anxiety sufferers are raised in families where feelings are not discussed or where they are actively discouraged. In some families, feelings are associated with out-of-control behavior. For these reasons, most people who develop anxiety disorders tend to be fearful of strong feelings. The onset of feelings can, therefore, signal danger and trigger the fight/flight reaction. Chapters 13 and 14 deal with feelings and anxiety, including techniques for safely identifying and expressing feelings.

Finally, there are a number of *thought patterns* that can trigger the fight/flight reaction, such as what-ifs, shoulds, perfectionism, negative thinking, worry, and black-and-white thinking. For example, "what-if" thoughts are negative anticipations about what might happen in the near or distant future: "What if the school bus goes off the road with my child on it? What if I forgot to turn off the oven? What if I have a panic attack in the mall? What if I have a serious but undetected illness?" The survival instinct, which takes no risks with danger, treats every "what-if" thought as an actual event. In the brain's *locus ceruleus*, where the survival center is located, a "what-if" thought is interpreted not as something that *might* happen but rather as something that definitely *will* happen. Therefore, the fight/flight mechanism is activated to deal with the "danger."

Perfectionism is another pattern of thinking that can trigger body reactions. Perfectionism—the idea that everything must be done just right—creates stress. People with perfectionistic thinking tend to push and drive themselves, often to the point of exhaustion. They function frequently at a high level of body activation as they strive to attain the elusive goal of perfection. And when they "fail," perfectionists often feel disappointed in themselves, or become depressed and self-critical. These negative feelings then add to the problem by creating more body reactions.

A related thought pattern is the *shoulds* that occur frequently in anxious persons. "I should be more productive, I should eat a healthier diet or lose weight, I should be a better parent, I shouldn't procrastinate so much, I should be in control of myself at all times," and "I should keep a cleaner home," are some common examples. Shoulds create stress and activate the body in much the same way as perfectionism. Some specific techniques for eliminating shoulds, as well as the other symptom-producing thought patterns, are offered in Chapter 11.

One additional thought pattern that contributes to body reactions is *black-and-white thinking*. This is a habit whereby everything is judged as good or bad—right or wrong—with nothing in between. If you did not do a great job, then you must have done a bad job. If I am not friendly to you one day, then I must be an unfriendly person. If you do not know what will happen, then it will probably be bad. If you make a mistake, then you are stupid. If you cannot learn something on the first try, then it is too difficult for you to learn no matter how hard you try. These examples of black-and-white thinking are common among anxious people, who frequently monitor the environment for safety and danger cues; if the cues are unclear, they prepare for the worst.

It should now be apparent that the fight/flight reaction is a natural response to actual danger, perceived danger, stress, strong emotions, and certain thought patterns. In some cases, such as danger and stress, body activation serves a useful, even lifesaving purpose. Except for actual danger, however, many anxiety sufferers do not recognize the logic of body activation as way of coping with the situations that trigger it. Furthermore, the anxiety personality *creates* stress with traits such as the need to be in control, difficulty setting reasonable human limits, high achievement needs, and perfectionism. In addition, lack of understanding of the mind–body relationship and the fight/flight survival mechanism, makes body activation frightening. As already discussed, the anxiety sufferer's fear of body activation creates a danger signal that further intensifies the body reactions, setting off a cycle of uncontrollable anxiety.

Anxiety can be understood as a vicious cycle in which the body's fight/flight reaction is set into motion by a number of conditions that are not dangerous but nevertheless affect us as though they were. The brain's survival center interprets these situations as threatening and activates the body. Due to their particular personality traits, many people stress themselves and frequently trigger the fight/flight reaction but then fear these body reactions. Among the personality traits involved in anxiety, the need for control is a key factor because once the fight/flight reaction is initiated it is difficult to control. People with this personality trait will, therefore, become more anxious during the fight/flight reaction, especially when it seems to happen for no reason. Fears of having a heart attack, going crazy, or losing control in public further feed into the anxiety cycle. It can also be confusing to distinguish among the many situations that might be triggering the body reactions. This is compounded by the anxious person's tendency to produce stress and other symptom triggers.

It might be helpful to distinguish between fear and anxiety. Fear is the instinctive reaction to danger. Anxiety is a learned, irrational reaction to fear—a fear of fear. Virtually all cases of anxiety begin with a negative experience in which initial fear seemed out of control. Sometimes this takes place when a person overreacts to a situation that would normally arouse fear in most people. In other cases, the anxiety consists of an intense reaction in a particular situation for no apparent reason. Once the frightening or traumatic reaction takes place, it develops into a persistent pattern of fear relative to the situation originally associated with it. A common denominator in most anxiety conditions is a strong fight/flight reaction to a place, thought, feeling, or situation, accompanied by an irrational fear of losing control, "going crazy," embarrassing oneself, or having a serious illness or dying.

Fatigue and depression are commonly associated with severe anxiety. Fatigue sets in when a person is frequently or chronically activated, due to energy loss and insufficient recovery. Depression is also common in anxiety due to inability to control body reactions, and as a result of the fatigue just mentioned. When the situation is chronic, depression is intensified by the discouraging belief that the situation cannot be changed.

A diagram summarizing the relationship between survival's fight/flight reaction and anxiety is shown in Figure 2–1.

FIGURE 2–1: SURVIVAL INSTINCT AND ANXIETY

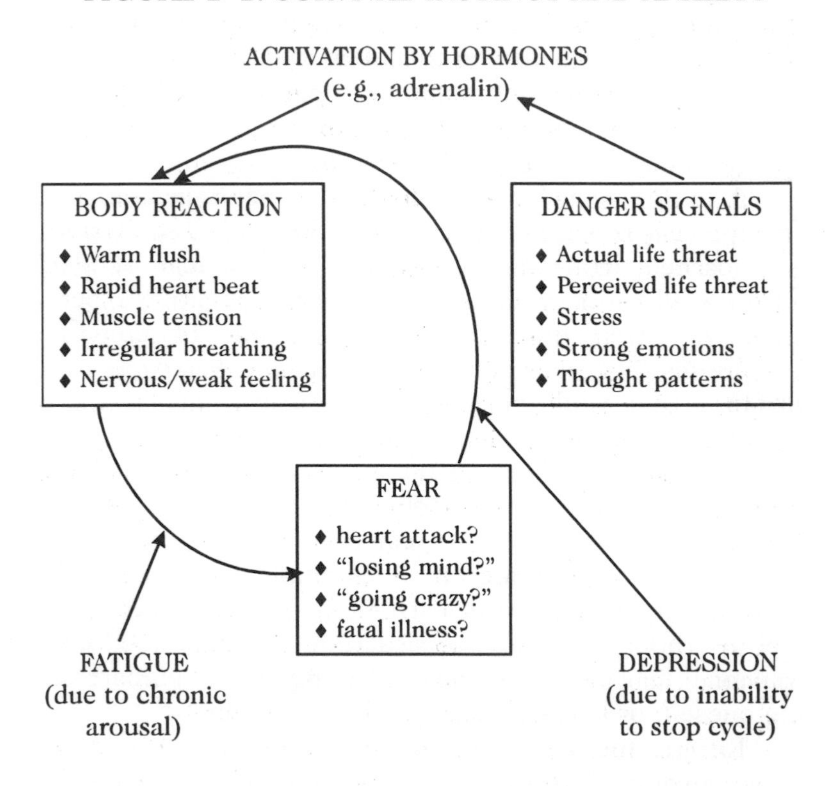

There are different forms of anxiety that develop as people attempt to cope with fear. Each of these anxiety conditions consists of a more or less distinct set of symptoms, and the condition can be diagnosed on the basis of those symptoms. These anxiety conditions are referred to as *disorders* to distinguish them from normal anxiety. In describing them, only the primary symptoms will be identified. For the complete criteria used in diagnosing the various anxiety disorders, the reader is referred to the internationally used *Diagnostic and Statistical Manual of Mental Disorders (DSM-IV)* (1994).

Until recently, child and adult anxiety disorders were listed separately, based on the belief that children do not experience the same type of anxiety as adults. We now know that children and adults do experience the same anxiety conditions. For example, contrary to old myths, children can experience panic attacks, and adults can suffer from separation anxiety. Therefore, in the recently revised *DSM-IV* (1994), there is no longer a clear distinction made between child and adult anxiety disorders. Nevertheless, because of circumstances unique to childhood, I discuss anxiety in children in greater depth in Chapter 6.

Panic disorder involves sudden episodes of intense anxiety—panic attacks—that occur when no real danger exists. With a panic disorder, you feel overwhelmed with terror as your body reacts with symptoms, such as heart palpitations or pounding, chest pain, shortness of breath or difficulty breathing, shaking, chills or hot flashes, weakness, sweating, numbness or tingling, nausea, and faintness. These experiences can be so intense that they are frequently accompanied by fears of having a heart attack, going crazy, or losing control. Typically, people who experience panic attacks seek help from a medical doctor or hospital emergency room but are told there is nothing physically wrong. Without proper help the condition progresses and agoraphobia may develop.

Panic disorder is illustrated by Harriet, who was referred to me for help by her physician after revealing her anxiety problem. Harriet was unable to come by herself to the first few appointments due to her fear of driving. She had frequent panic attacks associated with driving a car.

The condition had become so severe that Harriet required her husband to accompany her to any new situation. To get to work she would often offer to pick up a colleague who lived on the way, in order to avoid being alone in her car. During the day, she would panic just thinking about the drive home. Harriet spent considerable time anticipating and worrying about every trip out of the house. When I first saw Harriet, she was tearful and depressed about her inability to control her fear.

When a person begins to avoid places or situations associated with panic anxiety a pattern of *agoraphobia* may develop. This pattern of avoidant behavior is an attempt to prevent anxiety and to feel in control, and the avoided situations are usually places in which panic anxiety occurred in the past. Typical avoidances include driving, shopping, crowded places, standing in line, being alone, meetings, and social gatherings. These are the situations in which a person fears having an anxiety attack, losing control, or being embarrassed. Many remain in a painful state of anxious anticipation because of these fears. Some become restricted or even housebound, while others function normally but with great difficulty, often trying to hide their discomfort. Agoraphobia is both a severe anxiety condition and a phobia, as well as a pattern of avoidant behavior.

Daniel, a sensitive and thoughtful young man and father of two children, illustrates the agoraphobia pattern. At the beginning of his treatment for panic disorder with agoraphobia, Daniel was severely restricted and avoided shopping malls, large stores, and church (about which he felt extremely guilty). Daniel said, "Currently, everywhere I go and everything I do I need to think about how the anxiety might affect me during the activity. Fear has almost total control over my life and I feel that it has enveloped me and is smothering me. I do not want to spend the rest of my life with this fear." Daniel's successful recovery from panic disorder with agoraphobia is detailed in Chapter 21.

Generalized anxiety disorder consists of unreasonable worry about everyday occurrences, leading to a continuously high level of anxiety. People with this form of anxiety are constantly on the lookout for possible problems and "danger." Physical symptoms such as muscle aches, fatigue, difficulty sleeping, sweating, and dizziness are usually associated with this condition. Generalized anxiety disorder is illustrated by Lisa, who spent twelve to sixteen hours a day worrying and anticipating negative events. A homemaker and mother of three children, Lisa focused on all the bad things that could happen, and she felt she had little control over her life. Lisa often woke up feeling tired, as if she did not get enough sleep, no matter how many hours she slept. She was unable to relax or turn off her worry thoughts.

Social phobia involves a fear of situations in which a person feels exposed to scrutiny or judgment by others. The person typically fears that he or she may do something or act in a way that will be embarrassing or humiliating. The usual symptoms of anxiety are triggered by social situations, such as meetings, parties, and other situations involving interaction with people. This anxiety disorder is illustrated by one of my patients, Fred, who was painfully afraid of meetings, social events, and dating. Fred was convinced that he would say something foolish and that people would laugh or think he was stupid. Fred told me that he sometimes went for several days without interacting with another human being, even at work.

Although he felt more comfortable avoiding social contact, he revealed how lonely and isolated he was. Fred yearned for a special relationship, but his anxiety inhibited him from making any efforts.

A *specific phobia* is an intense and irrational fear associated with a particular object or situation, leading to an avoidance of that object or situation. Some common phobic situations are flying, driving, being alone, speaking in front of people, and certain animals such as dogs or snakes. Phobias are often part of other anxiety disorders, such as panic disorder and obsessive-compulsive disorder. Phobias are the most common anxiety disorder.

Maria, for example, wanted help eliminating her fear of flying. Approximately five years earlier, on an airplane trip to Florida, she experienced panic anxiety triggered by an extremely rough ride. "It was the worst experience of my life and when I got off that plane I vowed I would never fly again." After that, Maria could not even think about flying without intense anxiety and she avoided flying in spite of a love of travel. Before the incident, Maria had only one other instance of abnormal anxiety when facing surgery with general anesthesia. As a supervisor at work, Maria functioned effectively with people and job pressure. She had no other problems with anxiety but felt strongly that she was restricted by her fear of flying. Her goal was to be able to go on vacations with air travel again.

Adults can sometimes experience *separation anxiety*, which consists of intense fear of being separated from a security figure. Fears of losing control and not being able to function without the security figure characterize this anxiety disorder. Strong anticipatory anxiety usually emerges at the prospect of separation. For example, Jim, a competent special education teacher, functioned without anxiety on the job. However, he came to me for help because he experienced severe anxiety, including panic attacks, whenever his wife was late coming home from her job. His anxiety peaked whenever she was scheduled to travel on business, and Jim found it necessary to stay with a friend or have one of the adult children come home for the night. No one would have guessed that Jim suffered from this anxiety disorder, as he seemed to be in control whenever other people were around.

Obsessive-compulsive disorder involves repeated, intrusive, and unwanted thoughts (obsessions) that cause anxiety, often accompanied by ritualized behaviors (compulsions) that temporarily relieve the anxiety. Common obsessions include fear of germs or contamination, and fear of hurting someone. Common compulsions include excessive cleaning, double-checking, and hoarding things. The person suffering from obsessive-compulsive disorder usually recognizes that his or her behavior is irrational but is unable to control it. Trying to resist causes the anxiety to escalate, so the person learns to give in to the obsessive thought or compulsive behavior. One anxiety patient, Bruce, ate the same foods at the same time every day. He feared that if he changed his eating habits he would get food poisoning. Although Bruce complained that his diet was boring, he needed help to overcome the fear and add more interest to his diet and life in general.

Post-traumatic stress disorder develops when a person has experienced a trauma such as sexual abuse, violence, or injury that continues to affect his or her life. Common symptoms of this disorder can include reliving the trauma (disturbing dreams, flashbacks, distressing memories, strong physical and emotional reactions to reminders of the trauma), symptoms of increased arousal (sleep disturbance, impaired concentration, irritability, angry outbursts, difficulty relaxing), and numbing of general responsiveness (detachment from others, limited emotions, difficulty feeling love). One unusual case of post-traumatic stress disorder was Doris, who was referred to me by an attorney who was representing her in a lawsuit against a hair salon. Apparently, the hair stylist mismanaged the length of time and the type of chemical used to color Doris' hair. Her hair was so badly burned that it was necessary to remove virtually all of it. As she herself was a hair stylist, Doris felt ashamed and unable to face her clients. She reluctantly wore a wig but stopped working. Doris presented all of the symptoms of post-traumatic stress disorder.

Anxiety associated with a medical condition is a disorder just recently recognized in the *DSM-IV* (1994). The anxiety in this disorder is linked to fears about symptoms of an actual health problem or disease. Medical conditions involving pain, such as Crohn's disease, fibromyalgia, or migraine headaches, can trigger anxiety in certain people who tend to react strongly to physical symptoms and loss of control. However, the reverse can also occur; anxiety can cause a flare-up of the medical condition. This anxiety disorder is illustrated by Sandra, a petite woman, who had fibromyalgia involving intense muscle pain, especially in her chest. The tension and chest pain associated with fibromyalgia were similar to some of the symptoms of stress and anxiety. Whenever Sandra felt herself becoming tense, which occurred frequently under stress, she would panic and go to the hospital emergency room. Her first thought when tense was, "What if this is the beginning of a panic attack or a heart attack?"

I can personally identify with most of the anxiety disorders discussed in this chapter. Due to sexual abuse and near-death experiences as a child, for example, I suffered from symptoms of post-traumatic stress disorder for many years. My personality type also caused me to worry to an abnormal degree, causing symptoms of generalized anxiety disorder. As mentioned in Chapter 1, I also suffered from a period of panic attacks, and, because I had a fear of being alone, I desperately avoided it. These symptoms meant that I had elements of a panic disorder, a specific phobia, separation anxiety, and a pattern of agoraphobia. In some cases, such as mine, where there are features of several anxiety disorders, it is appropriate to designate the condition as an *anxiety disorder, not otherwise specified*. In addition, as I describe in my own anxiety story, I experienced some secondary depression due to my inability to control the anxiety.

Anxiety recovery begins with an understanding of what is happening in the body and the mind, and of what is triggering the anxiety reactions. It is important to realize that anxiety is not a life-threatening situation. Except for anxiety disorder associated with a medical condition, your medical doctor has probably ruled out a physical problem and you do not have a fatal illness. You are not losing your mind and you do not have a mental illness. You can change this learned pattern and recover from anxiety. May the rest of this book help show you the way out of anxiety.

3

Family Background

Those who forget the past are condemned to repeat it.
George Santayana

If you suffer from severe anxiety, you probably have a personality similar to mine. You are a sensitive, hard-working, dependable, and perfectionistic person who aims to please. Fearful of rejection and wanting to be liked, you tend to focus on the needs and feelings of other people, and you avoid conflict whenever possible. In going the extra mile, you have difficulty setting reasonable limits for yourself, and often feel stressed because you take on so much responsibility. In addition, you prefer to be in control, and you like structure and predictability. These and other related traits make us vulnerable to stress and anxiety. What causes this type of personality to develop?

In most cases, the anxiety-prone personality stems from an identifiable set of family and background experiences. It usually amazes anxiety patients to learn that their family backgrounds have so much in common. In this chapter, we will explore the background of people who, like you and me, developed the type of personality that makes us vulnerable to an anxiety condition. Then, in the next chapter, we will look more closely at this personality style and how it increases our chances for severe anxiety.

There are three basic ingredients in the development of anxiety: temperament, family background leading to a specific personality type, and stress. To begin our understanding of how anxiety develops, we must consider both the genetic factors and the family histories that shape our anxiety-prone personalities.

Our disposition to develop anxiety begins with two genetic factors, the first of which is *biological sensitivity*. We are unusually sensitive and tend to react intensely to both external stimulation, such as lights and sounds, and internal stimulation, such as our own body reactions and feelings. Due to our unusual sensitivity, we may react emotionally to many forms of stimulation, including vivid movies, other people's feelings and behavior, and even our own thoughts. This biological sensitivity is present at birth, but it does not mean we are born fearful or anxious. We are simply born with a sensitive temperament—a disposition towards reacting to stimuli with higher than average intensity. We are especially reactive to stress, which, as will we see later on, is the key to determining *when* we will become symptomatic with anxiety.

The second genetic factor is an *active mind*. Those who develop anxiety disorders tend to have at least average intelligence along with an active imagination. We tend to think visually—to form mental pictures as we think. Combined with our inborn sensitivity, our active imaginations lead to strong reactions to what we see, hear, smell, think, and feel. This turns out to be both an asset and a liability, because while sensitivity, intelligence, and imagination give us the capacity to interact effectively with the world, these traits also give us the ability to worry and scare ourselves with vivid imagery about all the things that can go wrong in life.

These inborn traits join forces with our childhood experiences, particularly those within our families, to shape our personalities. Some personality researchers emphasize the role of genetics in shaping personality, and I would agree insofar as anxiety sufferers seem to start out in life with an active mind and sensitive temperament. However, genetics is only part of the explanation. As my own anxiety story illustrates, early life experiences, particularly traumatic experiences occurring during the formative years of childhood, can have a profound impact on personality and subsequent behavior patterns. Our emotional and behavior patterns as adults are largely determined by our early life experiences.

Those of us who develop an anxiety condition tend to have similar family backgrounds. One of the first steps in anxiety treatment involves taking a client's family history, to identify the background experiences that contributed to the onset of an anxiety condition. The purpose of this step is to help each client understand that anxiety does not suddenly show up in adulthood—there is usually a history leading up to it. In most cases, clients in anxiety treatment will recognize the role played by their developmental history and conclude that the anxiety disorder was virtually "waiting to happen." As we will discuss later, anxiety is usually triggered by the way we react to certain situations, such as stress overload.

Anxiety disorders do not develop suddenly, although that is what many anxiety sufferers mistakenly believe. While the symptoms of anxiety may seem to appear "out of the blue," there is usually a developmental history leading up to the anxiety, beginning with inborn traits that combine with early family experiences to form an anxiety-prone personality. This personality type reacts strongly to stress. Furthermore, in sensitive people with this personality, strong reactions to stress often trigger a fear of the body's stress reaction, which creates more stress and more body reaction. This can form a pattern or cycle of anxiety. Anxiety can be also be triggered by traumatic experiences at any time, although in most cases the basic template for anxiety already exists as a result of background experiences and personality type.

The development of anxiety follows the sequence shown in Figure 3–1.

We can begin to fill in the details of anxiety development by focusing now on family background factors. As we review them, you might want to make mental notes of which seem to apply in your case. In the CHAANGE program, a developmental chart is provided that shows the common family background and personality traits associated with anxiety. The client in treatment can check each box on the chart that applies. This adds some structure to the process of learning how the condition developed in each case. In most instances, a pattern of factors leading to an anxiety condition is recognized. This can in itself bring some relief, because it provides a logical explanation for the anxiety. By taking the mystery out of anxiety,

FIGURE 3–1: SEQUENCE OF ANXIETY DEVELOPMENT

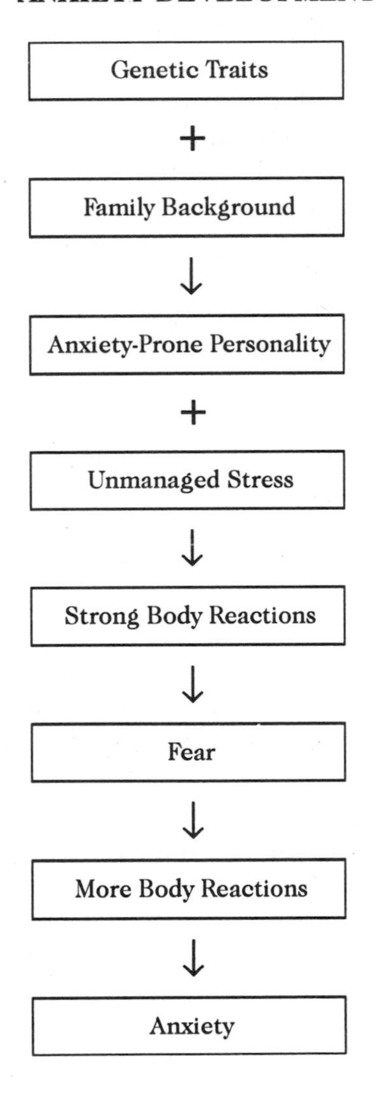

clients can begin to feel more in control and less fearful of the condition. The CHAANGE anxiety development chart is shown at the end of this chapter.

Looking back on their childhood, some adult anxiety sufferers can pinpoint episodes of *separation anxiety*, which is one of the first experiences in life that can make us feel out of control. For children, security is based on the emotional relationship and close proximity to parents, particularly with mother during the early bonding period. Unprepared for separation from their security base, children may experience symptoms of anxiety, such as accelerated heart rate, breathing difficulties, warm flush, and nervous stomach, along with fear of losing control, being ridiculed, or feeling embarrassed. The situations where such anxiety is most likely to occur are day care settings or preschool, sleep-overs at a friend's house, overnight camp, and hospitalizations. In addition, separation anxiety can develop as a result of inadequate emotional bonding, as will be discussed in greater detail in Chapter 6. Anxiety triggered by traumatic separation can become imprinted in our memories and interfere with a sense of security and independence. If you have experienced separation anxiety at some point in childhood, you are more likely to develop an anxiety disorder later.

Approval and love in some families are provided *on the basis of achievement*, more than on the essence or inner qualities of the child. This pattern teaches children to perform for acceptance and affection, and gives a subtle message that they are not intrinsically worthy of love and affection. This family pattern reinforces high achievement, perfectionism, and a tendency to focus on external accomplishments as the basis of self-worth. The pattern will create high stress later and make it difficult to set realistic goals and limits. Of course, it is important to praise children for their accomplishments, as this helps establish self-esteem. However, when approval, love, and praise are based primarily on achievement, the stage is set for problems with self-esteem and future stress.

In families where *feelings are not readily expressed or accepted*, children adapt by shutting down emotionally. In some cases, children may know their feelings but learn to hide them, or they may lose touch with their feelings. When feelings are frequently blocked, a pattern of *emotional armor*—muscular rigidity that further cuts us off from feelings—can develop. As a result, we may not learn the language of feelings, and we may become fearful of feelings because of the unfamiliar physical arousal they involve. Since anxiety involves strong feelings, those who are unfamiliar with feelings will tend to have more difficulty coping with it.

Problems with feelings contribute to anxiety in a number of ways. For example, one of the personality traits of anxiety sufferers is difficulty relaxing, despite a desire for peace and calm. Since we are most in touch with our feelings when we slow down and relax, we may have difficulty relaxing due to anxiety about feelings. Difficulty relaxing interferes with one of the most important skills for stress recovery and anxiety control. In addition, being able to read the early warning signals of stress—the trigger for anxiety—requires being in touch with feelings.

Frequent or severe criticism by parents is devastating to children's self-esteem. Children who are frequently criticized develop not only a poor self-image but also anxiety about taking risks as learners. In addition, children raised in families with critical parents may mistakenly believe that if only they tried harder or did better they would receive love, praise, and positive attention. This can create stress if the child, in a frustrated attempt to please and be accepted by critical parents, develops perfectionism and a high achievement drive. Furthermore, depression is likely to arise due to deprivation of love and attention.

Alcoholism in a family creates anxiety in a number of ways. Where an atmosphere of denial and unpredictability exists, children can become confused and anxious. Violence is another issue in many cases involving alcoholism. It is estimated that approximately 90 percent of all domestic violence is alcohol related. Violence and out-of-control behavior raise children's anxiety level by threatening their basic safety. Since alcoholic behavior patterns—including violence—are often unpredictable, children in alcoholic families may remain in a constant state of psychological arousal and fear. As "adult children of alcoholism," they may develop anxiety disorders as well as other emotional difficulties.

Families can be viewed as systems in which the behavior of one person affects the behavior of others. In alcoholic families, children may cope by adopting survival roles, whose purpose is to divert attention away from the alcoholism, or to compensate for it in some way. Wegscheider (1981) identifies a number of children's roles in the alcoholic family, such as *hero, scapegoat, lost child,* and *mascot.* The family hero, for example, acts out the myth that his or hers is a stable family, as demonstrated by a high-achieving child. The role of family mascot serves, like a court jester, to defuse family tension and anxiety. The lost child retreats into the background, adopting a passive style seen by others as simply well-behaved. The scapegoat, or troublemaker, acts out the family's feelings of abandonment, hurt, and anger. These are ways in which children cope with the anxiety engendered in an alcoholic family environment.

Families with sexual abuse, violence, severe marital problems, disorganization, or divorce can also create anxiety and affect children in similar ways. In any dysfunctional family, children must find ways to cope with instability and trauma and adjust to disruptions of normal development. In one case, an anxious woman with whom I worked was raised in a family with critical parents who had a tense marriage involving poor communication and virtually no affection. Arlene was the youngest of three children in the family, and was sexually abused at a young age on several occasions by her older brother, who threatened to hurt her if she told. There were several incidents, which took place in a bedroom closet. The lack of warmth and communication within the family, combined with the brother's threats, stopped Arlene from reporting the abuse. Arlene told no one about the abuse and repressed her feelings and memories of the trauma. However, Arlene developed a fear of authority figures, a pattern of pleasing others, difficulty relaxing, and many other traits common among anxiety sufferers. She initially came for help as an adult, following a period of stress, when she began to have panic attacks. Her trauma memories surfaced in therapy, but only after some emotional gains. In fact, she did not begin to recall the history of abuse until after she overcame her anxiety disorder using the CHAANGE program. Several months after completing the anxiety treatment program, Arlene contacted me to deal with her memories, which surfaced in a number of dreams.

It is surprising how frequently children come into adulthood with *limited knowledge about body functions, including sexuality*. Although knowledge of body functions and good health habits is included in most school curriculums, children will tend to practice what is modeled within the family. In families where body functions are not discussed openly, children may remain naive about the most basic health and stress management information. Regular exercise, good nutrition, familiarity with the body's systems, and knowledge about the effect of stress on the body can all go a long way towards anxiety prevention.

Sex is one of the most natural biological functions, and yet the subject is not handled comfortably in many families. Families that are unable to deal with sexual issues, such as masturbation, menstruation, or patterns of male and female sexual response, contribute to anxiety in their children due to confusion, lack of valid information, and uncomfortable feelings about their sexuality. Freud (1933) asserted that abnormal sexuality is responsible for anxiety and other emotional disorders, particularly in puberty when libido levels are high. Reich (1961, 1972) and Lowen (1975) also proposed that frustration of the sexual drive is the primary cause of anxiety. As I discuss in Chapter 15, sexual release is an anxiety-reducing mechanism, but this outlet may not be possible for those who are uncomfortable with their sexuality.

Parent–child role reversals occur in families when a child is placed in an adult role, such as caretaker or companion to a parent or surrogate parent to siblings. This can happen in families where there is a significant emotional or communication problem between the parents. In some families, one of the children may be drawn into a companion role with a parent who needs emotional support but is unable to meet this need in the marriage. In families with divorced parents, for example, a custodial parent may turn to one of the children to meet these frustrated needs. In other cases, an older child is expected to take responsibility for the younger children.

Parent–child role reversals can place inappropriate responsibility on children, interfering with normal development. Such children are likely to grow up as adults who feel responsible for the needs and feelings of other people at the expense of their own. In relationships, they may blame themselves for the problems of others. They may become stressed, or, as Elkind (1981) warns, too "hurried." Many anxiety sufferers have this personality trait—an overly responsible attitude and tendency to fill in for others at their own expense. One example was a woman who indicated that she could never take a day off from work, even when she was sick. A child-care worker, she would feel too responsible and guilty about burdening other staff with the workload. On one occasion, however, when she was so sick that going to work was just not possible, *she* sent flowers to her co-workers to cheer them up!

A *family secret* consists of information that is withheld from the children, due to shame or a desire to protect them. Suicide or mental illness of a relative, an extramarital affair, sexual abuse of a child by a parent, an out-of-wedlock child, adoption, alcoholism, or a crime committed by a family member are examples of family secrets. Such hidden information can contribute to anxiety in children when they intuitively sense that something does not fit together or is being avoided. Indeed, confusion and uncertainty are some of the most powerful anxiety producers.

Although not necessarily in the category of a family secret, some children are exposed to the idea that people can "go crazy" or "lose their minds." This may take place by hearing of people who were taken to a mental hospital or insane asylum. This idea can be frightening to children and become imprinted as a fear that under certain circumstances it could happen to them. This, of course, would add to the anxiety a person might experience later in life, especially when thought processes are out of control.

A family with *many rules and rigid patterns* creates an inflexible atmosphere that does not match up with the real world. Children who were raised with the idea that there is only one way to do things will have difficulty coping with situations involving choices or requiring flexibility. Such children may develop a problem with "shoulds"—a tendency to be compulsive about what must be done and how it is to be done. This can lead to stress and interfere with spontaneity and the ability to accept change.

Having reviewed these family background factors, you may now want to study the CHAANGE program's anxiety development chart, shown in Figure 3–2. Note those factors that apply to your family background, and see if your anxiety seems to have a developmental history.

We have now looked at the family background experiences that shape the personality of people who tend to develop problems with stress and anxiety. The combination of these biological and family factors results in a type of personality that could be called the "anxiety personality." In the next chapter, we turn to this type of personality to understand how it leads to problems with stress, fear, and anxiety. After the next chapter, you may want to return to the anxiety development chart and find those personality traits that apply to you.

FIGURE 3–2: CHAANGE PROGRAM'S ANXIETY DEVELOPMENT CHART

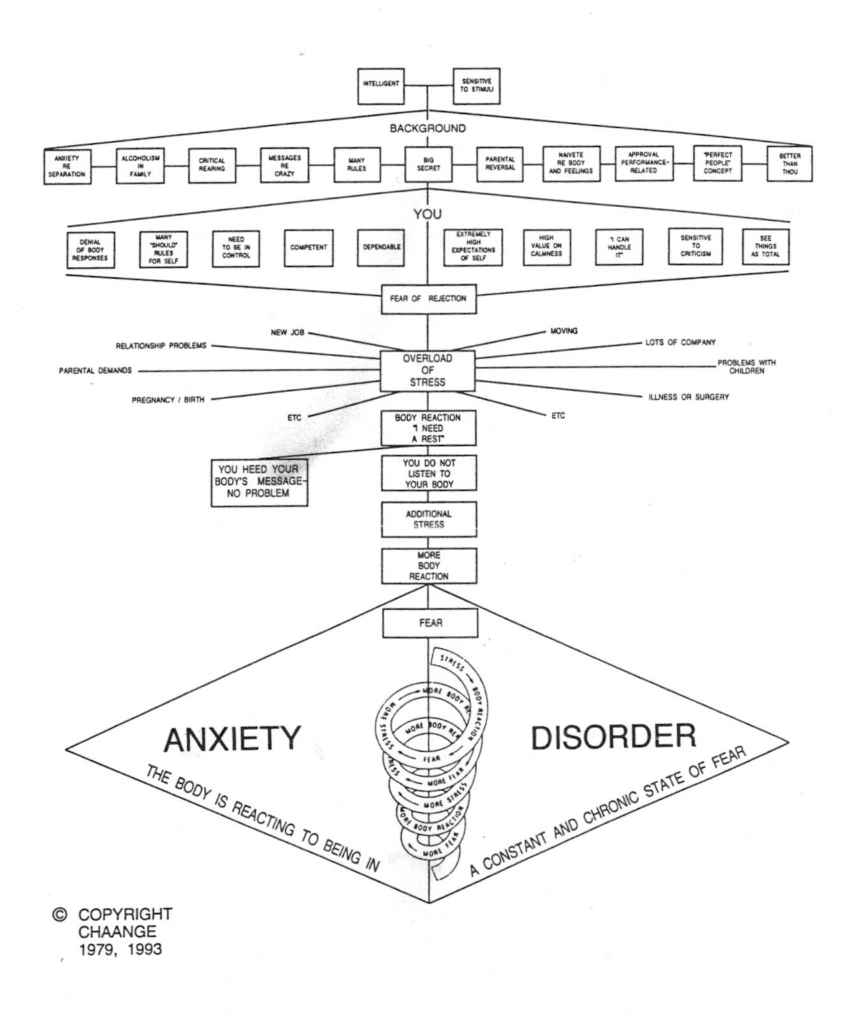

4

Anxiety's Personality

Are you in control of your personality,
or is your personality in control of you?

Personality is the combination of traits and qualities that makes each of us unique, yet there seem to be recognizable types of personalities—people who have certain traits in common. Some psychological tests attempt to determine an individual's personality "type," based on patterns of behavior, thought, and emotional style. In astrology, there are said to be twelve personality types based on their sun signs and other planetary conditions at birth. We all have experiences where we meet someone who seems to fit a particular type of personality, although we may not have a name for it. In this chapter we will explore the personality traits of people who become anxious, noting how this type of personality creates stress and anxiety symptoms. We will view both the positive and negative characteristics of people who develop anxiety.

This discussion pertains to my own personality, as well as to the millions of other people who acquired a particular set of traits as a result of their genetic and family backgrounds. If you identify with the personality type described in this chapter, you will recognize that in many ways you are predisposed to developing an anxiety condition. By the time you have acquired this type of personality, all it takes to trigger anxiety is an overload of stress.

The anxiety-prone personality develops from the combined effects of genetic factors and family background experiences. As one of the key ingredients that creates anxiety, this personality type increases the chances for an anxiety disorder, but only when all ingredients are present. Stress overload is usually the ingredient that determines *when* anxiety will occur in people who are predisposed due to their personality make-up.

Let's examine the traits found in the anxiety-prone personality, one by one. The anxiety-prone person is responsible, dependable, and hard-working. We can be counted on to do what we say and to do a good job. We are also loyal and reliable, and this makes us excellent and valued employees, as well as successful entrepreneurs when we are willing to take risks. Our values and ethics include keeping our word and fulfilling our promises. In part, we are dependable and hard-working because we do not want to disappoint others or let them down. This is related to another trait, our need to please others. Unfortunately, we are not good at setting reasonable goals and limits, or at taking care of ourselves. We often take on too many commitments and responsibilities. Therefore, our potential for burnout, resentment, and symptoms of stress is exceptionally high.

This personality type is perfectionistic. We have high standards and expectations for ourselves. We want to do well in everything, and we are willing to push ourselves to the limit in an effort to meet our own expectations and attain perfection. Combined with our dependability and strong work ethic, we usually achieve excellence in fulfilling our responsibilities, whatever they happen to be. For some, this trait may manifest in the way we keep house, while for others it will be apparent in the competence with which we do our jobs or perform in our professions. Since it is impossible to attain perfection at all times, however, we may find ourselves pushing even harder to reach this goal, or feeling frustrated or disappointed in ourselves when we fail to meet our unreasonably high expectations. It should be obvious that our perfectionism creates stress, but we find it difficult to control this deeply ingrained trait.

Related to high standards and expectations is a tendency towards many *shoulds*. Shoulds are self-imposed expectations about what we ought to do, and the way we ought to do it. Shoulds are usually the expectations our parents—or other influential people in our backgrounds—had for us that we have internalized as part of our personality. Shoulds control our behavior, even when they create stress. Shoulds are sometimes part of the way we try to be good, or to live up to a positive image of ourselves. "I should lose weight, I should read the newspaper more often, I should spend more time with my children, I shouldn't be so sensitive, I should make my bed before I leave the house," are some examples of shoulds. Some good-humored clients of mine will say that they "should on themselves" too much.

The anxiety-prone person seeks approval and reassurance from others. We have an excessive need to receive positive feedback in order to feel secure. Thus, we are "people pleasers," always willing to go the extra mile to be appreciated. At the same time, we are extremely sensitive to criticism and rejection. We try to avoid negative feedback by working hard to please and impress others. We try at all costs to avoid conflict with others, because we do not want anyone to be angry with us or disapprove. As a result, we tend to be somewhat passive in relationships, particularly with people who are in positions of authority, such as supervisors, managers, or anyone who is perceived as an authority. Our need for approval also interferes with our ability to be assertive, even when it is important and appropriate to speak up for ourselves.

Another trait found in the anxiety personality is a tendency to ignore our body signals. Our preoccupation with doing well, looking good and pleasing others, avoiding rejection and criticism, and so on, creates a great deal of stress, but we tend to deny these symptoms and keep going. When our bodies alert us with stress signals, such as fatigue, stress, even hunger or thirst, we may consider them annoying encumbrances. It may not be until our stress warnings intensify into severe physical symptoms that we begin to take notice, but even then we may not realize the connection between our personality style and our physical symptoms. We then focus on the symptoms themselves, often fearing loss of control or a life-threatening illness. This, of course, only makes matters worse by adding to the stress.

Difficulty relaxing is another component of the anxiety-prone personality. Despite our desire to relax, we find it difficult to calm down, take time out, and let go. We are physically active on a continual basis, and our minds are busy almost all the time. High gear is a habit, and it is hard to shift out of gear into neutral. In addition, there is no time to relax when we are busy proving our self-worth, taking care of others, avoiding criticism, and always doing a good job. Some feel anxious immediately upon relaxing because it threatens their sense of control and self-protection. Others simply cannot relax, or believe that relaxation is wasting time. There is, after all, always another item on the "should do" list. To truly let go and relax requires *being,* which is a different attitude from *doing,* as we will discuss in Chapter 8. When we cannot relax, we deprive ourselves of the stress recovery required to live without symptoms.

The need to be in control is a key issue for the anxiety-prone person. As one anxiety client put it, "I'll be the first to admit that I'm a control freak." Control gives us a feeling of power and safety, but in most cases it is based on lack of confidence in our ability to handle ourselves in ambiguous or unstructured situations. In order to feel in control we want to know what is going to happen in the future. But we also want options. We don't like to be pinned down because control means having the choice to leave an uncomfortable situation. On the other hand, we like structure and predictability, the conditions we usually did not have as children. In an effort to be prepared for whatever may happen, we try to predict the future. We worry a lot, as we try to anticipate what may happen in the future. We habitually "what-if," or second-guess the future. Naturally, we tend to focus on all the negative possibilities. It is as if we are continually preparing for threat or danger. Threat includes not just the sudden panic attack or anxiety feelings we fear, but the possibility of criticism, rejection, mistakes, or failure. This all keeps us in a continual state of arousal and fight/flight reaction. Inevitably, our need for control leads to anxiety.

Fear of strong emotions, such as anger, is another feature of the anxiety personality. As discussed in Chapter 2, feelings present a problem for many of us because we were reared in families with inappropriate or limited expression of feelings. Some feelings involve physical arousal similar to the fight/flight response, which contributes to the problem. In addition, anger, guilt, sadness, and other intense feelings—including fear itself—can all be frightening when our skills in handling them are limited. We may fear such strong feelings will take over, last indefinitely, or lead to out-of-control behavior. Anger, for example, may be frightening if in our family history it was associated with violence or out-of-control behavior. Anger also threatens us because we fear disapproval and rejection, and assume that relationships will be jeopardized by conflict or anger.

When feelings are denied or kept inside there is typically a buildup of physical tension. When that tension is not released, an internal pressure builds up. An accumulation of such pressure leads to anxiety, due to fears of losing control emotionally. That condition also triggers anxiety because of its physiological similarity to the fight/flight response, which is normally associated with danger. Thus, our personality creates a paradox in which we deny feelings to prevent anxiety but experience anxiety when we deny our feelings.

Our difficulty with strong feelings leads us to avoid situations that may trigger emotional arousal. Poignant movies, televised news—especially of violence, injury, or suffering—social events, and other stimuli may be avoided in order to maintain our sense of control. In our personal and professional relationships, we also avoid conflict or behavior that might lead to disapproval or rejection. We are careful to not offend, hurt, or anger others because of our extreme sensitivity to how others view us. Thus, we may hide our feelings or go against them, as we seek to keep peace and not make waves. In this way we are sometimes not true to ourselves, and we make choices that are not in our own best interests.

The anxiety-prone person is highly suggestible. This is due in part to our natural sensitivity, which causes us to react strongly to many stimuli, including the feelings and behavior of other people. Thus, we may find ourselves absorbing the concerns of others, or being easily influenced by their desires or needs. Combined with our excessive need for approval and fear of rejection, we are likely to be influenced by those around us.

Above all, we are skilled at hiding many of these traits from the eyes of other people. We cover up these aspects of our personality. We do not want others to be aware of our flaws or inadequacies because we fear they will think less of us or reject us. Our need to impress others to attain approval leads us to pretend we have it all together, whereas in truth we may be anxious or insecure. Many clients I see for treatment report that when they tell others about their anxiety problem, people are typically surprised: "You always seem to be in control. You do your job so well, and you always seem to have it all together. I never would have guessed you feel inadequate or insecure, or have a problem with anxiety."

One of the great ironies of this type of personality is that while we react strongly to stress, we create our own stress. For example, fear of rejection and strong need to please others—so they will like and accept us—causes us frequently to say "yes" when we feel "no." We work hard to earn acceptance and praise. We tend to focus on the needs and feelings of other people, often at our own expense. We typically take on too much and have difficulty setting reasonable limits for ourselves. Thus, these personality traits drive us to symptoms of stress. Then, given our sensitivity and need to feel in control, we may react fearfully to the body's reaction to stress, further intensifying the stress reaction and contributing to an anxiety condition.

For anxiety sufferers, it is usually the first panic attack or severe anxiety episode that draws attention to the link between personality and physical symptoms. The mind–body relationship becomes apparent when a person with anxiety symptoms goes to a medical doctor or hospital emergency room. The typical finding is that there is nothing physically wrong with the body—no organic pathology or diseases are found. Unfortunately, the treatment process usually ends there. While the person may be told that stress or anxiety seems to be the problem, often the anxiety disorder is not properly diagnosed and an appropriate referral to a mental health professional specializing in anxiety treatment is not made. This is tragic, since it is estimated that 80 percent of all complaints seen by physicians are related to anxiety. Although the first step taken by people with anxiety symptoms is to see a doctor, only 25 percent of anxiety sufferers take even this step. Thus, the vast majority of people with anxiety problems never receive the help they need. In part, this is due to the difficulty anxiety sufferers have in asking for help, since that runs against the grain of their personality. However, it is also due to lack of public awareness about anxiety and available treatment, and to inappropriate treatment for those who do seek help.

There is a positive side to this personality type. People with this type of personality tend to be sensitive, caring, nurturing, gentle, and kind. Compassionate and sensitive to the needs of others, we are good listeners and we make good friends. We care about the earth and other living beings, including animals and plants. These qualities may be found in the way we parent, provide community service, and maintain friendships. These traits stem from our innate sensitivity and attunement to our surroundings. Frankly, I would like to see more of these qualities in the world.

Such positive traits were seen in a client who participated in one of my anxiety therapy groups. Phyllis, a friendly and talkative woman, suffered from panic disorder with agoraphobia before she came for help. Her phobic situations were driving and crowded stores. One interesting thing about Phyllis was her ability to take any kind of plant, no matter how neglected and withered, and bring it back to health. She also loved animals. Phyllis would do many thoughtful things in group therapy, such as offering a kind word and remembering the birthdays of other members with a card or little gift.

Some other positive dimensions to this personality type are dependability, dedication, strong work ethic, competence, and high standards of achievement. The individual with this personality profile is typically a valued worker and responsible person. Achievement professionally and competence in home life are characteristic of this personality type, who is always striving for excellence.

Finally, the anxiety-prone personality tends to be spiritually oriented. While I cannot fully explain it, I notice that the majority of anxiety sufferers are people with spiritual inclinations. Surprisingly, many anxiety sufferers have faith in a higher power. This quality may be related to our sensitivity and empathy with all living beings. Perhaps we are spiritually inclined because we have a private inner life that we are reluctant to share with other people. Fortunately, spirituality is a great resource to be drawn upon in anxiety treatment, and I include a separate discussion of this issue in Chapter 20.

To help summarize this analysis of the anxiety-prone personality, I created a table of personality *assets* and *liabilities*. Table 4–1 lists the traits found in the anxiety-prone personality, as well as the positive and negative sides to this personality type.

Overcoming anxiety usually requires a thorough look at the personality traits that contribute to the anxiety condition. While it is not possible, or even desirable, to change our personality altogether, we can become aware of habits and traits that limit us or interfere with healthy behavior. In my own case, I take the view that my personality has many positive aspects, and that I want to modify the negative aspects. I want to be in control of my personality, rather than have my personality be in control of me. For example, I tend to be perfectionistic in everything I do. However, I know that this creates stress, especially when I do not have the time to do everything according to my high standards. I have learned to simply get the job done in some cases, and to be selective about which tasks or projects I will approach with utmost attention to detail. I strive for excellence rather than perfection, and accept

TABLE 4–1: THE ANXIETY PERSONALITY

Responsible/dependable/hard-working

Perfectionistic

High expectations of self

Likes to please others/approval seeking

Suggestible

Fearful of rejection

Sensitive to criticism

Need to be in control

Difficulty relaxing but wants to be calm

Denies body responses and signals

Problem with assertiveness

Black-and-white thinking

Many "shoulds"

"What-if" thinking

Assets	Liabilities
Caring/kind/supportive	Produces high stress
Loyal to friends	Overreacts to stimuli
Outstanding employee/worker	Difficulty setting reasonable limits
Good listener	Not assertive/can be exploited
High achieving	Fear of strong emotions
Spiritually oriented	Becomes resentful

that doing my best sometimes means working within less than ideal conditions.

As we go further into discussion about anxiety treatment, I will offer some techniques and skills for modifying the anxiety- and stress-producing aspects of our type of personality.

5

Dancing Around Anxiety

When we run from circumstances that feel dangerous, we generate additional fear and anxiety.
Wayne Muller, *Legacy of the Heart*

One of our most natural instincts is to run away from situations that are unpleasant or painful. The instinct to avoid is the ***flight*** part of the fight/flight reaction—a form of self-preservation. Because anxiety is unpleasant and painful, we want to avoid it wherever possible. Sometimes we may actually try to fight it—to not let it take control of us. This is the ***fight*** part of the fight/flight reaction, and certainly another form of self-preservation. In this chapter, we will explore a variety of ways in which we attempt to dance around anxiety. The focus will be on the coping patterns that develop before the anxiety sufferer receives proper help. Once anxiety treatment begins, a whole new set of skills can be learned to overcome the condition.

As discussed in Chapters 3 and 4, sensitivity is a key ingredient in the development of anxiety. Weekes (1978) focuses on this aspect of anxiety and offers an explanation for why and how we learn to avoid anxiety. Weekes, who was one of the first to offer hope and help to those suffering from severe anxiety, suggests that in sensitive people the reaction to a fight/flight response can become a greater source of fear than the stress originally triggering the fight/flight response. It is this sensitivity that accounts for the "unusual intensity and disconcerting swiftness" of certain people's reaction to stress. Directing her comments to those suffering from panic disorder with agoraphobia, Weekes explains:

> Most of us have felt the first fear in response to danger. It comes quickly, is normal in intensity and passes with the danger. However, the sensitized person's first fear is so electric, so out of proportion to the danger causing it, he usually recoils from it and at the same time adds a second flash—*fear of the first fear*. He is usually more concerned with the feeling of panic than with the original danger. And because sensitization prolongs the first flash, the second may seem to join it and the two fears are experienced as one. Hence the agoraphobic's bewilderment at the duration of the panic and his inability to cope with it. [p. 362]

In view of the "unusual intensity and disconcerting swiftness" of the sensitized person's fear of the fight/flight response, it is not surprising that anxiety is avoided wherever possible. Fears of losing control, going crazy, having a life-threatening illness, or public embarrassment are all part of the "second fear" triggered by everyday anxiety or stress. We dance around anxiety to avoid both the fight/flight response itself and the secondary fears that so readily follow. In Chapter 12, we will look at the opposite approach—facing our fears—as an essential step in overcoming anxiety.

Many everyday experiences involve the same body activation as the fight/flight response. Consider, for example, the autonomic arousal involved in sexual excitement: heart rate increases, breathing intensifies, body temperature rises, perspiration is profuse, muscles become tense, and the entire experience escalates during arousal until orgasm is reached. Another example is exercise, during which heart rate and respiration increase, perspiration is profuse, body temperature rises, and so on. These are virtually the same reactions as the fight/flight response, although they are not triggered by stress or danger. Most people do not perceive these body reactions as a sign of stress or danger, but for the sensitized person this type of reaction can trigger an anxiety cycle.

Some anxiety symptoms are actually attempts to avoid anxiety. Worrying, for example, is an attempt to anticipate events in order to prepare for what might happen and feel in control. Similarly, compulsive behaviors, such as double-checking and hoarding things, are ways some try to prevent anxiety. Avoidance of phobic situations—the distinguishing feature of agoraphobia—is another way to circumvent anxiety anticipated in driving, social gatherings, being alone, public speaking, standing on lines, or other situations. Some of these patterns do, in fact, succeed in warding off anxiety. Dancing around anxiety does provide a temporary feeling of safety and control, but there is also an ever-present fear of losing that control to anxiety.

On the other hand, the goal of anxiety therapy is to learn how to overcome the fear of fear. True anxiety recovery is achieved only when you no longer fear the body's reactions to stress. You must recognize these reactions for what they are, and develop confidence in your ability to handle them. Anxiety recovery allows you to flow with it, rather than fight it or fear it. When you overcome the fear of fear, you can dance *with* it rather than *around* it.

All anxiety avoidance mechanisms involve energy output and defensive activity. Being on the alert creates more stress and fight/flight reactions. In the sensitized person, these stress reactions tend to produce more anxiety. Dancing around anxiety, therefore, stimulates the very anxiety that it is designed to avoid.

The steps we take to dance around anxiety are known as *defense mechanisms*. The purpose of defense mechanisms is self-protection, or avoidance of unpleasant emotional experiences, such as feeling vulnerable or out of control. To a certain extent, we need to employ defense mechanisms to function effectively in daily life. For example, to be productive at work we may need to temporarily *deny* a personal problem, which might otherwise distract us and interfere with our concentration. In order to complete a boring or unpleasant task we may need to *suppress* our feelings about it, or use *distraction*. However, the ongoing fear of fear in the sensitized person leads to extreme use of defense mechanisms, interfering with performance in other areas of life. Excessive reliance on defense mechanisms can restrict emotional life, creativity, and intimacy in relationships. It can also lead to physical illness.

There are a variety of defense mechanisms used to protect ourselves from feelings of vulnerability. As we consider them, think about which defense mechanisms you use to protect yourself from vulnerability and unpleasant feelings, including anxiety.

Perhaps the most common anxiety defense mechanism is *avoidance* of situations in which anxiety is anticipated. If you are fearful of conflict, for example, you may avoid expressing your honest feelings, even when it is in your best interest to do so. If you anticipate anxiety or discomfort in social situations, you are likely to avoid gatherings of people, parties, or other social events. Similarly, any situation in which you anticipate feeling anxious or vulnerable may be handled by physically avoiding those situations. Avoiding an anxiety-arousing situation *is* often helpful in preventing unpleasant feelings, but only at the price of life restriction. Avoidance limits freedom and spontaneity, and often creates dependency on others in order to feel safe in certain situations. Depression also tends to develop from excessive avoiding as your comfort zone shrinks.

Frances, a 49-year-old woman who sought my help for panic disorder with agoraphobia, illustrates these issues. To feel in control, Frances avoided church, going alone far from home, driving over bridges, and driving on high, twisty roads. She was unable to do many things due to her travel anxiety, which was a problem even when she had someone with her. Her anxiety level was extremely high, and at the outset of treatment she reported an average of six panic episodes per week. At the beginning of therapy Frances commented, "My condition frustrates and aggravates me. It makes me feel helpless and hopeless because it hasn't seemed to respond to any of the many attempts I've made to understand or cure it. When anxiety isn't troubling me, I feel good—things are funny, life seems interesting and sweet. When anxiety is in control of me, I feel as if I'm descending into a pit. I feel like a helpless little girl and can't imagine how I'd exist without my husband. My feelings of dependence also make me feel depressed."

Intellectualization, another defense mechanism, involves separating and distancing feelings from thoughts. You can spot intellectualization by its emphasis on words, abstract knowledge, logic, and a retreat from emotions and interpersonal relationships. Intellectualization also allows "objective" focus on "theoretical" issues, rather than feelings. With this mechanism, you may say you are "probably" angry, sad, afraid, hurt, or depressed, without actually experiencing these feelings. With intellectualization, you are removed from feelings, even though you can still talk about them.

Intellectualization can be advantageous in coping with anxiety, because it puts uncomfortable feelings at a distance. However, intellectualization is not selective—all feelings are blocked by this defense mechanism. Therefore, the price paid for use of intellectualization is a loss of positive *and* negative feelings. Joy, pleasure, passion, love, and empathy are not readily available to the person who relies on intellectualization. In addition, excessive reliance on intellectualization interferes with intimacy and warmth in relationships.

Repression is involved to some extent in all defense mechanisms. In repression, uncomfortable feelings or thoughts are completely blocked out of awareness, resulting in an inability to identify what you feel or think about certain experiences. This mechanism can develop in people whose families prohibited emotional expression or frequently criticized a child's ideas. Repression is also responsible for people losing memory of painful experiences or traumas. Repression can be adaptive by putting childhood pain out of memory, but when used extensively it can become an emotional style that persists into adulthood where it no longer serves its original purpose. While repression may shield you from anxious feelings, it can make it difficult to have *any* feelings.

Feelings can be thought of as emotionally charged energy. When placed in storage by defense mechanisms, the emotional charge builds up as additional feelings are added. At a certain threshold, the emotional pressure reaches a critical level. Two options are then available. The first is an unregulated release of feelings, which may occur when more feelings are added to the existing overload. In this case, the expression of feelings may be out of proportion to the situation, and you may feel out of control. Moodiness, irritability, depression, impatience, and explosiveness result from this pattern.

The second option is a more gradual implosion of feelings, in the form of somatic symptoms such as indigestion, ulcers, muscular tension, headaches, and other physical ailments. The more successful you are at avoiding feelings, the more likely you are to develop physical symptoms having no apparent cause. This, too, will add to your anxiety.

A variation of repression is a defense mechanism known as *suppression.* Suppression consists of *conscious* stuffing and storing of feelings, putting feelings aside rather than facing them. Some reliance on defense mechanisms is necessary for daily functioning, and suppression is useful for this reason. For example, suppression can be adaptive when you ignore anxiety in facing a phobic situation. When suppression of feelings becomes a habit, however, it can backfire in the form of emotional and physical symptoms.

Another defense mechanism involving avoidance of feelings is *denial*. Denial consists of censorship of feelings, along with an effort to hide them from others. When feelings are denied, however, they are often apparent to others. You may deny that you are angry, for example, but your feelings may be apparent as you slam a door or shout at someone. Denial of anxiety is difficult to accomplish because of the intensity of physical arousal and secondary fears. Nevertheless, it is common for people with anxiety to hide their feelings from others. Dancing around anxiety often involves projecting an appearance of control, while inside feeling out of control.

Control, of course, is a core issue for the anxiety sufferer. The fear of losing control is what makes us feel vulnerable, frightened, and in need of ways to protect ourselves. Dancing around anxiety using defense mechanisms is trying to maintain control when we feel we may lose it. It should not be surprising, therefore, that *controlling* behavior is another defense mechanism. There are two directions controlling behavior can take. First, you may try to control your own feelings and behavior. You take few (if any) risks and you try to avoid making any mistakes. You may also avoid new experiences because you cannot predict the outcome. You want to know in advance what is going to happen, and you do not like surprises or changes. If you fear rejection and disapproval, you control your feelings so that no one will be upset with you. In short, you strive to be in control of yourself at all times. As with other defense mechanisms, too much control restricts your quality of life. With too much control, you gain safety and predictability at the expense of growth and development.

The second form of controlling behavior consists of attempts to control other people and the world around you in order to feel in control of yourself. If you are anxious or uncomfortable about traveling or shopping alone, for example, you may manipulate someone else into keeping you company, or you may do things for other people in an effort to have them need you. You may even reverse the dance by expressing disapproval, becoming angry, or withdrawing when others do not do what you want. There is a hidden desperation in your attempt to control others, as if your survival rests on being in control.

To achieve control, anxiety sufferers often use another defense mechanism, known as *reaction formation*. A variation of denial, this interesting mechanism involves disguising feelings behind their opposites. When you are angry, for example, you may act "nice." When you are depressed or sad, you may smile. When you feel inadequate, you may emphasize your competence. When you are feeling insecure, you may project self-confidence. When you are feeling anxious or out of control, you may present yourself as strong and in control.

There are several pitfalls in the use of reaction formation as a defense against anxiety. The first is increased pressure to keep up the appearance of being in control. After all, that is what others expect based on the image you project. As the discrepancy increases between what you feel inside and what you portray on the outside, your anxiety may increase. Second, you are less likely to receive the reassurance and support you need when no one knows how you really feel. Furthermore, if you hide your anxiety behind an appearance of having it all together, others will be less likely to offer help when you need it.

Projection is another mechanism by which we dance around anxiety. Schafer (1954) describes projection as "a process by which an objectionable internal tendency is unrealistically attributed to another person or other objects in the environment instead of being recognized as part of one's self" (p. 279). Projection is the basis of your judgmental or critical attitude towards others, whom you may perceive as inadequate, imperfect, stupid, or defective in some way. You may be critical of yourself, but project it onto others as a way of denying it in yourself.

You may also project your anxiety or fear onto objects in the environment. This happens in virtually all anxiety disorders. The internal sensations of fear are attributed to places or situations that are assumed to be responsible for the fear. As discussed in Chapter 2, however, it is not the situation or place that causes anxiety. It is the anticipation of fearful feelings in those settings and the prospect of losing control of yourself under those conditions that causes the anxiety. Projection contributes to the anxiety it is used to avoid.

One final mechanism, *sublimation,* deserves attention. Sublimation consists of channeling an uncomfortable feeling into an activity, drawing attention away from the troublesome feeling but at the same time giving expression to it. There are often elements of reaction formation and denial involved in sublimation. For example, the sensitive personality sublimates the fear of rejection and criticism by engaging in efforts to please others. Another example is when anxious feelings are sublimated into activities involving daring, risk, or courage. This defense mechanism was illustrated by Beth, a woman in her twenties with panic disorder and agoraphobia, who tried repeatedly to conquer her fear by going alone on wilderness camping trips. At home, she was often unable to get to the mailbox. When she asked me why her outward-bound strategy did not help her overcome her anxiety, I answered by asking what she experienced on those challenging trips. She said they were "torture," which explained the problem. Beth was not developing any skills or confidence from her wilderness trips. On the contrary, these experiences were making her condition worse by reinforcing her lack of control over anxiety.

One of the most intriguing aspects of the dance around anxiety is the resistance to change observed in many people during their therapy. Logically, it would be expected that anxiety sufferers would do whatever they could to overcome the condition, especially when following a step-by-step recovery program, such as CHAANGE. However, there is often a hesitation to recover, an ambivalence about succeeding, a resistance to change. I have identified several reasons for this paradox.

First is the fear of failing at recovery. This fear can be strong in perfectionistic people, who have lofty standards and high pressure to meet them. It is common for perfectionistic people to hold back or procrastinate, not only in anxiety recovery but also in other efforts, such as losing weight or studying in school. Second, the anxiety sufferer tends to be impatient, giving up easily when results are not immediate. This may be related to low self-esteem and belief that change is not really possible. Third, some anxiety sufferers experience frustration and difficulty with the relaxation phase of treatment. Relaxation is a problem for many anxiety sufferers because it requires learning to let go of control. Letting go may be equated with being out of control.

There may also be some *secondary gains* involved in some cases of severe anxiety. The anxiety sufferer may benefit in some subtle way from the impairment or limitations created by anxiety. For example, some sufferers receive caring, support, and attention from loved ones, which they fear may be lost as they recover and become more independent. In one case, a woman revealed a concern that her husband would no longer go places with her if she overcame her driving phobia. In other cases, an anxiety disorder may justify avoiding responsibilities, such as grocery shopping, managing money, answering the telephone, or attending parent–teacher conferences. These responsibilities would have to be faced if anxiety were no longer a limiting condition.

We have explored some of the mechanisms by which we cope with, or dance around, anxiety. In many cases, the defense mechanisms do protect us from anxiety, bringing temporary relief. In most cases, however, dancing around anxiety only postpones the recovery process. Sacrificing intimacy and warmth in relationships due to excessive intellectualization, for example, is a high price to pay for avoiding feelings of anxiety. Developing a physical illness due to frequent stuffing and storing of feelings is another unreasonable consequence of the avoidance dance.

What is the alternative to dancing around anxiety? Are there more effective methods for dealing with it? Anxiety can be overcome through learning the right skills, such as relaxation, dealing comfortably with feelings, changing internal dialogue, effective communication, and developing confidence and faith in your ability to handle whatever may happen in life. All of these methods and skills share one common denominator. They are based on learning how to face anxiety rather than dance around it. When you acquire the necessary skills, you can dance without fear.

6

Anxiety in Children

Anxiety cripples learning and the growth of intelligence.

Joseph Chilton Pearce, *Magical Child*

Some experts call today's children the "shell-shocked" generation. Traumas such as divorce and family breakdown, crime and violence, drug abuse, AIDS, and a failing school system are affecting our children and producing anxiety in many cases. Fifty years ago, there were no known suicides under the age of 14, but today a child attempts suicide every 78 seconds, with cases as young as 3 years of age. One hundred thirty-five thousand children carry guns and thirty children are hit with bullets every day, leaving ten of them dead on a daily basis. A million children are hospitalized each year due to physical abuse by their parents, and each year another five thousand children are actually killed by their own parents.

An estimated three million children and teenagers suffer from anxiety severe enough to affect their school attendance, academic motivation, learning ability, memory, concentration and attention, and sleep. Severe anxiety in children is a far-reaching problem because it diminishes intellectual, emotional and social development. Many learning-impaired children have anxiety disorders, and many children and adolescents with behavior problems are suffering from the effects of stress and anxiety. Without appropriate help, most of these children and adolescents will grow up to be anxious adults.

Left untreated, most children with anxiety will continue to show anxiety as adults, although not all adults who develop anxiety showed anxiety as children. When the backgrounds of adult anxiety sufferers are considered, a common pattern of predisposing childhood experiences is evident, as discussed in Chapter 3. While these background factors predispose children toward anxiety disorders later in life, in many cases the anxiety begins to manifest in childhood. In this chapter, we will take a closer look at how and why anxiety develops in children, and how child anxiety can be diagnosed and treated.

The mental health field is beginning to realize that there is a continuity in anxiety disorders from childhood to adulthood. Anxiety disorders that are identifiable in children, such as school phobia or separation anxiety, may appear to be different from anxiety disorders in adults, but the basic disposition towards anxiety begins in childhood and continues throughout the life cycle. The ingredients that cause an anxiety disorder to develop—biological sensitivity, a specific personality style shaped by family background, and stress—are the same for children and adults.

Only the *form* or *expression* of anxiety varies with age and maturation. It would, therefore, be useful to think of the disposition towards anxiety as continuous across the life-span, even though the expression of fear and anxiety may appear to be distinctive from one stage of life to another. Indeed, it is now understood that children and adults are equally susceptible to many of the same anxiety disorders, such as post-traumatic stress disorder, panic disorder, obsessive-compulsive disorder, phobic disorders, and acute stress disorder.

The continuity in anxiety from childhood to adulthood was recognized in the most recent revision to the *Diagnostic and Statistical Manual of Mental Disorders* (1994). In this internationally used guide for diagnosing emotional disorders, anxiety conditions are no longer different for children and adults, with one exception. All of the anxiety disorders, except separation anxiety, apply to both children and adults, using the same symptoms and diagnostic criteria. This refinement represents a major step in our understanding of children's anxiety because it recognizes that children react physically and emotionally to stress in the same ways as adults, and because it recognizes that adult anxiety has its roots in childhood. This implies that adult anxiety can, to a great extent, be prevented by changing the way children are reared. Another implication is that we can help heal adult anxiety by filling in what should have occurred in childhood, such as building self-confidence, teaching certain social and self-control skills, mind–body education, and allowing relaxation and play.

Anxiety in children involves the same mind–body dynamics as anxiety in adults. Stress produces physical arousal reactions, such as elevated heart rate, higher blood pressure, muscular tension, and increased glandular and hormone activity. Chronic stress produces chronic arousal, leading to the next stage of warning signals: difficulty concentrating, memory impairment, fatigue, physical complaints, fears and phobias, and difficulty relaxing. In school, these symptoms may show up as low motivation, deterioration in academic achievement, or school avoidance.

Child development unfolds in stages, a pattern recognized by virtually all child development theories as well as by common observation. Each stage of development involves new learning, building upon the foundation of skills and experiences acquired during previous stages. This was recognized by Freud (1935) in children's emotional development, by Erikson (1950) in children's social development, by Piaget (1952) in cognitive development, and by Steiner (1947, 1975) in spiritual development. Through child study and brain research we know that nature provides a template for child development, a predetermined sequence of stages during which specific input must occur for successful growth. Within each stage, the brain develops new structures—additional brain cells and connecting pathways—that allow for new learning, and in each stage there must be appropriate stimuli, experiences, and models for development to reach its highest potential.

Virtually all human skills and capacities develop according to this basic plan. Hearing, speech and language, motor development, self-confidence, trust, abstract reasoning, imagination, moral development, and spirituality all develop in stages, each requiring appropriate input at the appropriate times. A simple illustration is the development of speech and language. A child who is biologically ready for speech input between the ages of 1 and 4 or 5, will acquire the language of the models to whom he or she is exposed. Thus, a French-speaking family produces a French-speaking child, and a Japanese family produces a Japanese-speaking child. Animal research has demonstrated that if young songbirds are separated from mature songbirds during their language acquisition stage, they will miss the learning opportunity and *never* acquire birdsong, even after being reunited with mature singing birds. In humans, certain skills are more readily learned during certain stages of development because the human brain has specific agendas at specific stages according to a basic plan for survival of the species.

The stages of child development are called *critical periods*, because the match between biological readiness and environmental input is a relatively narrow window of opportunity. Within each stage, the required environmental input must coincide with developing brain structures for the child to acquire new skills and abilities. If a developmental stage is not successfully completed, the development of abilities in subsequent stages will be jeopardized. On the other hand, if development is disrupted at any stage, it may be possible to compensate later, though generally not to the full potential.

Anxiety in children begins when nature's plan for development is disrupted or mismanaged. Our first concern is with the stage of bonding between mother and child, which begins in utero. During embryonic development, mother and child are intimately connected in a biological relationship in which the child depends on the mother's body for oxygen, growth nutrients, disease prevention, and so on. "Communication" between mother and child also takes place during pregnancy, long before verbal interaction occurs. Such communication occurs at a cellular level, through the sympathetic pulsing of the heart cells of mother and embryo. This has been demonstrated in the laboratory: if two living heart cells are placed a distance apart on a microscopic slide, they will pulsate randomly, each at its own rate. However, if moved closer together (they do not have to touch) they will arc the gap between them and "communicate" with each other by pulsing in unison, as one heart. At another level of communication, the infant in utero responds immediately with body movements to sounds from the mother and the surrounding environment. Those movements, it turns out, match precisely the mother's sound inputs in a predictable one-to-one pattern. Thus, the bonding process between mother and child begins long before birth.

The embryonic stage ends with birth, an event which all too often destroys the mother–child bond and marks the beginning of anxiety in children. Nature accounted for the separation of mother and child at birth in a number of ingenious ways. One is the length of the umbilical cord, which averages 26 inches, just the right length to allow the infant to be held to the mother's breast without damaging this reserve lifeline. The umbilical cord not only provides for continued supply of blood and oxygen during the transition from womb to world, but also allows for continuity of bonding through uninterrupted physical contact between infant and mother. Premature separation of the child from the mother disrupts the bonding process and sets the stage for anxiety, as is often the case in contemporary childbirth practices where the umbilical cord is cut almost immediately after birth, followed by separation of mother and child.

Breastfeeding is another one of nature's mechanisms for protecting and enhancing the bonding process. Unfortunately, in many cases this is a missed opportunity, particularly in families with working mothers. In an effort to shorten the period of infant dependency and enable the mother to return to work from her brief maternity leave, breastfeeding may be replaced by formula feeding, and physical contact may be replaced by day care. Deprivation of physical contact between infant and mother (or primary caretaker) sacrifices a basic requirement for the development of security and trust, and contributes to anxiety in children. Economic pressures on working parents may thus be one of the first causes of separation anxiety in children. On the other hand, the bonding process can take place with consistent caretakers other than a biological parent. This is a major cultural issue, considering that about 70 percent of all preschoolers spend five days a week in day-care settings.

It is interesting to note that in Sweden working mothers receive a government-guaranteed maternity leave for one year with full pay, so that they may remain in close proximity to their children during the critical period for security and trust. Recently, this guarantee was extended to fathers as well. In that country, it is apparently recognized that a financial investment by the government in preserving the crucial parent–child bond will pay off through prevention of the costly consequences of breaking the bond prematurely. Those consequences include symptoms of stress and anxiety, which require medical and psychological treatment as well as other costly social services required in a society with many "unbonded" citizens. In the United States, we have begun to move in this direction with flexible job hours, part-time employment, job sharing, and day care for children at the workplace.

The birth experience is a child's first encounter with all-out arousal and stress. Nature programs the infant for this potentially traumatic event through the timed release of adrenal steroids, those same fight/flight arousal hormones that are released in response to fear. This activates and prepares the infant for the first, and perhaps greatest, survival challenge in life. The instinctive fight/flight response prepares the infant for the short but stressful descent down the narrow birth canal, by contracting its body for efficient passage. At the same time, other hormones are released to prepare the brain for new learning during the next stage after birth.

What about the various methods of delivering children into the world, and their potential for producing anxiety and fear? In societies that are more in touch with nature, childbirth tends to be a routine event performed within the family or tribal setting, with continuity of contact between mother and infant. There is virtually no separation of child from mother in these instances. For example, Pearce (1977) reports that the Australian aboriginal mother retreats from tribal activities, digs a hole in the sand, delivers her baby, puts her infant against her breast, and rejoins her tribe. She is gone approximately 20 minutes. Similarly, Pearce observes that the Ugandan mother follows her usual routines until a few minutes before the baby emerges, retires to a place of privacy, squats, delivers her young with the help of a midwife, and resumes her ordinary activities with her baby on her back within the hour.

In stark contrast, the American practice of childbirth has been medicalized to the point where it is treated like a disease. Historically, childbirth became a hospital-based procedure within the past 50 to 75 years, in conjunction with the rise of industrial-technological society. Before World War II, 97 percent of all childbirths occurred at home, but now the same percent of childbirths take place in hospitals. In some states, home births are illegal. Strangely enough, however, hospital births are no safer than home births, and some studies even suggest that there is a greater percentage of complications and deaths associated with hospital births in spite of their technological advantage. As Arms (1975) reports, the entire procedure of childbirth is often delayed and complicated by the use of drugs, particularly anesthetics, which counteract the action-oriented surge of adrenaline naturally produced by the mother and used by the infant to assist in moving efficiently through the birth canal to delivery. As a result, the delivery process may become seriously prolonged and, therefore, more extended in its painfulness. The situation frequently spirals into an anxiety-ridden experience for both mother and infant, a crisis that is often managed by additional medication. The birth experience may be further complicated by the use of mechanical interventions, such as forceps and suction devices, which are risky to the fragile brain casing of the newborn infant, or by surgical procedures such as episiotomies that are risky for the mother. Birth is potentially traumatic under the best circumstances, but when natural childbirth is replaced by institutional childbirth, the results can be disastrous as far as anxiety is concerned.

Perhaps the most anxiety-arousing aspect of an unnatural childbirth is the separation of the mother and child at birth, a common practice in hospital-based delivery until recent years. Because nature's timing is highly specific, such separation interferes with signals for the child's relaxation and recovery from the stress of birth. The immediate contact of the infant with the warmth and heartbeat of the mother's chest triggers the relaxation response. Without that contact and relaxation response, the first disruption in nature's developmental plan takes place, along with the beginning of the child's anxiety template. Fortunately, hospital-based childbirth has come a long way in many communities, where birthing rooms are set up to create a more natural and comfortable environment, and where mother and child, as well as family and friends, can remain together.

Physical contact with the newborn child has crucial biological purposes. In the animal world, if an infant is separated from its mother for any length of time, the mother will not recognize the infant when it is returned and may refuse to nurture it. If the separation occurs at birth and lasts for more than a few hours, the infant will probably not survive. With cats, the licking of kittens by their mother stimulates the development of a brain structure called the reticular formation. Without the licking stimulation, the reticular formation does not fully develop, development is jeopardized, and the kitten will be unable to process sensory information.

As a parent, I felt strongly enough about these issues to want the birth of my two children to take place at home. Due to my anxiety about going completely natural, my first child was born at a birth center, where I participated in delivering our baby. After removing her from her mother's body, I stared with awe into her eyes and whispered her name, placed her on her mother's breast, and at the appropriate time, cut her umbilical cord. Our second child was born in our bedroom at home, under the supervision of a midwife and with the support of close friends. I believe that direct participation in childbirth connects parents in an irreversible way to their children. In my case, that connection—a deep emotional bond—persists strongly to this day and I cannot imagine it diminishing. This profound bond helps me deal with the stress of raising children and keeps me motivated when the going gets rough. I believe that if all parents participated directly in the birthing of their children, child abuse would be reduced, the divorce rate would drop, and much anxiety in children would be prevented.

At birth, there is only one thing a child can visually recognize (besides light and dark) and that is the human face. This is another example of nature's plan for human survival. Studies indicate that the face needs to be within 6 to 12 inches of the child's eyes to be recognizable. This requires the mother or caretaker to be at close range, within a foot of the child, to maintain the bonding process. During the early stages of bonding after birth, the child spends up to 80 percent of his or her waking time focused on that human face, if it is present, and can track its movements around the room. Deprive the child of the recognizable stimulus of the human face at close range and he or she will show symptoms of anxiety and distress. This bonding mechanism is reciprocal. As the parent responds to the child's eye contact, a repertoire of cooing and attention-giving behaviors on the part of the parent is activated.

Face recognition is only one of nature's mechanisms for bonding, as is evidenced by the fact that blind children can bond to their parents. Another mechanism is skin-to-skin, physical contact between child and parents. This may be the most crucial requirement for bonding, security, trust, reassurance, and anxiety prevention.

The developing child's agenda is to acquire knowledge about the world and the self. Strong and positive bonding helps the child to know the world and human relationships as safe, predictable within limits, and worthy of trust. To a great extent, successful bonding immunizes the child against future anxiety. Furthermore, successful bonding is the foundation for the child's identity as lovable, worthy of attention, and powerful. This is the basis for self-esteem, and without it all future praise and positive reinforcement will leak through this hole in the bucket.

On the other hand, an unhealthy degree of attachment between parent and child occurs in some cases, which interferes with normal development and fosters anxiety. Due to separation anxiety on the part of parents, or their concern about a child's ability to function independently, normal exploratory behavior and interaction with the world may be discouraged. When a parent projects his or her own insecurity, vulnerability, or need for protection onto the child, the child absorbs that anxiety, with resulting fear and guilt about growth and independence. Such unhealthy attachment is common in single-parent families, particularly custodial parents following a divorce, who may turn to one of the children for friendship and companionship. This puts a burden of responsibility on the child, who is likely to develop stress symptoms and anxiety.

All developmental stages require appropriate environmental input for normal physical, emotional, and intellectual growth of the child. Experiences and input must match the child's stage of readiness and ability to assimilate and accommodate. When environmental input is not appropriate—if it is overwhelming or exceeds the child's capabilities—the child is stressed and anxiety results.

This issue is most apparent in the schools, where learning demands do not always synchronize with the developmental capacities of children. In a typical classroom of twenty or more children, it is unrealistic to expect all of them to be at the same point of readiness for the same tasks and learning activities. Some children will naturally be slower than others, not necessarily due to lower intelligence, but because they are not developmentally ready for the tasks presented. Stress and anxiety result from expecting children to perform intellectual tasks that are beyond their current capacities. Premature learning produces anxiety, and anxiety in turn cripples learning. Anxiety interferes with learning because it blocks short-term memory and shuts off attention and concentration ability. Children with anxiety fall behind in school, further reinforcing their anxiety and lowering their self-esteem.

Before the age of 7, the developing child does not have the ability to think abstractly because the required brain structures, such as the *corpus callosum*, have not yet formed. In many schools, however, reading and conceptual math are introduced in kindergarten, despite evidence that the human brain is not prepared for the skills involved in these complex tasks until approximately 7 years of age. The practice of teaching math and reading to kindergartners, and in some cases to preschoolers, contributes to anxiety in children. Although it is possible to teach some 4- and 5-year-olds these skills, the imaginative and magical elements of childhood are sacrificed in the process. Studies by Piaget (1952, 1962) and others have demonstrated that a wide, rich imaginative life is the foundation for language and other conceptual skills. The best way to assure that children will gain higher cognitive skills is to work on them indirectly through motor skills, imaginative play, and artistic expression until approximately age 7.

In addition, the developmental tasks of kindergarten children revolve around social interaction and group play. Introducing cognitive demands directly at this age can interfere with acquisition of social skills, which are essential for learning in groups and future participation in work teams. Successful preparation of children for life requires going through nature's developmental stages, with appropriate input at the predetermined pace.

Anxiety blocks learning in a number of ways. All learning involves moving from the known to the unknown, from the familiar to the unfamiliar. To make this shift, the brain must have the necessary structures in place, and the personality must be secure enough to take risks. Assuming that the brain is sufficiently developed for a new learning task, the child must be comfortable with trying something new, with stretching beyond known abilities. In addition, the child must be willing to make errors and mistakes, since that is a necessary feedback mechanism in all learning. The secure child, who has established a sense of basic safety and self-confidence, can face new learning without anxiety.

When the outcome of a new learning task is unknown, the brain signals a "danger" situation, and the hormone system responds with adrenaline to activate the learner to rise to the challenge. Within limits, this adrenaline reaction is necessary and helpful, as it prepares the learner by increasing energy, alertness, attention, and concentration. However, beyond that helpful limit arousal interferes with learning, as the fight/flight response focuses on survival. In the survival mode, all resources are reserved for combating the "enemy," which for many children is the learning environment itself. For the insecure child who has experienced abandonment, uncertainty, and frustration of basic needs, this can become a chronic state that paralyzes learning.

Some educational systems recognize these risks and have developed curriculums with greater sensitivity to the stages of child development. Such programs slow down the introduction of certain skills and tasks, and focus on nurturing the basic capacities of social trust, imagination, and artistic expression. One example is the Waldorf school system, an international movement with over 600 schools (160 in North America). In this approach, children are educated gently through a sequence of learning experiences that parallel the history of man. First there is storytelling, followed by drawings, in which the imagination is given expression on paper. Reading and writing are taught in a series of stages that correspond to oral teachings, pictographs, and finally to written language. In contrast to most curriculums where reading is introduced in kindergarten or even in preschool, Waldorf education introduces reading in the first grade. It has been found that children in this system not only catch up to their public school peers but are spared the frustration, school anxiety, and learning difficulties so common in schools today. In addition, Waldorf education discourages television viewing in the early years because it interferes with the development of visual thinking and imagination, the capacities that are so crucial to reading, problem solving, and other cognitive abilities. Technology is also postponed until basic reading, writing, and arithmetic reasoning skills are in place, again corresponding to human evolution. This approach to education extends childhood and allows a slower unfolding of abilities, which reduces the risk of anxiety.

Another example is the Williston Central School, a public school in Vermont that offers an innovative approach to education based on a "developmentally appropriate learning" philosophy. In this model, each child is viewed as an individual and assisted in learning along a continuum of skills without comparison to other children. In fact, there are no numerical grades from kindergarten through eighth grade. The program acknowledges that children do not develop at the same rate, and that even within the same child intellectual, physical, social, and emotional development do not always unfold at an even rate. Children are, therefore, grouped into multi-age "families of learners," consisting of four grades in each "house," and permitted to learn from one another by watching, listening, and modeling. This structure also allows teachers to spend several years with each child and the family, fostering bonding and a long-term view of development. Instead of direct teaching of information to students, the "facilitators" guide students in using resources to seek, access, and apply knowledge. Each child has a personalized educational plan based on "essential learning behaviors," such as the abilities to think creatively and critically, communicate, cooperate with others, function independently, take risks, exhibit self-confidence, and make choices. The entire program reflects the school district's goals, expressed in its mission statement:

> We believe that each individual, regardless of age or experience, is capable of learning and that every learn-

> er can master the behaviors, skills, and knowledge essential for a contributing member of a democratic society. The mission of Williston Central School is to create empowered learners who have a clear understanding of and ownership for their learning, have a positive self-concept and global understanding, and who have acquired the behaviors and skills to become life-long learners (Mission Statement 1994).

Understandably, some parents find these new educational approaches to be threatening because they cannot readily translate their child's progress into familiar terms. In seeking a familiar method of evaluating their children's progress, parents usually look for comparative grades, and expect schools to introduce, as soon as possible, subject matter that appears to be important to success in high school, college, and adult life. This puts tremendous pressure on schools and students, and it is one of the biggest sources of anxiety in children. Parents may also be anxious about their children's ability to compete for college acceptance and financial aid (the average cost of a four-year private college is approaching $20,000 per year, enough to make most families anxious). In addition, innovative educational approaches are difficult to fully evaluate and some parents fear their children would be test cases with uncertain results. However, my prediction is that innovative educational approaches, as represented by the Waldorf movement and Williston Central School, will proliferate because they are based on what we now understand about development in children, and because traditional education appears to be failing. Furthermore, these educational approaches make learning in school a more positive experience, and eliminate the anxiety that accompanies traditional education for so many children. To prepare for success in a rapidly changing and uncertain world, children must learn to be flexible, adaptable, and independent. They must be able to take risks, function with self-confidence and without anxiety, and view education as a lifelong process.

Television is another source of anxiety in children. The violent content of many programs is often viewed by children before they have developed the ability to distinguish between acting and real life. Couple this with the fact that children learn by imitation, and consider the consequences. Children's impulses are stimulated, and they may find themselves acting out what they have witnessed on television, without the capacity to understand or control their behavior. There is also evidence that television viewing before age 7 deprives the brain of developing visual thinking and imagination. By combining visual and auditory input, television usurps the brain's practice at forming visual imagery to correspond with auditory input. Considering that American children watch an average of five to six hours of television per day, their powers of imagination can be significantly impaired. Without visual thinking and imagination, children will be handicapped in learning skills such as reading. They will also have less capacity for mentally releasing their feelings—such as anger—through imagery, leaving them with anxiety about emotional self-control.

Even without these risks, children are simply not mature enough to understand many of the things they see on television. In addition to program content, children also view an average of twenty thousand commercials per year. Advertisers spend approximately $600 million each year on television commercials specifically directed towards children as consumers. Research has shown that in many cases, children cannot distinguish between television programs and commercials. This stresses children by exposing them to pressures they are not developmentally equipped to handle. Television also confuses identity formation in children who are already struggling to define themselves.

Stress is inherent in child development. School pressures, social development, and even physical growth itself are all part of the stressful nature of growing up. To measure stress in children, Elkind (1981) adapted the adult Life Change Scale. Common stresses include events such as birth of a sibling, moving to another city or another part of town, receiving or losing a pet, starting a new extracurricular activity, threat of violence in school, trouble with a teacher, school change, friendship changes, and so on. When abnormal family stresses are added, such as divorce, alcoholism, domestic violence, or child abuse of any kind, severe anxiety almost inevitably develops in children. Reiter and co-authors (1992), found that children and adolescents with high anxiety have a greater number of environmental stressors than peers with low anxiety. Stress is likely to produce anxiety in children who already have "anxiety personality" traits, such as sensitivity, emotional inhibition, need to please, perfectionism, need for structure, high achievement needs, and related characteristics.

Children learn primarily through imitation of role models, and it is estimated that 95 percent of such learning takes place unconsciously. Virtually all learning occurs without awareness as children imitate what they see and hear. Not surprisingly, parents and teachers are the primary role models, profoundly influencing the emotional, cognitive, and social development of children. The most significant influence on the formation of the child's personality is the parents' style of dealing with feelings, communication, sexuality, and relationships. This bears directly on how anxiety develops in many children. As discussed in Chapter 3, children reared in families that do not deal openly with feelings, or where there is a divorce, stepfamily adjustment, child abuse, alcoholism or drug abuse, or violence are more susceptible to anxiety.

For example, in families where conflict and tension exists, or where abuse of any kind is occurring, children protect themselves through the fight/flight mechanism. They either respond with autonomic arousal, in which relaxation is impossible, or they adapt through psychological defense mechanisms. As we know, chronic arousal in the body and difficulty relaxing are the physical basis of stress and anxiety. In order to function on a day-to-day basis and avoid physical breakdown, children in high-stress family situations may shut down some or all systems, using defense mechanisms such as repression of feelings, social withdrawal, and even denial of reality. While these solutions enable day-to-day functioning, such children will be handicapped in coping with other demands and stress and will be at risk for additional anxiety.

Children who are frequently criticized in the family will suffer damaged self-esteem and low self-confidence. They will fear failure, hesitate to take risks, and have difficulty succeeding academically and socially. Low self-esteem can lead to learning problems and academic underachievement, making school an anxiety-arousing situation. Low self-esteem often leads to passivity in relationships, rendering the child vulnerable to manipulation and control by others and making the world of relationships a source of anxiety.

Children with high pressures from parents to perform in school or sports, or who are rewarded more for achievement than for who they are, are likely to experience stress and anxiety symptoms. Children adapt to such pressures by overachieving and by measuring their self-worth in terms of their accomplishments. This increases their risk for future anxiety. Perfectionism and compulsiveness are also likely to develop in children who are high-achieving, and whose agenda is to live up to high expectations. Such children will have difficulty setting reasonable limits for themselves, which will create more stress and anxiety.

Children are also likely to develop perfectionism and compulsive traits if their role models are rigid, demanding, controlling, or establish arbitrary rules. A compliant and passive personality style is likely to develop in children reared by such role models. They may have difficulty thinking independently because they are accustomed to following the rules and doing what they have been told. Emotional dependence is another likely outcome. These personality traits increase the risk for anxiety because life will inevitably present new situations, challenges, and problems that require self-reliance and an ability to think for oneself. In addition, perfectionism and compulsiveness lead to anxiety due to the stress and frustration they create. One adolescent I worked with was unable to complete his schoolwork and homework because of an excessive concern with producing perfect results. His perfectionism had grown into a school phobia with panic anxiety, and in spite of exceptionally high intelligence he was unable to attend school.

In families where feelings are not expressed openly, children adapt by shutting down emotionally. This occurs in families with parents who are uncomfortable with feelings or who do not have the skills to verbally express feelings. "I love you," "I'm upset with you," "I need your help," "I'm sorry for what I said," may never be heard by the child in an emotionally repressed family. In addition, warmth and physical affection are likely to be absent in such a family. As a result of this kind of emotional environment, strong feelings of any kind may produce anxiety. I work with many adult anxiety patients for whom feelings themselves are the feared situation. In these cases, virtually any strong feeling or state of emotional arousal is threatening and produces anxiety. Invariably, these individuals were raised in emotionally repressed families.

The potential for anxiety in children is increased if their parents do not model good health habits and knowledge of body functions. Knowing how to take care of oneself physically is essential to anxiety prevention. Regular exercise, proper diet and nutrition, and good sleep habits are the most basic stress management practices. Taking cues from the body by recognizing its signals of stress, and making accommodations as needed, are also part of taking care of oneself and preventing early warning signals from escalating into anxiety symptoms. Remembering that children learn primarily by imitation, parents can impart these skills by taking care of their own health.

Sexuality is related to health and body functions, but is rarely recognized as an issue in anxiety disorders. In families where parents are uncomfortable with their own sexuality, or where open discussion about sexuality with the children does not take place, children are likely to be uncomfortable with sexual matters. Parental anxiety about teen pregnancy, for example, is often handled with an authoritarian approach to the subject or by simply avoiding it altogether, yet sexual concerns are high on the agenda for most adolescents. Concerns about masturbation, sexual feelings, dating, intimacy, and falling in love are all normal but often confusing and anxiety-arousing. These concerns do not necessarily end in adulthood, and the child who is not prepared for sexuality in adolescence is likely to be unprepared for a fulfilling experience of sexuality later in life. Furthermore, as the work of Reich (1961, 1972), Lowen (1975, 1990), and others have shown, a significant cause of anxiety is frustration of the sexual drive, an issue that we will explore in more depth in Chapter 15.

More than half of all marriages break up, leaving millions of children with the task of adjusting to loss and the stress of divorce. Even before a divorce occurs, a period of tension and conflict between parents, if not outright violence, is typically experienced. This would be sufficient to produce anxiety in most children. However, the stress of divorce often continues well beyond the acute crisis and separation of the parents. Custody and visitation arrangements are frequently unstable, and conflict between divorced parents can linger or even intensify over a period of many years. Stepfamily adjustments also become another source of stress, and half of all children who have been through the trauma of divorce must face a second divorce of at least one of their parents.

The effects of divorce on children are far-reaching, and vary with their age at the time a divorce occurs. Separation anxiety and fears of abandonment, for example, are common in children under age 5. The fear of loss is quite realistic if one parent fades out of the child's life, further reinforcing the fear of abandonment by the other parent. Between the ages of 5 and 8, children of divorce are usually overwhelmed by feelings—loss, rejection, guilt, loyalty conflicts, and sadness—all of which can create anxiety due to inability to handle these strong feelings and concerns. In addition, they also tend to have school performance problems due to the distracting effect of these issues. Many young children, who are dealing with the disruptiveness of visitation and frequent transitions between divorced parents, also develop symptoms of an acute stress disorder (an anxiety condition). A composite example of this disorder is the 4- to 10-year-old child who exhibits angry outbursts, sleep disturbance, difficulty relaxing, and regressive behaviors such as bedwetting and soiling, all of which may be most evident shortly before or after visits with the non-custodial parent. Children between the ages of 9 and 12 also have problems with feelings, especially anger, and are likely to develop behavior problems as their feelings are acted out. Adolescents, who need a family structure to help set limits on sexual and aggressive impulses, are likely to respond to divorce with anxiety. They may also develop fears about commitment and intimacy. Regardless of age, however, the effects of divorce last much longer than usually believed. In a ten-year study of one hundred divorced families, for example, Wallerstein and Blakeslee (1989) found that some effects do not show up until young adulthood, when children of divorce face issues of intimacy, marriage, and having children of their own.

Alcoholism and drug addiction in the family pose a special risk for anxiety in children, for several reasons. First, the behavior patterns of a chemically dependent parent can be unpredictable, making it difficult for the children to anticipate what to expect, as well as interfering with family stability. Second, violence and out-of-control behavior are often associated with alcoholism and drug dependence. In fact, it is estimated that 80 to 90 percent of all domestic violence is linked to alcoholism. Violence in the home, of course, frightens children by threatening their safety and security, as well as by strongly activating their survival mechanisms. Third, the typical parental relationship in an alcoholic family consists of a chemically dependent adult and an enabling spouse. The enabler typically covers for the impaired partner by filling in the lapses of responsibility and keeping the family intact. The enabler is controlled by the spouse's chemical dependency. These are the adult models in a chemically dependent family. Anxiety is likely to develop as the child realizes that both parents are in denial and that neither parent can deal effectively with the problem. Furthermore, the child's intuition—that important sensing mechanism and survival skill—is often damaged in a chemically dependent family, where the obvious may be minimized or denied.

Alcoholism and drug abuse are often kept within the family walls as a secret. There are other family secrets that can increase the risk for anxiety in children, now or later in their lives. Any information that is hidden because it is considered by parents to be shameful or embarrassing, or because it might reflect poorly on the family, qualifies as a family secret. This can include out-of-wedlock pregnancies, suicide of an extended family member, mental illness of a family member, or trouble with the law. The relationship to anxiety is that family secrets foster shame and discourage openness. Thus, when a child (or later an adult) experiences feelings that seem to be socially unacceptable, such as anxiety or fear, he or she may hide them from others. This perpetuates anxiety and interferes with seeking appropriate help.

Each year in this country, one million children are hospitalized due to brutal physical abuse by their own parents. Another five thousand children between the ages of 2 weeks and 2 years are actually killed by their parents. One out of every three to four girls, and one out of ten boys, are victims of sexual abuse by age 18, often within their own families. Where abuse of a child occurs, anxiety is virtually guaranteed. All biological and psychological systems are damaged in cases of physical, sexual, or emotional abuse. Where the abuse occurs within the family, the most obvious damages are the betrayal of trust and break in bonding, with their vast implications for anxiety, especially if the abuse is kept secret or not stopped by an informed adult. Post-traumatic stress disorder—or acute stress disorder if the symptoms are evident within one month of the abuse—is the severe anxiety disorder that invariably develops as a result of abuse. Until recently, post-traumatic stress disorder was believed to occur only in adults. However, it is now known that children and adolescents can have this anxiety disorder, and that the symptoms are similar to those seen in adults. The symptoms of this anxiety disorder include acute anxiety upon exposure to reminders of the abuse, with reactions that include fear, helplessness, nightmares, irritability, angry outbursts, numbing of feelings, and high autonomic arousal that interferes with sleep, concentration, and ability to relax. Abused children are also likely to experience symptoms of depression. The effects of abuse can stay with the victim for many years, or a lifetime, if proper help is not received.

Many of the family influences on a child's personality will have their full effect later in life, when an overload of stress tests the limits of adjustment and ability to cope. Severe anxiety is triggered when the personality formed in childhood combines later in life with stress. Most adults who come to therapy with anxiety disorders are unaware of how much stress they are under because it has been a normal part of life since childhood. They lack an objective perspective on stress because they have never lived without it, or because they have somehow managed to remain in control in spite of it.

Children's anxiety is also stimulated by the transitions between, and tasks within, the developmental stages. Standing on the line between the known and the unknown, and sensing the approach of new challenges, children ask themselves, "What is this new situation? What is expected? Can I handle this?" These are normal concerns, and they must be distinguished from severe or abnormal anxiety. It has been estimated that normally about 50 percent of children have some six to seven signs of anxiety, which include fears of animals, thunder or lightning, and medical procedures such as injections. Typical children's fears, of course, vary with their age and developmental level. What may be a typical fear for a 2-year-old child, therefore, may be an abnormal or irrational fear for a 10- or 12-year-old. The severity of children's anxiety is determined by the degree to which the anxiety interrupts learning and social development, the persistence of anxiety symptoms, and the amount of emotional distress experienced by the child.

Table 6–1 shows some of the common and normal fears of childhood and adolescence, displayed according to age.

TABLE 6–1: COMMON FEARS IN CHILDREN AND ADOLESCENTS

Age	Common Fears
0–6 months	Loss of support, loud noises
7–12 months	Strangers, sudden movements or large/ looming objects
1 year	Separation, toilet, strangers
2 years	Separation, dark, animals, loud noises, large objects, changes in house
3–4 years	Separation, masks, dark, animals, noises at night
5 years	Separation, animals, "bad people," bodily harm
6 years	Separation, thunder and lightning, supernatural beings, dark, sleeping or staying alone, bodily injury
7–8 years	Supernatural beings, dark, fears based on television viewing, staying alone, bodily injury
9–12 years	Tests, school performance, physical appearance, thunder and lightning, bodily injury, death
14–15 years	Family and home issues, political concerns, preparation for future, personal appearance, social relations, school

Adapted from Last, C. Copyright © 1992. Anxiety disorders in childhood and adolescence. In Reynolds, W., ed. *Internalizing Disorders in Children and Adolescence*. Reprinted by permission of John Wiley & Sons, Inc.

In viewing the chart of common fears in children and adolescents, notice that separation anxiety is normal throughout the preschool years, when the bonding process is taking place. As children mature, normal anxiety shifts to school and social concerns.

How is abnormal anxiety expressed in children? As with adults, there are a number of anxiety patterns and types of fear, which are grouped into *anxiety disorders*. An anxiety disorder is a severe anxiety condition, with a more or less distinct cluster of symptoms, that is persistent or interferes with normal development and day-to-day functioning. Children can develop severe anxiety in the form of separation anxiety disorder, avoidant disorder, overanxious disorder, phobic disorders, generalized anxiety disorder, post-traumatic stress disorder, obsessive-compulsive disorder, and panic disorder.

Separation anxiety disorder is considered to be exclusively a condition in children, although I frequently see aspects of this condition in adults with anxiety problems. In separation anxiety disorder, severe anxiety symptoms develop in anticipation of separation from a security figure. As distinguished from normal separation anxiety in children, this disorder consists of excessive, persistent, and unrealistic worry about separation from either the mother or primary attachment figure to the extent that the anxiety symptoms are very painful and cause a significant impairment in one or more important areas of the child's functioning. Although mothers are frequently the attachment figure, a father or sibling can also be the focus of security. Children with separation anxiety are often brought to therapy by parents who are distressed by their child's inability or reluctance to separate from them. Separation anxiety disorder often occurs in combination with school phobia or school avoidance; approximately 75 percent of children with separation anxiety disorder have difficulty going to school. The condition tends to come and go over time, and is usually activated by new situations involving separation that are normally encountered in adolescence and adulthood. The condition is diagnosed when three or more of the following symptoms persist for at least two weeks, beginning before age 18:

1. Persistent, unrealistic fear that a destructive event will befall the attachment figure, thereby preventing his or her return, or fear that the attachment figure will leave permanently
2. Fear of a destructive event occurring to the child such as kidnapping or having an accident that will maintain the child's separation from the parent
3. Persistent refusal or reluctance to sleep without the presence of the attachment figure or to sleep away from home
4. Persistent avoidance of being alone as manifested in clinging and shadowing behaviors
5. Somatic symptoms on many school days or in anticipation of a separation with symptoms including headaches, stomach aches, nausea, and vomiting
6. Repeated signs of distress or complaints of distress such as temper tantrums, crying, and plead ing with parents not to leave in anticipation of a separation
7. Repeated signs or complaints of distress when separated, such as needing to call parents or return home

Overanxious disorder is the children's version of generalized anxiety disorder. This anxiety condition is characterized by unrealistic worry over future and past events, excessive concern about performing competently, and excessive self-consciousness. Children with this form of anxiety often seek reassurance from others, and may limit their involvement to activities in which they feel confident of success and positive feedback. Performance-oriented activities, such as playing a musical instrument or participating in sports, are often avoided. Due to their excessive need for reassurance they easily feel slighted and are sensitive to criticism. They also tend to have physical complaints during periods of increased anxiety, such as stomach aches and headaches. Teachers are often unaware of the anxiety because such children tend to be quiet but precocious in their behavior. Parents often describe such children as excessively nervous. A diagnosis of overanxious disorder may be made if the child or adolescent experiences four or more of the following symptoms for six months or longer:

1. Excessive or unrealistic worry about future events
2. Excessive or unrealistic worry about the appropriateness of past events
3. Excessive or unrealistic concern about competence in one or more areas including academic, athletic, and social
4. Somatic complaints with no established physical basis
5. Excessive self-consciousness
6. Excessive need for reassurance about many things
7. Difficulty relaxing and high level of tension

Avoidant disorder consists of excessive fear of being around unfamiliar people, including both children or adults, to the extent that social relationships are impaired. Children with this anxiety disorder desire and generally have warm relationships with family members, but do not warm up to other people. Typically, such children exhibit isolation from peers, lack of assertiveness, and low self-confidence. The condition is less common than separation anxiety disorder, and differs by its focus on avoiding unfamiliar people rather than fear of separation from an attachment figure. Unlike overanxious disorder, which is also more common, avoidant disorder is focused on a more specific source of fear. The criteria for diagnosing avoidant disorder in children include:

1. Excessive avoidance of contact with unfamiliar people to such a degree that social functioning is impaired for a period of at least six months
2. Desire for and involvement in warm relations with family and familiar people
3. Age of onset no younger than 2½ years

Currently, phobic disorders are divided into two types of fears, specific phobia and social phobia. A *specific phobia* is an excessive and persistent fear triggered by the presence or anticipation of a specific object or situation, such as flying, heights, darkness, animals, loud sounds, people in costumes, receiving an injection, and so on. The presence of the feared object or situation usually leads to an immediate anxiety reaction, which may appear as a panic attack or in the form of crying, tantrums, freezing, or clinging by the child. Children with specific phobias do not necessarily recognize the unrealistic nature of their fears. With children's anxiety disorders, it is important to distinguish between abnormal anxiety and developmentally normal fears, which are experienced temporarily by most children. If the child's phobia is age-appropriate, but his or her reaction is severe enough to interfere with daily functioning, then a diagnosis of specific phobia is justified.

Social phobia, or social anxiety disorder, is characterized by a marked fear of social or performance situations in which the person is exposed to unfamiliar people or to possible scrutiny by others. The child (or adult, as the case may be) fears that he or she will act in a way that will be humiliating or embarrassing, such as showing anxiety symptoms or blushing. The most common fears among children with social phobia are school and public speaking. Avoidance of feared situations is usually the first line of defense against the anxiety. If the phobic situations cannot be avoided they are experienced as extremely stressful, and the anxious anticipation escalates, further interfering with ability to cope. As with specific phobias, the child with social phobia may not be aware of the unrealistic nature of the fear.

Until recently, *post-traumatic stress disorder* was believed to occur only in adults. However, it is now known that children and adolescents can have this anxiety disorder, and that the symptoms are similar to those seen in adults. The condition is most commonly seen in reaction to physical and sexual abuse, and is often accompanied by depression and other symptoms. The term *acute stress disorder* is used if symptoms are apparent within a month of a traumatic event. The symptoms of post-traumatic stress disorder include the following:

1. Exposure to a traumatic event involving threat or actual injury
2. Response to the trauma involving intense fear, helplessness, or horror, which may be expressed as disorganized or agitated behavior
3. Persistent re-experiencing of the event, such as distressing memories, disturbing dreams, acting or feeling as if the event was recurring, reenactment of specific aspects of the trauma, and strong physical or emotional reactions to reminders of the trauma
4. Avoidance of reminders of the trauma
5. Numbing of general responsiveness, such as detachment from others, limited emotions, and difficulty feeling love
6. Symptoms of increased arousal, such as sleep disturbance, impaired concentration, irritability, and angry outbursts

Obsessive-compulsive disorder is an unusual form of anxiety. In this condition, unwanted obsessions (thoughts, impulses, or images) create anxiety because they cannot be controlled, and the child or adolescent feels compelled to engage in repetitive behaviors aimed at preventing or controlling anxious feelings. The primary concern of the person with this condition, as with most anxiety disorders, is control. The lack of control over obsessive thoughts or compulsive behaviors is threatening and anxiety-arousing. The obsessive thoughts and compulsive behaviors usually have more power over the person than the person has over them. Usually, the child or adolescent with this condition knows that the thoughts and behaviors are exaggerated and unreasonable but is unable to stop them. Shame and secrecy about the problem cause children to hide it, resulting in delays until adulthood before help is sought.

Obsessive-compulsive disorder is illustrated by Becky, an intelligent 16-year-old adolescent, who was failing her first-period biology class in high school because she was always late or absent. She set her alarm for five o'clock in the morning, hoping to get to her 8:30 class on time. She spent the next three hours taking a long shower, followed by changing clothes repeatedly until it "felt right." She then packed and repacked her books until they were just right, opened the front door and prepared to walk down the front steps. She went through a ritual of pausing on each step for a particular length of time. Even though she realized that her thoughts and behaviors were irrational, she felt compelled to complete her rituals. Once she completed these rituals, she would make a mad dash for school and arrive when the first period was almost over.

Panic disorder is still considered by many to be an adult anxiety disorder, but children and adolescents do experience panic attacks. In adults, panic disorder may occur with or without a pattern of avoiding situations in which panic is anticipated. This distinction may also apply to children, although it is more likely that children will be found with panic disorder in combination with social phobia or a specific phobia, such as fears about school, dark, certain animals, and so on. Panic anxiety involves the following symptoms:

1. Heart palpitations, pounding heart, or accelerated heart rate
2. Sweating

3. Trembling or shaking
4. Shortness of breath or smothering (or choking) sensations
5. Chest pain or discomfort
6. Nausea or abdominal distress
7. Feeling dizzy, unsteady, lightheaded, or faint
8. Feelings of unreality
9. Fear of losing control, going crazy, or dying
10. Numbness or tingling
11. Chills or hot flashes

The criteria for diagnosing anxiety disorders in children are included above to help readers recognize typical signs and symptoms, and to help identify the type of anxiety that might be involved in specific cases. However, formal diagnosis of anxiety in children is best performed by an experienced therapist, who can help distinguish between normal and abnormal anxiety and confirm the diagnosis.

The diagnostic procedure used by therapists usually consists of an interview with parents to obtain a developmental history and background information, as well as one or more visits with the child. In addition, there are a number of psychological tests that can be used to help identify an anxiety disorder in children. One example is the Revised Children's Manifest Anxiety Scale, a questionnaire completed by the child and scored by a psychologist for indications of an anxiety disorder. Another measure, the Children's Separation Inventory, is an excellent screening test for children whose parents are separated or divorced. This test determines the extent to which a child may be fearful of abandonment, as well as other issues such as hopes for reconciliation, self-blame, and fear of peers knowing about the separation or divorce. The Achenbach Child Behavior Checklist, a behavior rating instrument completed by teachers and parents, is another test offering pertinent scales such as anxiety, attention problems, school performance, social withdrawal, and somatic complaints. Some projective tests, such as the Thematic Apperception Test and the Sentence Completion Test, ask children to make up stories or sentence endings, and can be helpful in identifying anxiety based on a child's feelings and concerns. Finally, the Wechsler Intelligence Scale for Children, Third Edition, measures a dozen different cognitive abilities, some of which are known to be directly affected by anxiety.

Most anxiety disorders in children can be treated effectively within a few months, with the exception of abuse cases where treatment is usually long-term. About 80 percent of anxiety disorders can be treated successfully without medication. In my opinion, effective therapy for children's anxiety must involve a combination of ingredients. *Positive rapport*, for example, is important for developing trust and credibility with a child. An educational phase must be included to demystify anxiety. *Relaxation training* is necessary to counteract and control anxiety. *Cognitive change*, involving identifying and restructuring attitudes and beliefs and teaching how to change self-talk when anxious, is also necessary for successful treatment. *Working with the family system* is, in many cases, necessary to reduce family stress and alleviate the child's symptoms in context. Finally, for children who have developed patterns of avoiding certain anxiety-arousing situations, or who need to change nonproductive habits, *behavioral training* and *desensitization* may be necessary.

An excellent anxiety treatment for children is LifeSkills, a ten-session process that can be guided by a trained therapist, school guidance counselor, or parent. The program is interactive, using cassette tapes and a workbook, and provides structured learning activities to be practiced by the child. This format can supplement office therapy, and it appeals to children who are not comfortable with the idea of therapy. Content of the program includes "skill builder" lessons about stress, mind–body connection, relaxation, anger, assertiveness, self-talk, imagery, risk-taking, self-esteem, and other skills. These are the skills and knowledge needed by children to overcome anxiety and cope effectively with stress. Although the LifeSkills program stands on its own, it is best used as a reinforcement to professional therapy, where treatment can be individualized and monitored responsibly. Parents, therapists, school personnel, and others interested in this approach to anxiety treatment for children should contact CHAANGE (see Appendix B). This anxiety treatment center will send free information about the LifeSkills anxiety treatment program.

Medication is sometimes used in the treatment of anxiety in children. However, there are few well-controlled studies of the value of medications for children and adolescents with anxiety disorders. The best studies have been done on the effect of the antidepressant imipramine on school-phobic children. Gittelman-Klein and Klein (1980), for example, found this drug to be helpful in facilitating school return and decreasing separation anxiety. On the other hand, the side effects of this drug can include drowsiness, decreased frustration tolerance, and risk to the child's cardiovascular system. Similar concerns apply to other drugs, such as benzodiazepines, whose side-effects include sedation, cognitive performance deficits, or abuse and dependency on the drug. Although the benzodiazepines have been used in adult anxiety cases, little support exists for their use with young people. Considering the fact that about 80 percent of children with anxiety disorders can benefit from therapy without medications, my opinion is that drugs should be used as a last resort, with an awareness of side effects and risks.

Let us consider the treatment of some actual children with anxiety. The first case is Michelle, aged 14, who was referred for help because she refused to go to school. An interview with her parents revealed that she was always self-conscious about her appearance and somewhat shy and inhibited. Her concerns intensified in junior high school, where she became so anxious about interacting with other children that she began to make excuses for avoiding school and social events. In working with Michelle, it became apparent that certain situations triggered her severe anxiety: the school cafeteria, which involved socializing; English class, where she had to read aloud; and gym, where she had to undress in front of others.

Treatment of Michelle's social phobia involved several stages, beginning with developing rapport and teaching her some basic mind–body information. She was trained in self-relaxation, which was then combined with systematic desensitization to help her overcome her social anxiety.

As part of her therapy, Michelle was asked to make a list of all situations that made her anxious or panicky, and number them by degree of difficulty. She then worked on each situation, starting with the least threatening, by relaxing and imagining herself in the situation. Whenever she became anxious, she would stop, relax, and start over, until she was able to visualize herself being reasonably comfortable in the situations on her list. At that point, Michelle was encouraged to enter the feared situations, again starting with the least threatening, for a few minutes at a time until her comfort level expanded.

Michelle was also taught how to change her inner dialogue from negative to positive "self statements," such as "I did this in the past, I can do it again," "I can handle this," and, "The other kids in the cafeteria are not there to stare at me. They will be busy doing their own thing." In addition, some work on assertive communication and self-esteem was included. Michelle was taught about the importance of eye contact when communicating with others, and she practiced accepting compliments by saying "Thank you" while maintaining eye contact. The process of anxiety recovery for Michelle took about four months to complete.

Another example of successful treatment with an anxious child was Nicholas, a 9-year-old boy, who was referred by his school for help with learning problems. He was identified by the school as deficient in reading and written language skills, and it was also known that his parents were undergoing a divorce. My first task was to conduct an evaluation to determine Nicholas' cognitive abilities and the extent to which the family situation might be impacting on his academic functioning. A complete psychological evaluation was performed, and the resulting behavior profile indicated that Nicholas was an emotionally sensitive and withdrawn boy who was easily frustrated and often sad, as well as having a need to please and a tendency to worry. An intellectual assessment indicated that Nicholas' overall cognitive abilities were in the superior range (top 7 percent of the population in his age range). However, his scores were low on several subtests that are sensitive to the effects of anxiety. The projective tests revealed that Nicholas was preoccupied and distressed about his parents' divorce process. On the Sentence Completion Test, for example, he said, "I get sad when . . . *my mom and dad fight*," and "I don't like it when . . . *my mother fights with my dad*." Given three wishes, Nicholas' first wish was, "My mother and father were back together." On the Children's Separation Inventory, Nicholas showed self-consciousness about the parental separation, hesitancy about others knowing what was happening at home, and a mild degree of self-blame about the divorce. Finally, additional tests suggested that Nicholas suppressed his feelings. He was not a risk taker, and he preferred to stick to the known aspects of new or unstructured situations. Nicholas was unable to learn effectively in school, and showed low frustration tolerance. Taken all together, the psychological evaluation indicated that Nicholas was an intellectually bright and creative child who was highly anxious about the divorce at home. His ability to concentrate and sustain attention at school appeared to be related to his emotional distress and anxiety. Psychotherapy to help Nicholas cope more effectively was one of my recommendations.

Nicholas had a successful therapy experience, consisting of fourteen sessions over a six-month period. Initially, he was despondent and uncommunicative but responded well to mime games and play, which drew him out and enabled him to become more talkative, warm, and friendly. Following this period of establishing rapport, Nicholas was taught about anxiety and mind–body principles. He was then taught how to practice relaxation, as well as a number of other anxiety control techniques, such as changing his inner dialogue and confining his anxiety to a specific "worry time."

Although Nicholas was not a verbally expressive boy, some time was also spent discussing his feelings about the changes that were taking place within his family. Contact with the parents provided opportunities to make some recommendations for how they could be helpful to Nicholas' anxiety recovery and divorce adjustment. Fortunately, the parents were mature enough to put his needs high on their priorities.

Shortly before the last scheduled session, Nicholas reported, "My worrying has been cut in half since we met last time." In his final therapy session, he stated, "My worrying is gone! What helped the most was telling myself that worrying wouldn't help and the what-if thoughts went away."

7

The CHAANGE Program for Anxiety Recovery

> *Words can't express the relief with which I listened to the first couple of CHAANGE tapes. I had thought I was the only one who acted in those "shameful" ways, who lived in constant fear—of driving over a bridge, sitting in a crowd, going on a trip. I couldn't believe recovery could be that simple—there had to be a catch. It wouldn't work for me, I thought, because I had anxiety in some form or other since 1972 and it was now 1994.*
>
> Elizabeth, age 46

The CHAANGE program for anxiety recovery is a holistic, step-by-step process for overcoming severe anxiety without medication. The program deals with causes, not just behavior change, and teaches the skills necessary for overcoming anxiety and for lifelong recovery. The effectiveness of the CHAANGE process has been proven with more than fourteen thousand individuals, who have regained their freedom from the limitations of severe anxiety. My own recovery from anxiety would have taken far less time if CHAANGE had been available to me. What makes this unique approach so successful?

The CHAANGE program is *structured.* This is important for people with the anxiety personality who have a preference for organization and structure. The program has a beginning, middle, and end, and deals with all the issues and skills that most experts agree are necessary for anxiety recovery. The materials are presented in a step-by-step sequence of audiotapes and readings containing information, instructions, and prescribed exercises and activities. People undergoing the CHAANGE program can be involved seven days a week in their recovery by doing the daily homework. Ideally, the program is administered by one of the CHAANGE-affiliated therapists across the country—and internationally as recognition of the program grows—but it is also designed to be taken on an in-home basis.

Another unique feature of the CHAANGE program is that it was *created by patients* who recovered from severe anxiety. Ann Seagrave and Faison Covington were two anxiety sufferers who recovered under the guidance of their therapist, Lou Owensby, in Charlotte, North Carolina. Ann, Faison, and Lou organized all of the components of the recovery process and created the CHAANGE program, as well as the Center for Help for Anxiety and Agoraphobia through New Growth Experiences. Ann's and Faison's recovery experiences using CHAANGE were publicized in their book, *Free From Fears*, and they appeared on national television as guests on the *Oprah, Larry King Live*, and *Regis* talk shows. It is essential for anxiety sufferers to believe that recovery is possible. The CHAANGE program is credible because it is taught directly by two people who overcame their anxiety with this therapeutic method.

Those who identify with Ann and Faison can be assured that they, too, can overcome their fears. An atmosphere of support and encouragement, combined with the interactive tapes by Ann, Faison, and Lou, add immeasurably to the program's effectiveness.

The CHAANGE program is different from other approaches in that it is based on the conviction that severe anxiety is a *learned* condition, and that it can be *unlearned.* The thought processes, personality style, and behavior patterns involved in anxiety are learned over a period of time, often beginning in childhood. Anxiety is considered to be primarily a psychological condition that can be reversed, rather than a biochemical disorder that must be managed. While medication can play a role in some cases by controlling symptoms, its usefulness is in allowing learning to take place. Drugs are not recommended as a long-term solution or to correct a "chemical imbalance."

The CHAANGE program consists of sixteen lessons that can be completed in sixteen weeks. Although complete recovery from severe anxiety can occur within this period of time, it is more realistic to think of the program as an opportunity to acquire the information and skills required for recovery. What remains is the need to practice the skills until new attitudes, habits, and behavior patterns become automatic. Thus, the actual length of time required for recovery will vary with other influences, such as a person's motivation, learning style, and stress level at the time of program participation. Co-existing issues, such as relationship problems or medical conditions, can also affect the length of recovery time. However, the length of suffering with anxiety before starting the CHAANGE program does *not,* in itself, determine length of treatment. I have personally witnessed remarkable recoveries within the sixteen-week program in people who have suffered with anxiety for many years.

The CHAANGE program focuses on overcoming the fear of fear by decreasing a person's sensitization to the fight/flight reaction. At the same time, CHAANGE helps eliminate the thought and behavior habits that create anxiety. It is not sufficient to focus on the phobic situation—the thing or place—associated with anxiety. Thus, even if a person has not had any anxiety episodes for months, or even years, he or she would not be considered recovered as long as there is a fear of relapses. A person is considered recovered when it no longer matters whether anxiety occurs. Paradoxically, when it no longer matters, anxiety is much less likely to occur.

These goals are accomplished by the CHAANGE program using education, insight, and skills, presented in overlapping phases. In the *education phase*, a person learns about anxiety, how it developed in each person's case, the body mechanisms involved, the role of stress in anxiety, and other pertinent information and concepts. The purpose of the education phase is not only to give the recovering person an understanding of his or her condition but to help counteract fear of the condition. Since most anxiety sufferers react fearfully to their own body reactions, understanding what is happening is the first step toward gaining control. Knowing there is a name and explanation for the condition, and that others have recovered from the same problem, is a reassuring stage of recovery.

Relaxation training begins immediately and continues throughout the program. Several relaxation techniques are used, including progressive muscle relaxation, breathing exercises, and visualization. I sometimes add training in yoga and meditation. Yoga is helpful because it is active, yet gentle, and fills a gap between muscle relaxation and aerobic exercise. In addition, yoga involves movement, which is helpful for those who initially cannot sit still. Meditation is helpful for controlling the mind, particularly in relation to fear-inducing and stress-creating thoughts.

Anxiety sufferers tend to have many nonproductive thought habits, such as worrying, negative thinking, and many "shoulds," as discussed in Chapter 2 and Chapter 11. The *cognitive phase* teaches skills for replacing such habits. This is accomplished by identifying nonproductive thoughts, and replacing them with more productive and reassuring self-statements. In the CHAANGE program, this process is referred to as "changing your inner dialogue." The specific techniques are discussed in Chapter 11. Recovery would not be possible without these changes because the nonproductive thought habits are largely responsible for creating and maintaining anxiety and stress symptoms. Without these changes, anxiety recovery would be like trying to fill a leaking bucket—the effect would never hold.

Another phase consists of *desensitization,* a procedure for helping the anxiety sufferer re-enter phobic situations without fear. This phase is essential for those who have developed a pattern of avoidant behavior or phobias. Desensitization builds on the previous phases of recovery by combining relaxation, positive inner dialogue, and visualization to mentally practice fearless behavior. When prepared, the person then actually faces the feared situations and, using other acquired skills, learns to handle them with greater comfort. While support persons or assistants can be helpful to the anxious patient, dependency on such support is not encouraged. In the CHAANGE program, it is believed that recovery is enhanced when people can personally "own" their success and accomplishments.

Many people who seek help for severe anxiety have, at one point or another, taken medication. CHAANGE has no objection to people beginning the anxiety treatment program while taking medication, but believes that long-term medication is not necessary to live without fear. Generally speaking, anxiety sufferers are uncomfortable with drugs because of their need for control and an innate sensitivity to the effects of drugs. On the other hand, the desperation felt by some sufferers makes this option attractive. Medication has a role to play in the short run for those who may need help to improve concentration, self-control, and sleep, in order to participate in a therapy program. In virtually all cases, anxiety sufferers who use medication wish to discontinue, and most do within the sixteen weeks of program participation. I consult routinely with doctors who are prescribing medication for patients, and I always advise patients to contact their doctor for input on tapering and discontinuing medication.

The CHAANGE program is suitable for a wide range of anxiety conditions. The most successful use of the program is with individuals for whom severe anxiety is a major component of their psychological difficulties. While the program is most appropriate for individuals who are experiencing anxiety directly, it can also benefit persons who have developed maladaptive patterns of avoiding anxiety, such as obsessive thinking and compulsive behavior. Individuals suffering with agoraphobia, panic disorder, generalized anxiety, social phobia, post-traumatic stress disorder, specific phobias, and anxiety associated with medical conditions can all benefit from the program. Additional techniques may be added where necessary for complete resolution of some conditions, such as obsessive-compulsive disorder, post-traumatic stress disorder, and social phobia. Nevertheless, CHAANGE serves well as the core of treatment for virtually all anxiety conditions and disorders.

Special attention needs to be devoted to the presence of depression associated with anxiety. When a person's limitations are primarily caused by depression, the CHAANGE program is not likely to be helpful. However, it is common for people with severe anxiety to become discouraged, negative, and depressed. Where depression arises as a secondary complication from an anxiety disorder, the program is likely to be appropriate and quite valuable.

The CHAANGE program is available through a network of licensed therapists who receive special training in use of this treatment approach. In cases where a CHAANGE-affiliated therapist is not within a reasonable distance, the program can be taken on an in-home basis with telephone consultation provided by one of the affiliated therapists or regional coordinators. The basic requirement for successful use of the program is fluency in English (a version is now available in Spanish and there are plans for French and Italian versions), and ability to read at an eighth-grade level. Motivation to overcome anxiety, a willingness to take the time and do the work—about 45 minutes each day for sixteen weeks—is also necessary for successful results. Anyone interested in receiving a free information packet on the CHAANGE program, which includes an audiotape and a list of affiliated therapists, is invited to contact the national office (see Appendix B). Psychotherapists interested in joining the network and receiving training in the CHAANGE program are also encouraged to contact the national office.

The success rate of the CHAANGE program is in line with outcome data published by the National Institute of Mental Health (NIMH). NIMH reports a success rate of approximately 80 percent for anxiety disorders when appropriate treatment is used. In a study of results achieved by CHAANGE graduates at the sixteen-week mark, 78 percent rated themselves as "completely improved," "much improved," or "improved," in their anxiety level. Another 11 percent reported a "slight improvement" within the sixteen weeks. Rating their degree of disturbance by phobic symptoms, 81 percent felt "completely improved," "improved," or "much improved," with another 16 percent who felt a "slight improvement." Finally, 78 percent of graduates discontinued their avoidant behavior to a moderate to significant extent within the sixteen weeks. It should be kept in mind that these results were reported by CHAANGE graduates after only sixteen weeks, typically without medications. With continued practice of skills learned in the program, recovery progresses further and then stabilizes. I have kept in contact with patients for up to six years and have found that, indeed, recovery is usually maintained. In isolated cases, relapses after recovery occurred because the individual discontinued regular practice of the acquired skills. When this happens, the person has only to return to the program to reinforce his or her previous improvement and to continue to improve.

One benefit of the CHAANGE program is the opportunity for participants to go through the therapy process more than once. The materials can serve as a lifelong resource for participants who, like reading a book more than once, may derive more information and skills through periodic review of the program. In fact, at the end of the program a checklist is provided for this purpose. In this way, freedom from anxiety can continue to increase with time.

The CHAANGE program has been shown to save money on unnecessary health care. It is known that people with anxiety symptoms over-utilize medical services and spend many health-care dollars in an attempt to diagnose and overcome the condition. The cost of a hospital emergency room visit, for example, can range from fees for a basic physical exam to costly, hi-tech diagnostic tests. Doctor visits, lab tests, medication, and even ambulance services can all be part of the unnecessary expense of anxiety disorders that are misdiagnosed or improperly treated.

A cost–benefit study on the CHAANGE program was conducted at San Diego's Rohr Industries, which employs about 6,500 workers. The company's in-house team of health-care professionals refer to the CHAANGE program any employees, or their dependents, who are identified as experiencing symptoms of anxiety. In a study of nine employees who recovered from severe anxiety through the program, a 54 percent reduction in health-care expenses was found during a one-year period following the program compared to the year before. The actual dollars saved were $2,639 per year for each employee treated with the program. This expense reduction is even more impressive considering that the cost of the CHAANGE program—including materials fees and sixteen therapy sessions—was *included* in the one-year period following the program.

The power of the CHAANGE program is illustrated by thousands of successful recovery stories, a few of which are shared in Chapter 22. The progress of all of the patients whose stories are reported occurred by the sixteenth week of their program participation. I will share just one example here. Harriet was a 37-year-old married mother of three children, with an elementary-school teaching career, who was referred by her physician after revealing her severe anxiety condition. She was unable to come by herself to the first few appointments due to panic attacks associated with driving. Harriet's condition had become so intense that she required her husband to accompany her to any new situation, including her initial appointments with me. To get to work, she would offer to pick up a colleague who lived on the way to school to avoid being alone in her car. During the work day, Harriet would become panicky just thinking about the drive home. Like many anxiety sufferers, she spent considerable energy anticipating and worrying. Her physician prescribed Xanax, 25 milligrams per day, upon learning of Harriet's anxiety condition.

When she first came in, Harriet was tearful and depressed about her inability to control her fear. On the CHAANGE pre-program evaluation Harriet wrote, "Presently, this condition is making it difficult to focus on daily activities. I am nervous about driving nearly all the time so I am often uncomfortable and scared I'm going crazy. In addition, I feel depressed, which triggers its own set of anxieties."

Just sixteen weeks later, Harriet wrote on her post-program evaluation, "At present, I feel 85–90 percent recovered. I am driving everywhere I need to drive without panic and I am beginning to drive other places a little at a time. I am finding myself using the relaxation techniques when I start to feel anxious. Deep breathing seems second nature now. I am without doubt more comfortable in my work environment. I can sit through meetings and lunch with co-workers and practically relax!"

A summary of progress made by Harriet during the sixteen-week program is presented in Table 21–2 in Chapter 21. The table shows that Harriet experienced a significant reduction in anxiety symptoms and depression and an increase in self-control. She was more comfortable and able to resume normal driving. Harriet also discontinued her medication during the program.

The CHAANGE anxiety treatment program requires a commitment to recovery and a period of hard work. Effort is necessary because old habits of thought and behavior are difficult to replace. However, the re-learning process is enjoyable for most participants, and it is certainly rewarding for all who complete the program. Here is a comment from just one of more than 14,000 who are dancing without fear as a result of completing the program: "CHAANGE provided me with the tools to develop my self-esteem and free myself from fear and anxiety. I now have the confidence to drive over a bridge, fly, take a long trip, say 'no' if I want to, and pursue my lifelong dream of singing, dancing, and acting."

8

Sitting Still

Be here now.
Ram Dass

Be still and know that I am God.
Holy Bible

There once was a time when sitting still was necessary for human survival. Before agriculture and the development of long-range weapons, we were hunters, dependent on catching prey for food, clothing, and tools. At that point in history, the only way we could get close enough to throw a rock or spear at living animal targets was to sit quietly and patiently, awaiting their arrival and close proximity. We had to blend into nature to avoid detection by equally cunning prey. Sitting still for many hours was a natural survival mechanism.

Sitting still is as necessary for survival now as it was in prehistoric times, but for very different reasons. In today's technological society, we are relieved of many basic survival tasks, which are conveniently performed for us by machines and devices. For most of us, the raw materials for living are readily available, and our food, clothing, tools, and shelters are no longer grown or fabricated by our own hands. Theoretically, we have the luxury of more leisure time, greater control, and less stress. But how many of us have replaced those survival tasks with the gift of more leisure time? How often do we sit still and appreciate what we have? Instead, we have filled our extra time with more tasks, activities, and commitments, and we have increased our speed of living. In spite of modern conveniences and the promise of more free time and an easier life, we are often rushed and we have more stress. As a society, we are "stressed out" and have difficulty slowing down. Our survival now depends on our ability to cope with stress and minimize the damage it causes.

The anxiety sufferer's personality style adds to the stress of life. Impatience, a desire to please others, difficulty relaxing in spite of a desire to be calm, trouble setting reasonable limits or saying "no," and a need to feel in control are some of the traits that create stress and anxiety symptoms. Anxiety symptoms are warning signals, indicating a need to slow down and reevaluate our thinking and behavior. In this chapter we will explore just how to accomplish this, in spite of some tenacious obstacles.

We have two tasks in learning to sit still. First, we must address the personality style that drives us to anxiety symptoms. We can begin by changing our attitudes about taking time out for relaxation and stress recovery. This is not easy for the anxious person who tends to view relaxation as nonproductive, and who fears becoming lazy or not being able to resume productive activities after slowing down. This is, of course, black-and-white thinking, another personality trait to be changed.

The second task is to learn the skills of relaxation, meditation, and related practices. This is also a difficult task for the anxiety sufferer, whose personality is impatient with anything other than immediate relief, and who is easily discouraged when results are not immediate.

I have worked with many patients for whom relaxation training was the most difficult aspect of anxiety recovery. A number of issues account for some people's resistance to relaxation in spite of their intellectual recognition of its importance and even their desire to relax. In some cases, the resistance stems from an underlying belief that taking time out from work or household chores will mean the job won't get done. There may be a compulsive quality to this attitude, in which taking time out is outweighed by a need to keep busy. Fear of stalling—of not being able to get going after slowing down—may also make relaxation difficult. In some instances, where a person is tired from chronic anxiety, fear of collapsing may have an actual basis, although never to an irreversible degree. Naturally, if relaxation is mistaken for laziness or not being productive, it is likely to be resisted. It is important to realize that relaxation actually improves productivity because it enhances efficiency and restores energy, a point to be discussed further.

Resistance to relaxation also stems from a fear of giving up one of the most common defense mechanisms against anxiety—keeping busy. As a form of distraction from uncomfortable feelings, keeping busy serves to avoid anxious thoughts and internal sensations. By focusing on outside tasks and activities, attention is diverted away from anxiety. In this case, slowing down or sitting still risks a face-to-face encounter with fearful thoughts and anxious feelings.

Frequent stress and anxiety cause the body to remain in a state of tension and arousal that is resistant to relaxation. Reich (1972) used the term *body armor* to describe this pattern. Reich indicated that an armored person is unable to completely relax. Relaxation threatens that person's protective layers of muscular tension. For the armored person, relaxation can produce feelings of vulnerability, which are picked up by the survival center as a danger signal, activating the fight/flight reaction. For those who have a long history of stress or anxiety, which often begins in childhood, relaxation may be experienced as a threat to personal security. In other words, our body adapts to our emotional attitude. Like the hard shell of some animals, the body molds itself into the patterns of muscular tension that are associated with anxiety. Repeated over and over, such tension can become the normal body experience. Therefore, in beginning to relax, the anxious person may feel threatened or vulnerable, and, as the survival instinct responds to these danger signals, the fight/flight reaction is triggered.

Another issue is the need to be in control, discussed in Chapter 4 as a common personality trait in anxiety sufferers. Being in control usually requires an alert, watchful, guarded, and tense state of being. Preparing to cope with anxiety on a moment's notice, a chronic fight/flight stance is adopted, with continuous arousal. Relaxation, on the other hand, requires letting down your guard, trusting, and "opening" to the universe. This may threaten your sense of control and self-protection. As relaxation softens the boundaries of separateness, the line blurs between your individual self and the world around you. In relaxation, you "open up" and interact more flexibly and permeably with others. For sensitive people, who are fearful of rejection or whose self-esteem is weak, this is anxiety-arousing.

You cannot be relaxed and activated at the same time. As a result, your survival instinct must choose between the two, and, as a conservative defense mechanism, it will always choose the fight/flight option. If you have rigid body armor, a strong need for control, concerns about safety and vulnerability, or strong needs for achievement, you may have to train yourself to enjoy the benefits of relaxation.

To sit still and relax we must face another formidable obstacle, the mind's agendas. Mind and body are intricately connected, and the body responds in some way to virtually every thought. When our thoughts go unrestrained, relaxation is difficult, because the stimulation and stress caused by our thoughts keep us activated. We each have between 30,000 and 50,000 thoughts every day, an average of approximately one thought per second. Relaxation requires shutting off our thoughts, or at least curtailing our reactions to them. In one Buddhist form of meditation, the goal is to attain "no-mind," a peaceful mental state where there is nothing on your mind.

Controlling what we think about is a key part of relaxation. Every thought affects our bodies in some way, but the actual effect depends on specific thoughts. Worry thoughts, for example, activate the fight/flight response, because our survival instinct interprets them as danger signals. Although worrying is usually irrational, and the danger is only in our own minds, we react in a real and physical way.

Other thought patterns also activate the fight/flight response, making relaxation difficult. For example, in believing that people will like you only if you please or impress them, you are likely to work too hard, take things too seriously, and push yourself beyond reasonable limits. Based on this belief, you may have difficulty relaxing, especially around other people. Another example is *shoulds*, thoughts that cause physical stress as you push yourself to do what you "should." High expectations and achievement needs are another source of stress, if you push yourself beyond reasonable limits to fulfill them. On the other hand, pleasant thoughts can have a soothing effect on the body, helping to restore relaxed equilibrium. Once you learn to relax, just the thought of relaxing can have a calming effect.

The power of thoughts to affect us physically can be demonstrated by this simple experiment: take a moment to focus with your eyes closed on a bright yellow lemon. Visualize the lemon being sliced sharply in half, and then squeezed into juice. Imagine tasting the juice as you smell its pungent aroma. Most people will begin to salivate in response to this thought, making it obvious that the body responds readily to thoughts.

Since the mind and body are intertwined in one organic system, relaxation can be approached from either aspect of this relationship. It is possible to relax the body by calming the mind, as well as calm the mind by relaxing the body. The CHAANGE program recognizes this by providing, as its very first assignment, a relaxation training tape with two procedures. One is a physical relaxation procedure, called "progressive muscle relaxation." The other is a visualization, or mental relaxation procedure. By using both forms of relaxation, there is a greater chance for acquiring this vitally important skill. In one case, a woman who practiced these skills during the program said at the end of her therapy, "Relaxation is second nature now. Whenever I begin to feel tense or anxious, I automatically take a few deep breaths and relax, without even thinking about it." Another program participant reported, "I am finding myself using the relaxation techniques when I start to feel anxious. Deep breathing seems second nature now."

We all experience relaxed moments, when our attention is fully engaged in a single activity. Sitting quietly by the fireplace, knitting, reading, or boating on a sunny summer afternoon are examples of such activities when serenity replaces the internal chatter of thoughts. Under these conditions we are quiet and content, and the concerns of daily life are transcended. However, these activities bring us only temporary peace during the time they absorb our interest, or perhaps for a short lingering period afterwards. Once the mind returns to its "normal" state, we are once again activated by one thought after another.

Because relaxation requires an integration of mind and body, and a reconciling of disturbing thoughts, slowing down can be a growth opportunity. In fact, some relaxation methods, such as meditation, involve processes and goals similar to psychotherapy. In order to achieve peace of mind, you must face your inner self with all its fears, beliefs, and feelings. Freud (1935), in pioneering psychological therapy, asserted that the goal of psychoanalysis was to render the unconscious conscious. Freedom would come from a conscious awareness of what motivates us, and from making choices based on self-understanding. While psychoanalysis has waned since Freud's time, most therapy approaches still involve facing the inner self as a step in healing. This is essential to anxiety recovery, which requires facing fears and learning to handle them. The technique of "floating through anxiety," developed by Weekes (1978) and discussed in Chapter 12, involves relaxing into fear and staying open while it passes. In facing fearful thoughts and situations, anxiety is experienced, but by learning and applying the right skills, self-confidence and courage grow. Relaxation is the foundation of these new skills and attitudes.

Defense mechanisms use up mental energy. This was observed by Gardner and colleagues (1959) in their studies of cognitive behavior. Gardner and colleagues noticed that some people had more mental energy and could handle uncertainty better than others. They referred to this resource as "conflict-free energy," which was found to be more abundant in people with fewer emotional conflicts and concerns. Anxiety was singled out as a significant drain on energy resources because it requires so much defensive activity. Scanning the environment for situations that might trigger anxiety, constantly categorizing things as safe or unsafe, monitoring other people for signs of rejection or acceptance, are all examples of defensive activities that use up mental energy. Relaxation training helps to free up energy resources by producing feelings of safety and well-being. When relaxing, there is a letting down of the guard—less defensiveness—and a release of bound-up energy. The more relaxed, the less anxious, and the less anxious, the more free energy.

Mental energy, and its role in anxiety, can be compared to the memory resources of a computer. The defensive activities required to control anxiety use a lot of random access memory (RAM), which leaves less of this resource for other tasks. A shortage of RAM slows the system down, rendering it less efficient at performing other work. Regular practice of relaxation would, to complete the analogy, free up memory, as fewer defensive activities would be necessary to maintain feelings of control and safety.

Inherent in every person is a natural state of peace, which can be experienced when all is calm. Some other terms for this are "equilibrium" and "homeostasis," which imply a state of balance at the core of life. On a day-to-day basis, as well as during the course of a lifetime, our equilibrium is disturbed by various crises and the general stress of life. If we know the skills, and practice them regularly, we can restore our equilibrium and stay in touch with inner peace. However, if we do not know how to recover from stress, a chronic fight/flight response will lead to an emotional or physical health crisis, such as a severe anxiety disorder.

Restoring relaxed equilibrium is necessary for biological and psychological health. During relaxation, damaged cells are replaced, the immune system is re-powered, and, through a variety of other healing processes, organ systems are helped to recover from the effects of stress. Stress is not necessarily destructive, but lack of stress recovery is. Without relaxation, physical symptoms and disease are sure to develop. This issue will be explored in more depth in Chapter 16.

Psychologically, relaxation is necessary for restoring mental efficiency, problem-solving abilities, creativity, peace of mind, and general enjoyment of life. Furthermore, without relaxation the anxious mind remains in turmoil, and, in severe anxiety cases, leads to a fear of losing control or going crazy.

Relaxation is necessary to overcome anxiety for a number of other reasons. We already noted that relaxation and anxiety are incompatible states—the more relaxed, the less anxious. In addition, training yourself to relax raises the threshold of stress required to activate the fight/flight response. At baseline relaxation, it takes more of a truly life-threatening situation to activate a defensive reaction, whereas if you are tense and up-tight it takes much less stress to raise your already elevated defensiveness. Also, once an anxiety reaction is set in motion, relaxation can help to counteract it, although it still takes time to recover from an adrenaline surge.

Benson's (1975, 1984) extensive research on the healing benefits of relaxation helps to establish its importance in anxiety recovery. Benson finds that the body has an inborn capacity to enter a special state characterized by lowered heart rate, decreased rate of breathing, lowered blood pressure, slower brain waves, and an overall reduction of the speed of metabolism. The changes produced by this "relaxation response" counteract the harmful effects and uncomfortable feelings of stress. As Benson puts it, "In this relatively peaceful condition, the individual's mental patterns change so that he breaks free of what I call worry cycles. These are unproductive grooves or circuits that cause the mind to play over and over again, almost involuntarily, the same anxieties or uncreative, health-impairing thoughts" (Benson 1984, p. 5).

Benson recommends a simple four-step procedure for eliciting the relaxation response. This technique represents the essence of many forms of relaxation, such as meditation, hypnosis, autogenic training, yoga, and progressive muscle relaxation. The four components are: (1) finding a quiet environment, (2) consciously relaxing the body's muscles, (3) focusing for ten to twenty minutes on a mental device, such as a special word or prayer, and (4) assuming a passive attitude toward intrusive thoughts. In his most recent work, Benson (1984) adds one other element, the *faith factor*. The faith factor is a person's deeply held positive beliefs or spiritual convictions. By combining the relaxation response with the faith factor, the possibilities for self-healing are almost unlimited. Indeed, Benson reports an astounding list of physical and emotional disorders that can be eliminated or significantly reduced using this approach. The list includes headaches, angina pain, high blood pressure, insomnia, backaches, and high cholesterol. He reports, for example, that 80 percent of angina pain can be relieved by relaxation combined with positive belief. Benson also indicates that most symptoms of anxiety, including panic attacks, anticipatory worry, GI distress (nausea, diarrhea, irritable bowel syndrome, constipation), hyperventilation, and irritability can be alleviated with regular practice of relaxation combined with positive belief.

I personally had difficulty relaxing, and could not sit still for many years until I made a commitment to learn how to slow down. As a doctoral student in clinical psychology, I spent a training year in San Francisco, where I lived with a friend named John. When I first met John, he immediately impressed me as one of the most gentle, patient men I had ever encountered, and I envied the peacefulness he exuded. One evening, shortly after we became roommates, John announced that he was going into his room to meditate, and he added, "Don't call me, I'll call you." I was interested in meditation, which had a mysterious, almost secretive quality, but I knew nothing about the practice. Fortunately, John offered to be my meditation teacher.

I was surprised to learn how simple, yet difficult, was the practice of meditation. When I first sat still to meditate, I was up within seconds responding to the call of nature and basic needs such as thirst. When I resumed sitting, I was up again quickly with a need to change my clothes and "prepare" myself. That was the sum total of my first meditation session. The next day, I performed all my preparations in advance, but to my dismay, sitting was again interrupted by a list of things that could not wait to be done. After a few days of this agitated sitting, I recognized a pattern of resistance, traceable to my mind's difficulty with letting go. This was frustrating but, fortunately, I was reassured by my meditation teacher that I would overcome this hurdle with further practice. Persisting with the practice, I became comfortable with sitting still and looked forward to my meditation sessions. Within a few months, I experienced a new awareness and inner peace that permeated other areas of my life. I continued to incorporate meditation into my life, benefiting from it in many ways. I credit meditation with improvement in my concentration ability, energy level, clarity and steadiness in thinking, and deepening understanding of myself and of life's secrets and mysteries.

Meditation as a science was developed in ancient India and spread to Egypt, China, Japan, and recently to the West.

Although there are numerous methods of meditation associated with different spiritual traditions, all share some common elements. In fact, virtually all meditation practices involve the components identified by Benson in his study of the relaxation response. Let's focus on those aspects of meditation that are appropriate and helpful for anxiety recovery.

The process of meditation consists of choosing an object of concentration and maintaining a focus on it, letting all other thoughts dissolve into the background. What is difficult is letting go of other thoughts, which compete vigorously for our attention. Normally we identify with our thoughts, taking them seriously and reacting emotionally to them. In everyday life, the mind moves actively from thought to thought, often wandering haphazardly: "I'm hungry. I should call my mother. The children need my attention. What's for dinner? Where's my pen?" The essence of meditation is learning to let all these thoughts, which demand attention and energy, fade into the background while you concentrate on the one point. At first, you may become distracted by your thoughts, or feel compelled to respond to them immediately. However, by gently letting go of thoughts and returning to the point of focus, you will slowly strengthen your concentration ability. With steady practice, you will succeed in emptying your mind of all thoughts and, as even the object of concentration fades away, you will experience the quiet peace behind thinking.

As you sit still and meditate, a number of sensations may occur. You may notice that certain thoughts are repetitive, like an old, scratched record that keeps playing the same passage over and over. What is the purpose of such thoughts? Perhaps they are unfinished items needing a disposition before you can let them go. Make a mental note of them, as well as a commitment to deal with them so that they will not disturb you next time you sit. You may also notice that your mind is reluctant to let go of certain thoughts and resists your efforts. That is natural, since the anxious mind is conditioned to be alert for danger and vulnerability. Stay with the practice, reminding yourself that all new skills, such as learning to play a musical instrument, require consistent practice over a period of time in order to be mastered.

In meditation, attention is directed toward the present moment, whatever is chosen as the object of concentration. This counteracts anxiety and worrying, which is typically focused on what might occur in the future. Anxiety anticipates the future, based on the past. It is concerned about "there and then" rather than "here and now." Ram Dass (1971) emphasizes this aspect, inviting us to "be here now" as we meditate. I advise my patients to periodically stop and ask, "How am I doing *right now*?" During periods of high anticipatory anxiety, this question can be asked frequently, on a moment-to-moment basis if necessary, to help with staying in the present. Typically, even the anxious person is in control *in the present moment*. It is fear of losing control in the future, under certain anticipated circumstances, that arouses anxiety.

Meditation is relevant to anxiety recovery because in practicing this skill you must deal with many of the thought processes that create and maintain fear. Worrying about the future, "what-ifs," "shoulds," judging, difficulty concentrating, restlessness, and so on are all anxiety habits that must be faced and dissolved in order to attain the goals of anxiety recovery. These goals include relaxation and inner peace. Below I offer some exercises to help attain these goals.

EXERCISE: LEARNING TO RELAX

Learning how to relax is similar to developing any new skill. It requires proper instructions, combined with a commitment to learn and dedication of some time and energy to practicing on a regular basis. Take several breaks each day when you can devote 10 to 20 minutes to practicing relaxation. Use of a cassette tape with recorded instructions is often helpful. Play it several times a day, during relaxation breaks. Several more times each day, think about relaxing while you are doing other activities that do not require intense concentration, such as washing dishes, folding laundry, or straightening up your office or home. In addition, consider learning how to meditate as a way of slowing down your mind and eliciting the relaxation response. Be patient with these practices, and remember that you are replacing old, well-established habits and patterns. Also, remind yourself that slowing down and relaxation are safe, good, and necessary for survival and health.

EXERCISE: CULTIVATING PATIENCE

Select a simple, everyday situation that has its own time requirement. Water boiling for tea, hand lotion being absorbed by the skin, food cooking on the stove with a timer, or waiting for someone who is running late are all good examples of situations requiring a few minutes of waiting. Practice cultivating an attitude of patience by sitting still, relaxing, and waiting peacefully. Surrender gracefully to such situations, and transform them into opportunities for enjoying a few minutes of silent meditation.

MEDITATION INSTRUCTIONS

Choose a time when you can be relatively free of outside distractions. The quiet times of dawn and dusk are ideal, but any time that fits your lifestyle is appropriate. Set aside approximately 20 minutes for meditation, once or twice each day.

Set up a special place for meditation, such as a corner of a room, where you can build up a peaceful atmosphere to help quiet your mind. Of course, you can meditate anywhere, including a park bench or while waiting in a parked car.

Sit straight but not rigidly, with head, neck, and back in alignment. Face north or east, if possible. It is also important to be relaxed, warm, and comfortable in order to minimize distraction. If necessary, stretch or exercise before meditation.

Close your eyes and begin with relaxed breathing, pulling in your diaphragm to fully empty your lungs as you exhale. Establish a natural, deep breathing rhythm, with approximately 3 seconds each of inhalation and exhalation.

Let your mind wander initially as you regulate your breathing, then gradually focus on the sensations of breathing. Next, gently bring your attention to the focal point of your choice. This can be a blank screen, a mental picture, a steady sound such as flowing water, or the rising and falling of your breathing. You may also try gazing steadily at an object, such as a candle flame or an inspiring picture.

Hold your concentration on the one focal point, gently returning to it each time your mind is drawn away by passing thoughts. This is the essence of meditation practice. Do not be frustrated by the frequency of losing focus. Cultivate an attitude that does not judge your thoughts, but instead detaches gently from them.

Keep a notebook handy for stubborn or compelling thoughts, and release them by jotting them down. Then close your eyes and return to concentration on the focal point or the space between thoughts.

Rise calmly upon completing your session, and remain connected to the thin and delicate thread of awareness. Carry the serenity of meditation into your daily life, and continue your practice on a regular basis.

9

Food and Fear

If doctors of today will not become the nutritionists of tomorrow, the nutritionists of today will become the doctors of tomorrow. There simply could be no healing without proper nutrition.

Paavo Airola

Many aspects of food, eating, and nutrition can produce anxiety symptoms and strong emotional reactions in sensitive people. To understand the relationship between food and fear, recall that as a sensitive person you react strongly to external and internal stimuli. This includes what, when, and how much you eat. Your anxiety level is influenced by these factors, and you may need to modify your eating patterns as part of your anxiety recovery.

One of the most basic food-related conditions you face on a daily basis is fluctuations in your blood sugar level. Blood sugar is a factor in determining your energy level, and it is influenced largely by the timing of your meals and the type of foods you eat. Sharp rises in blood sugar, resulting from intake of simple carbohydrates, such as white bread, and heavily sugared candy, cakes, and cookies are associated with increases in adrenaline—the activating hormone in anxiety symptoms and fear. Low blood sugar, resulting from missed meals or eating large amounts of simple carbohydrates, produces symptoms such as fatigue, irritability, headaches, blurry vision, mental confusion, and weak or "strung-out" feelings. These symptoms are also commonly associated with anxiety.

Both high and low blood sugar levels can be caused by a diet that is high in sugar and simple carbohydrates. Such foods cause the pancreas to release larger amounts of insulin, the blood sugar regulator, to ensure that the sugar level doesn't get too high. But often the amount of insulin released will exceed what is needed to lower the blood sugar. This is one of the body's safety mechanisms, but it can sometimes go too far in lowering blood sugar. When this happens, the liver releases glycogen to increase blood sugar level. Such fluctuations in your blood sugar can cause a host of physical, emotional, and mental symptoms. Low blood sugar level, of course, can also result from an inconsistent eating schedule. Therefore, it is important to eat regularly, and perhaps more frequently (four to six small meals per day), to maintain a consistent blood sugar level. In addition, a diet emphasizing complex carbohydrates such as whole grains, breads, pasta, vegetables, and grains is advised. These foods have plenty of fiber, which helps the digestive system break down foods slowly and absorb sugar gradually.

Also consider how you react to the taste, smell, texture, temperature, and immediate biological effect of foods. Hot and spicy foods, for example, can raise body temperature and cause flushing, which are anxiety symptoms in some people. Monosodium glutamate (MSG)—the ingredient used to enhance flavor in some foods—can also cause a flushing reaction that serves as a stimulus for panic reactions in some people. Stimulants, such as the caffeine in coffee, chocolate, and many sodas will "rev up" your body, another typical symptom of anxiety. Depressants, such as alcohol in wine, beer, and liquor, have mood-altering effects that can trigger anxiety in sensitive people. Caffeine and alcohol, of course, are drugs with the potential for addiction and other pitfalls for the biologically sensitive person. Therefore, it may be necessary for you to avoid certain foods and drinks as part of your anxiety recovery. In this chapter, we will explore the food and fear relationship, and identify appropriate changes for proper nutrition and eating habits.

Your response to food begins even before it enters your body. How and under what conditions you eat are the first considerations. For example, your mental state and degree of physical relaxation at the time of eating have a significant influence on your response to food. If you are rushed and under pressure while eating, your energy is not available for the more subtle task of food metabolism. In this case, eating is not enjoyable and digestion is less efficient. In some instances, when you eat by the clock or when it is simply convenient, you may not even be hungry. In other instances, you may be hungry but unaware of it because you are too stressed or busy. These conditions can trigger anxiety, and eating under stress is likely to stimulate the stress–fight/flight–anxiety cycle.

Your attitude toward and past experience with foods also affect your response to them. Just the thought of certain foods may make you nauseated or weak, while the thought of other foods may give you energy, strength, or a relaxed feeling. As with anxiety, conditioning plays a central role in your physical and emotional responses to food. Your feelings about most foods are based on past experiences with them, including childhood experiences. Therefore, changing what and how you eat will require experimentation, patience, and new conditioning.

Another issue is your beliefs and expectations about food. A vegetarian may avoid animal foods, based on health concerns or moral convictions, while a meat-eater might delight in the same fare. At a conference I attended some years ago, a panel of experts were asked their opinion on taking vitamin supplements. The response of the panel's physician emphasized the power of belief in diet and nutrition: "If you believe you need vitamin supplements and don't take them, you'll probably develop symptoms of vitamin deficiency. On the other hand, if you believe you do not need them, you'll probably show no deficiency symptoms without them."

While this may seem like a radical position, there are many examples of the power of belief in health and healing. Pelletier (1977) concludes, after an extensive review of mind–body research, that the mind has great powers in alleviating stress and preventing stress-induced illness. Siegel (1986), Borysenko (1987), Kabat-Zinn (1994a,b), and others further demonstrate the healing mind–body relationship. These health practitioners have shown how the power of belief can help alleviate or prevent symptoms of cancer, high blood pressure, gastrointestinal disorders, headaches, heart disease, and other physical conditions.

I believe that proper nutrition and eating habits are a form of preventive medicine, and that they can have healing powers. Furthermore, you can significantly enhance your anxiety recovery process with proper nutrition and eating habits. The guidelines and recommendations offered later in this chapter are based on this belief.

Why do we eat? Normally, we eat to sustain our energy and continually rebuild our physical body. However, sometimes we eat for emotional nourishment, rather than to meet our body's requirements. This, of course, is part of the joy of eating, but not when it conflicts with health. Eating to cope with feelings such as boredom, anger, anxiety, or depression may result in eating too much or consuming addictive substances such as alcohol and caffeine. The most obvious consequences of unhealthy eating are physical: obesity, heart disease, low energy, poor skin and hair condition, and other signs of health deterioration. In addition, there are emotional consequences, such as depression, poor self-image, and shame. For the sensitive person, all of these consequences of improper eating may stimulate anxiety as a secondary reaction.

One of the most important issues for anxiety is *control.* Anxiety almost invariably develops when you feel out of control, whether it is about losing control of your eating behavior, your emotions, or your health. Therefore, as long as you are not in control of your health or eating behavior, you are at risk for developing anxiety symptoms. In the case of drugs and alcohol, the problem with control is easily recognized. However, you can also develop control problems with certain foods. For example, you may develop a psychological addiction to particular foods, such as chocolate, potato chips, or candy, in which case you will sense a degree of being controlled by your need for them. This leaves you with subtle feelings of powerlessness or weakness, often coupled with shame or guilt about giving in to your impulses or going against your own health. On the other hand, this does not mean you must never indulge in these treats. The issue is control: Are you in control of your eating or is your eating in control of you?

In addition to control issues and food addictions, anxiety is sometimes associated with "emotional eating." One example is *overeating* or *binge eating* to compensate for unpleasant emotions. Unpleasant emotions can include anxiety; feelings of loneliness, emptiness, or rejection; lack of interest in work; frustration; unexpressed anger; loss; and disappointment in some aspect of your life. To cope with these unpleasant experiences, you might use food as a tranquilizing medication. Eating is, in fact, tranquilizing due to blood being temporarily withdrawn from the brain and other extremities during digestion. This yields a lightheaded and relaxed feeling. However, "emotional eating" often becomes chronic overeating, with resulting weight gain or obesity. Weight problems, of course, can create additional health risks, such as heart disease, back and joint disease, diabetes, lower stamina, and breathing difficulties. In addition, being overweight often lowers self-esteem and creates social anxiety. Anxiety, therefore, can both *cause* overeating and *result from* overeating.

Another eating pattern is *undereating* due to body image problems or a wish to lose weight. Intentional undereating in order to lose weight is common among people whose eating behavior or life circumstances are out of control. Usually, this is done in the form of dieting. Dieting is reinforced by the social stigma of being overweight, as well as the cultural value placed on being thin. For others who are not overweight, especially for many women, problems with distorted self-perception of body size and shape, as well as low self-esteem and concerns about social acceptance, may lead to undereating. A woman who sees herself as overweight, even when she is at a normal weight by objective standards, may resort to habitual undereating to correct her "deficiency." Another strategy may be a pattern of purging after eating, an eating disorder known as bulimia.

Undereating and bulimia increase the risk for anxiety in a number of ways. First, blood sugar level decreases when eating is inconsistent or insufficient. Low blood sugar level is experienced as weakness, irritability, visual fluctuations, impaired attention and concentration, headaches, and fatigue, all of which can be signals for an anxiety reaction in the sensitized person. Second, the shame, frustration, guilt, and other feelings typically associated with undereating and bulimia may create an anxiety state. Such feelings are unpleasant and anxiety-arousing, raising the need for defense mechanisms such as denial. Third, these eating patterns are often compulsive, leading to anxiety about not being in control of oneself or "going crazy."

Related to undereating is a less frequent but intriguing problem for anxiety, namely fasting. Fasting, or intentional abstinence from food, can have powerful therapeutic effects. Fasting is cleansing and rejuvenating to the body, and it is usually associated with increased mental clarity and "high" feelings. Many spiritual texts espouse the benefits of periodic fasting, and some religious holidays, such as Lent and Yom Kippur, involve food abstinence. You should, in fact, fast every day for approximately ten hours between your evening and morning meals (individuals with a tendency towards low blood sugar should consult their doctor for advice on intervals between meals). Indeed, the morning meal, breakfast, literally means "breaking fast" or ending the fast. During the daily fast, your body detoxifies itself and your digestive system has an opportunity for rest and recovery. It is important to "break-fast" properly, and then resupply your body with food. Skipping breakfast is a set-up for anxiety, due to the likelihood of low blood sugar later in the day. Simply break your daily fast with diluted fruit juice, herbal tea, or fresh fruit. After an assimilation period of 30 to 60 minutes, eat a whole-grain complex carbohydrate, such as cereal or bread.

I have personally used more extended fasting for both health benefits and spiritual development. Obviously, fasting involves some risks, particularly in terms of its impact on blood sugar level. I have had to be careful with this practice because my total body fat is approximately 6 percent, leaving me with little stored energy reserves. An excellent alternative to total abstinence is a juice fast, a period of time during which you drink only diluted fruit and vegetable juices. This approach helps to maintain blood sugar level and energy, while providing the benefits of fasting. Fasting is best done within a contemplative time and place, away from strenuous activities or work. If you are interested in the benefits of fasting, I recommend that you learn more through reading and seek guidance from a nutritionist for fasting longer than one day.

There is yet another food-related issue to be addressed, in spite of its being almost too obvious to mention. Your body composition is primarily water, and water is required for almost every biological process, including blood and lymph flow, hormone production, digestion, and excretion. When your water level drops too low, you experience signals of dehydration in the form of thirst, loss of concentration and attention span, and in later stages, headaches, fatigue, and weakness. These signals are virtually identical to the some of the more common symptoms of anxiety. You may confuse dehydration symptoms with anxiety, leading to fear of an impending panic attack or episode of severe anxiety. It is important to drink plenty of pure water throughout the day, preferably between meals. Two quarts (about eight glasses) per day is the standard recommendation.

Health is a necessary part of anxiety recovery, and proper nutrition and eating habits are essential to health. One of the best ways to improve and maintain health is to eat a healthy diet, choosing foods that are closest to nature and that provide good nutrition. Healthy cells, organs, and body systems require high-quality raw ingredients derived from the foods you eat and water you drink. This usually means more grains, fresh fruits, and vegetables.

My own diet evolved towards vegetarianism some twenty-five years ago. I found that a vegetarian diet was more suitable to my digestive system, as well as more compatible with my beliefs and environmental awareness. For example, I was sensitive to world hunger and learned that it took approximately five pounds of beans and grains fed to cattle to yield one pound of meat, and that those foods could efficiently serve the nutritional needs of more people. I also knew that while meat is a source of complete protein, it is higher in fat than a grain-based diet. I was attracted to a healthy lifestyle with ecological benefits.

A number of writers over the years influenced my diet and attitudes toward food. Lappe (1971), for example, impressed me in *Diet for a Small Planet* with a discussion of the politics and ecology of food. In *The Book of Tofu*, Shurtleff and Aoyagi (1975) helped me recognize the potential for a vegetarian solution to world hunger. I became interested in the diets of people known for their health and longevity, such as the Seventh Day Adventists and the Hunzas. I must also mention the impact of my visits to The Farm, a spiritual community in Tennessee, where up to twelve hundred people lived a no-animal-products lifestyle from food to clothes. The Farm diet was based on soybeans, a virtually complete protein source. I am still fond of The Farm's *Ice Bean* products, which are sold today in health food stores as a soy-based alternative to ice cream.

For a number of years I was somewhat rigid and moralistic about my diet, denying my occasional desires for meat and sweets. In addition, my former black-and-white approach to a vegetarian diet interfered with my ability to adapt to a relocation from Southern California to Vermont, where I was unable to keep warm until I allowed some meat and fish into my diet.

Each of us is physically and emotionally unique, and even our individual nutritional needs vary from day to day based on activities and stress level. Therefore, I avoid rigid rules and formulas in making recommendations about nutrition and eating patterns. Instead, I offer principles and guidelines, and encourage you to learn and experiment with what works best for you. Consultation with a nutritionist is also a good idea, to help individualize what you learn. With those qualifications, I offer:

FOOD PRINCIPLES AND GUIDELINES FOR DANCING WITH FEAR

Eat on a regular basis with a natural rhythm.

Your body will develop habits and expectations about meal times, just as it does with your sleep cycle. Hunger, food metabolism, and elimination are most natural when they correspond to regular daily cycles. On the other hand, your hunger and nutritional needs vary with changes in activity level, stress, seasonal changes, and other factors. Therefore, leave room for flexibility and spontaneity in your eating rhythm.

Eat small meals four to six times a day to maintain a level blood sugar.

Your blood sugar level is more likely to be steady when you eat slow-burning foods that prevent sudden changes in blood sugar level. A meal can be light, consisting of complex carbohydrates and a small amount of protein, fresh fruit or vegetables, cereal, a salad, crackers and cheese or bean dip, bread and soup, rather than the more traditional and hearty idea of a meal. Main meals should have a balance of protein, carbohydrates, and a small amount of fat. Including some protein or carbohydrate at each meal will help ensure steady energy.

My typical daily eating schedule begins with fresh fruit or diluted fruit juice, followed by a carbohydrate breakfast. I eat again about mid-morning, having another carbohydrate snack of bread, muffin, bagel, or banana and dried fruit. A light lunch at midday might consist of a sandwich, or leftovers from the previous night's dinner. In the afternoon, I snack on crackers and cheese, more leftovers, apple and dried fruit, or cereal. My main meal is dinner, where I emphasize grains, beans, and vegetables. I generally keep a supply of food at my office, and carry healthy snacks when I travel, so that I can maintain my blood sugar level and energy wherever I am.

Allow a daily fast period of eight to twelve hours between dinner and breakfast.

In experimenting with an eating schedule that works best for you, pay attention to your body's need for a rest-and-repair period once a day, at night or during your sleep cycle. Your sleep may improve if you quiet your body and relieve it from digestion beginning two to four hours prior to bedtime. Break your daily fast with diluted fruit juice, herbal tea, or fresh fruit to help cleanse the toxins that are released during the daily fast.

Drink an adequate supply of fresh water on a regular basis.

Avoid symptoms of dehydration while supplying the most essential requirement to your body. Remember that your body's chemistry, circulation, and metabolic functions, as well as mechanical functioning of muscles and joints, all depend on an adequate supply of water. Drink approximately two quarts of water per day (about eight glasses), more if you're active. Any drink other than pure water will need to be filtered and purified by your body. Why make extra work for your body by drinking fluids requiring filtering, such as sodas, unless they have real food value?

Unfortunately, you can no longer trust the quality of water in many locations. My community, for example, supplies drinking water from Lake Champlain, the site of treated sewage, public swimming, and gasoline-powered boating. Therefore, you may need to purchase your drinking water, or filter your tap water for drinking. The most cost-effective option is to install a simple charcoal-type filter on your drinking water supply, to remove impurities and chemical agents such as chlorine. Don't pollute your body with drinks other than pure water.

Be aware of your hunger level when eating and let hunger guide your eating rhythm.

As you learn to relax and approach eating with awareness, you will be guided by your natural hunger signals as to when, what, and how much to eat. Try some of the methods for increasing awareness and eating consciously that are offered later in these guidelines. To develop an intimate sense of your hunger mechanism, rate your hunger level on a ten-point scale, with ten representing "weak and starving" and zero representing "uncomfortably full." Rate your hunger before and after you eat, as well as periodically during the day to increase hunger awareness. Eat when your hunger rating is about seven, and stop when your hunger rating is about four. By synchronizing your eating schedule with your hunger cycle, your energy level will be more consistent and your health will improve.

Eat primarily whole, minimally processed foods with the most "life force."

Fresh foods possess the highest nutritional value, which cannot be improved by preserving, processing, flavoring, or coloring. Foods do not need to be "enriched" or "improved" unless they have first been devitalized by processing. In general, be informed about what you eat by reading and understanding food packaging labels. Avoid chemicals such as preservatives, artificial flavors, and artificial dyes as much as possible.

Avoid caffeine, and discover alternatives to coffee, such as herbal teas and grain-based brews.

The advisability of eliminating caffeine as part of anxiety recovery was discussed earlier in this chapter. There are many alternatives and substitutes to explore. One option is grain-based hot drinks that provide a hearty aroma and dark, rich taste. There are a number of such products, with brand names such as "Pero" and "Inka," typically available at health food stores. In addition, there are several blends of herbal teas that have a dark, rich flavor. My favorites are "Roastaroma" (Celestial Seasonings) and "Take-A-Break" (Lipton). In addition, there are countless other caffeine-free herbal tea blends available, and you can even blend your own favorites. Consider the use of iced herbal teas, particularly the fruity flavors, as an alternative to sodas. Also be aware that many soft drinks contain caffeine—they should also be discontinued.

Avoid sugar and learn to use fruit for sweets.

Sugar can affect sensitive people as if it were a drug. In fact, reliance on sugared foods for energy can lead to sugar addiction, and long-term use can weaken the organs involved in sugar regulation. When your body cannot properly regulate blood sugar level, you are likely to experience sugar fluctuations as irritability, lethargy, headaches, mood changes, mental confusion, impaired attention and concentration, and visual problems. These symptoms put you at risk for anxiety due to body and mood changes that may occur for no apparent reason. Excess sugar on a continual basis also puts you at risk for diseases such as adult-onset diabetes. The best solution for maintaining steady blood sugar level is to eat complex carbohydrates from natural sources, such as grains, vegetables, and fruits. Foods high in protein—beans and legumes—will also help regulate sugar level in the blood. If you have a "sweet tooth" as I do, learn to use fresh and dried fruit as a snack. My favorites are raisins, dates, and figs, which should be eaten in moderation. As you eliminate simple carbohydrates and sugared foods you will probably find that fruit tastes sweeter, and that it can satisfy your sweet tooth without the health risks associated with those foods.

Use the U.S. Department of Agriculture's (USDA) "pyramid chart" as a nutritional guideline.

In 1992, the USDA updated its dietary recommendations in the form of a Food Guide Pyramid, a chart depicting the amounts and types of foods needed for health. The Food

Guide Pyramid, which emphasizes grains as the basis of a healthy diet, shows the recommended number of servings from each food group. You can obtain a copy of the Food Guide Pyramid by a sending $1.00 (check made out to "Superintendent of Documents") to: Consumer Information Center, Department 159-Y, Pueblo, Colorado 81009.

Eating according to these guidelines will probably mean decreasing your consumption of animal foods and increasing grains, vegetables, and fruit. Also, decreasing sweets and fats is likely to be an adjustment. Keep the words "balance" and "moderation" in mind as you modify your nutritional lifestyle, and make changes gradually. Building a healthy nutritional lifestyle takes time, because it involves changing your eating, shopping, and cooking habits.

Learn the creative art of cooking and develop some favorite healthful dishes.

Since eating is a basic necessity, learning how to prepare food for yourself is a basic skill. Empower yourself by learning how to select and prepare food that is appetizing and healthful. Cookbooks are helpful; seek those that are health-oriented and provide nutritional information as well as recipes. Two excellent examples are Levitt, Smith, and Warren's (1980) *Kripalu Kitchen: A Natural Foods Cookbook and Nutritional Guide*, and Robertson, Flinders, and Godfrey's (1976) *Laurel's Kitchen: A Handbook for Vegetarian Cookery and Nutrition*. For those who have little time for cooking, an excellent choice would be Ponichtera's (1991) *Quick and Healthy Recipes and Ideas*. However, do not be bound by recipes. Learn from them, and gradually create your own. Keep it simple, and be guided by basic health principles. For example, avoid excess oils in cooking by using steaming and pressure-cooking methods. When you do cook with oil, choose polyunsaturated and monounsaturated oils like olive, canola, and sunflower. Your self-esteem is likely to improve as you develop skills and competence in cooking.

If you are interested in a vegetarian diet, eat a variety of foods each day to ensure adequate nutrition.

If you are making a transition to vegetarianism from meat and dairy foods, the most immediate concern is to obtain complete protein from vegetable sources. While meat and dairy protein generally contain complete protein, vegetable foods are not complete in terms of the presence of all required amino acids. Therefore, it is necessary to eat a good balance of foods each day to acquire complete protein. Most foods contain important protein elements and eating a balanced diet is likely to meet your nutritional requirements. On the other hand, the amount of protein consumed by Americans is excessive, and may even be harmful to health. The recommended protein requirement is approximately 0.36 grams per day for each pound of body weight. This would mean about 61 grams of protein per day for a 170-pound person, and about 46 grams for a 128-pound person. However, like other nutrition requirements, your protein needs may vary significantly due to factors such as age, activity level, and stress. A food chart, such as the one provided by Robertson, Flinders, and Godfrey (1976), will give you the protein and other nutrient contents of most foods.

Read, learn, experiment, and expand your awareness of nutrition.

There is a vast amount of information about diet and nutrition, and it could take a lifetime to fully understand all the intricacies of the subject. Indeed, one of my recommendations is to adopt an attitude of lifelong learning about your body, health, diet, and nutrition. Do not assume that you learned what you need to know about these issues in school or in your family. Some specific areas of importance are: understanding the digestive system and how food is metabolized into energy, reading and understanding food packaging labels, learning about your body's nutritional requirements, and knowing the nutrient contents of various foods. Some cookbooks have excellent sections on nutrition. Two of my favorites were mentioned earlier. Libraries, bookstores, classes/workshops in your community, health centers, and state and federal health departments are also good sources of information.

Love your body and develop an intimate relationship with it.

Your body is the vehicle that carries you through life. Caring for your body will encourage it to serve you with reliability and grace. Spiritually, your body is also the temple, or physical home, for your spirit; nurturing your body is part of nurturing your soul. One of my greatest joys in life is experiencing physical health and high energy, which I attribute to my caring relationship with my body. Eating the most alive and healthiest food available, and staying in touch with the effects of food on my energy level, are part of this relationship. You will have less fear and anxiety if you develop this type of intimacy with your body, because there will be few surprises and you will be aware of early warning signals before they become symptoms.

Exercise aids digestion and food assimilation, and it is essential for your health.

Airola, a European nutritionist with whom I studied, once said he would rather eat junk food and exercise regularly than eat well and not exercise. His point was obvious: exercise plays a vital role in food digestion. Exercise is important because it helps regulate hunger, metabolism, and elimination. In addition, the lymph system depends on muscle movement as the only mechanism for stimulating the flow of lymph. Lymph is the cleansing fluid for detoxification and removal of bacteria. Exercise is also the key to reducing stress, a requirement for anxiety recovery.

As part of your anxiety recovery, exercise is also important for other reasons. Exercise improves self-esteem, sleep, energy level, mood, and mental concentration and attention span. Exercise stimulates the brain to produce hormones, known as "endorphins," which are associated with feelings of well-being. Physical strength and stamina are improved through exercise, which elevates emotional power for dealing with stress and anxiety. Finally, exercise counteracts depression, which we discussed in a previous chapter as a common secondary symptom in anxiety disorders. Recommendations for exercise as part of your anxiety recovery will be found in Chapter 10.

Eat consciously and dialogue with your body in determining what works best for you.

The entire subject of food and eating is difficult to address because each of us is unique in our physical and emotional needs. Furthermore, even our individual requirements vary from day to day based on our activities and stress levels. Therefore, you are the best judge of food and eating policies, based on what works for you. I recommend that you learn to tune in to the wisdom of your own body, and take responsibility for your diet and health. Develop a keen awareness of your body's nutritional needs and reactions to food. Here are some specific suggestions:

1. Several times a week, eat in silence, listening attentively to your body before, during, and after you eat.
2. Relax before and during eating, and eat in peaceful surroundings. Eating outdoors in a natural setting is conducive to conscious eating. In a restaurant, choose a quiet table or booth if possible.
3. Before eating, close your eyes and take a few deep breaths. Think about energy: what it is, where it comes from, and how food is transformed into energy. Be aware that you are part of an energy exchange, and focus on what you will do with the energy you receive from your food.

4. Concentrate your attention and senses on the process of eating. Eat slowly and chew thoroughly. Take the time your body needs to eat and digest food. Remember that digestion begins with the sight and smell of food, followed by digestive enzymes in your saliva. Liquefy the foods in your mouth as part of digestion and release of energy. Avoid rushing, and allow yourself to experience the taste, aroma, and consistency of your food. Eating slowly also helps you feel the subtle signal of fullness, and prevents you from overeating.
5. Develop an attitude of thankfulness and reverence for the foods you receive. The energy and health you derive from food is a blessing. Begin each meal by acknowledging your gratitude. When my children were young, we gave thanks with nature-oriented meal blessings, such as: "Dear Earth, dear Sun, by you we live. Our loving thanks to you we give. Blessings on the meal." Another nature-oriented grace was, "Blessings on the blossoms. Blessings on the fruit. Blessings on the leaves and stems, and blessings on the root." We now use more formal meal blessings from our spiritual tradition to thank God for providing the food we eat.

Discover sources of emotional nourishment, other than food.

Although food and eating should be a source of joy and pleasure, they are not a substitute for true emotional fulfillment. Your eating patterns are most likely to be natural and under control when you have other sources of emotional satisfaction. Satisfying interpersonal relationships and intimacy are, perhaps, the most important sources for emotional nourishment. Make sure you devote time to developing and nurturing your social relationships. In addition, identify those activities that bring you joy, pleasure, or satisfaction, and make sure you make time for them on a regular basis. These may include hobbies, outdoor recreation, socializing with friends, spending time with family, or spending quiet time by yourself.

10

Take a Deep Breath

Anxiety is excitement without breath.

Fritz Perls

Although breathing is a matter of life and death, many people do not breathe properly and suffer a loss of vitality and health. Breathing is often taken for granted and considered a simple, automatic function that cannot be controlled. Breathing is also overlooked as a reflection of a person's emotional condition and state of mind. However, proper breathing is essential for physical, emotional and mental self-regulation, which are the basis for stress recovery and for overcoming anxiety. In this chapter we will explore breathing as an essential anxiety recovery skill, and discover some techniques for developing natural, deep breathing.

A full breath begins, not with an inhalation, but with a complete exhalation that empties the lungs and allows a new supply of air to fill in from the bottom to the top of the lungs. The action of the diaphragm compresses the lungs during exhalation and releases the pressure as air is drawn into the lungs. The result is a full expansion during inhalation, which can be felt in the stomach and chest. In natural breathing, the lungs function like a bellows, collapsing purposefully to release air followed by a vacuum effect that sucks in a new supply of air as they expand.

You can evaluate your breathing pattern with two simple exercises. In the first exercise, place one hand on your chest and the other hand on your diaphragm (just above the stomach). As you breathe, notice whether both areas expand and contract, or whether one—or both—holds still. In natural breathing, the full participation of diaphragm and chest is involved, and a maximum amount of air is absorbed and released.

The second exercise for checking the condition of your breathing is to make a continuous "ah" sound in your normal voice while watching the second hand on a watch or clock. If you cannot maintain the sound for at least twenty seconds, you are not breathing fully or you have some respiratory difficulty.

Some other indications of inhibited breathing are frequent sighing or yawning. Sighing is a valuable clue, since it is a response to unconsciously holding the breath. Frequent sighing is the body's attempt to more fully release the lungs, which may be locked by tension in the abdominal and chest muscles. Yawning, on the other hand, involves taking in air. Frequent yawning is a sign of being tired, bored, or sleepy, and occurs when our energy needs replenishing. Yawning is the body's attempt to revitalize itself by activating deeper breathing and increasing oxygen supply.

When I am stressed, I feel tension in my chest, neck, shoulders, and back, and my breathing becomes shallow and inhibited. These are the early warning signals of stress overload, or needing a break from concentrated work. Since it is muscle tension that restricts the spontaneity of my breathing, I respond with stretches that release the tension and help restore my deep breathing pattern. I also regularly practice relaxation and yoga, including a number of breathing exercises. In addition, I have some automatic cues for instant relaxation and deep breathing. One cue, for example, is red traffic lights. Whenever I am stopped by a traffic light, I accept it as a gift from the universe and pause for a moment to breathe deeply and remember my purpose in life. I chose this particular cue because stoplights used to frustrate me, causing tension. To appreciate what a difference even a moment of deep breathing can make, pause for a moment and perform this simple exercise:

EXERCISE: SIMPLE STRETCH FOR DEEPER BREATHING

> Lean back, raise your arms, and breathe deeply several times. This stretches the chest and back muscles, which permits the lungs to expand and breathe more deeply.

Children breathe, cry, and laugh with their whole bodies. There is a fullness noticeable in the abdominal region, where the stomach seems to be involved in these activities. But this natural pattern is often replaced by learned habits, such as inhibiting the urge to cry or holding in the stomach. In adults, it may be considered shapely to have a flat stomach, which appears to emphasize the chest and create the illusion of fitness. This, of course, reduces the fullness of breathing, limiting air intake to a fraction of lung capacity. Respiratory movements in this case are limited to the chest, forcing the lungs to expand sideways, rather than downward, when a person tries to take a deep breath. This places a strain on the body, since expansion of the thoracic cage requires more effort than expanding the abdominal muscles that are designed for this purpose. Holding the stomach in requires more work to breathe and results in less oxygen for the effort.

There is also a relationship between breathing and feeling. To breathe deeply is to feel deeply. Normally, the abdomen is involved in deep crying and laughing. We speak of "belly crying," a "belly laugh," and "laughing until your stomach aches." When we suppress feelings, however, we hold our breath and limit breathing to a shallow, constricted pattern. By holding in the abdomen, we can cut off the painful feelings of sadness and hurt, but at the same time we lose the ability to breathe fully. Anger, fear, and sadness, for example, are often controlled by breathing narrowly through the nose. When we give up control of feelings, however, breathing opens up. In sexual arousal, for example, breathing opens up to deep breaths through the mouth.

We breathe normally approximately fifteen times a minute. A little arithmetic will indicate that this means approximately four seconds for each inhalation–exhalation cycle, or two seconds for each in-breath and out-breath. Unfortunately, although our lungs have a capacity for about ten pints of air, most people take in much less—one pint in an inhalation is not unusual. This pattern deprives the body of potential energy and oxygen, resulting in loss of vitality, strength, and health. Deep breathing, on the other hand, can significantly increase the amount of inhaled air. In addition, deep breathing has a calming effect on other body systems, such as heart rate and digestion. Furthermore, as both yoga breathing practices and research on the relaxation response demonstrate, the mind is disciplined and calmed by deep breathing. These beneficial effects of deep breathing have an obvious role in reducing anxiety.

Should we breathe through our mouths or our noses? Breathing through the nose—nasal breathing—activates the air passages in the head, heightening the senses, especially the sense of smell. The hairy lining of the nostrils also performs a filtering function in nasal breathing. Alertness is increased through a steady flow of air through the nose, and a person's face looks more alive when breathing nasally, compared to a duller countenance when breathing with the mouth open. In sleep, however, the jaw frequently drops and breathing takes place largely through the mouth. In addition, breathing through the mouth is natural during strenuous exercise or physical activity because of an increased need for oxygen. It is apparent that both nasal and oral breathing are natural, depending on the circumstances. Therefore, it is important to allow your breathing to take its natural form based on the situation and your body's needs.

Many people have forgotten how to breathe properly. Their breathing is shallow, and their oxygen uptake is at a fraction of lung capacity. The resulting low oxygen level can result in symptoms such as fatigue and drowsiness, poor concentration, loss of vitality, headaches, and weakness. Furthermore, shallow breathing results in atrophy of the muscles involved in deep breathing—the diaphragm and chest muscles—rendering them inefficient when deep breathing is required. In fact, re-learning how to breathe properly can be initially uncomfortable or even painful for those who have lost their natural breathing ability.

Difficulty breathing can lead to chest pain and breathlessness, which are common symptoms in anxiety. These symptoms can be frightening to the sensitive, anxiety-prone person, who may interpret them as indications of a serious medical problem, such as a heart attack or prelude to fainting. Indeed, Bass (1992) reports that chest pain and breathlessness are the most common complaints seen in outpatient care, comprising some 12 percent of all medical complaints. However, an overwhelming 91 percent of such complaints are related to emotional problems, such as anxiety, and not to heart or other medical problems.

Anxiety has an immediate and noticeable affect on breathing, typically by increasing the number of breaths per minute and decreasing the amount of air taken in. Muscle tension in anxiety contracts the lungs, limiting their expansion. At the same time, the fight/flight response calls for maximum oxygen supply to all systems. Two incompatible conditions are created in anxiety—a need for more oxygen and difficulty breathing. The result is a pattern of rapid but shallow breathing. In high anxiety episodes, hyperventilation—a rapid, shallow breathing pattern with unpleasant body symptoms—may occur.

The interaction between anxiety and breathing is illustrated in Mary's case. Mary, a passive 45-year-old homemaker and mother of two children, referred herself for anxiety treatment after hearing my radio show on panic anxiety. Although she presented with typical symptoms of severe anxiety—nervous stomach, shakiness, rapid heart beat, worrying, "what-if" thinking, avoidance of situations in which anxiety was anticipated—she also identified an unusual problem with her breathing. Mary described her breathing problem on the CHAANGE pre-program evaluation as follows:

> I feel as though my body has turned against me. In the past nine months, I've lost ten pounds, I've been on medication for high blood pressure caused by my anxiety, and I am currently experiencing a breathing problem which my allergist believes would be helped by reducing the stress caused by my panic attacks. My panic attacks and resulting agoraphobia and breathing problem have totally sapped my energy and confidence because they started at a time in my life when I was feeling strong and making future plans, despite the fact that there were several external stresses with which my family and I were dealing. I feel that I cannot proceed with my life until I can learn to deal with my anxiety and fears and overcome them.

At the halfway point in the program, Mary wrote,

> I feel that I have much more control over my panic and my reactions to it. I don't think I'm afraid of my panic anymore. When I'm in a situation in which I feel panic coming, I'm able to flow with it, knowing that it will pass. . . .When I began the CHAANGE program, I had a problem with my breathing because I was feeling so much anxiety. I couldn't take even a short walk without feeling anxious and getting a tight feeling in my chest. The relaxation has really helped me with this problem. I am now able to take walks in my neighborhood, and I'm working on increasing their length each

> time. I have more confidence now that I will be able to get over this condition.

At midpoint, Mary had also discontinued the medication prescribed for her anxiety. At the end of the program, Mary evaluated her progress by stating,

> At this point, I don't even consider things like driving, going grocery shopping or to malls, or going to restaurants and other places as being fearful situations for me. I can do these things comfortably. . . .

In addition to eliminating her avoidant behavior, Mary was able to walk freely for exercise, with no breathing impairment. She developed the deep breathing habit, and was able to take deep breaths without chest pain or discomfort. This reinforced her ability to relax through anxiety until it no longer mattered.

It is estimated that at least 25 percent of all people hyperventilate frequently. Hyperventilation, a form of rapid, shallow breathing, reduces carbon dioxide in the blood, triggering a number of chemical reactions. Whereas carbon dioxide is often thought of simply as a waste product of breathing, this compound keeps the blood's pH, or acid–alkaline level, in healthy balance. In rapid breathing, carbon dioxide is exhaled before it can perform this job. The resulting alkalinity of the blood and other body fluids sets off a chain reaction that changes the calcium balance in muscles and nerves, heightening their sensitivity and making you tense, nervous, and shaky. Fingers and toes can feel tingly and cold, and skin can feel warm and flushed.

In addition, shallow breathing can reduce oxygen to the brain by as much as 20 percent, causing lightheadedness, dizziness, and headaches—symptoms that can add to anxiety. When such a pattern persists, the diaphragm and abdominal muscles lose their tone and strength, making it difficult to resume healthy breathing. Anxiety symptoms, such as tension, nervousness, and lightheaded sensations, can then occur for no apparent reason.

Sudden alterations in breathing pattern caused by anxiety are part of the "first fear"—that aspect of anxiety consisting of the adrenaline-charged fight/flight response. For many anxiety sufferers, the emotional reaction to this response—the "second fear"—consists of fear of life-threatening breathing problems, such as choking, suffocating, or fainting.

One of the most important aspects of breathing, as far as anxiety recovery is concerned, is that it is the key to self-regulation of the entire body. Normally, body systems such as the cardiovascular, respiratory, digestive, and glandular systems are regulated by the autonomic nervous system, whose brain control center is located in the medulla. The autonomic system consists of two complementary sub-systems, sympathetic and parasympathetic, which, as their names imply, work in opposition to each other. The parasympathetic system slows things down and the sympathetic system accelerates them. Heart rate, for example, is regulated by the complementary action of these two systems.

The main nerve of the parasympathetic system—the system that slows things down—is the vagus nerve. This nerve travels from the medulla at the base of the brain down the spinal cord, through the neck, chest, and abdomen, where it makes contact with the lungs. The vagus nerve is actually stimulated by the movement of the lungs as they expand and contract. Breathing rhythm, therefore, influences the action of organs in the body through its effect on the parasympathetic nervous system. Slow/deep breathing calms the body, and rapid/shallow breathing activates the body. This ingenious arrangement allows us to modify heart rate, digestive activity, and other so-called involuntary processes, and to gain control over the entire body. This is essential to overcoming anxiety.

Deep breathing is associated with the relaxation response. As discussed earlier in Chapter 8, the relaxation response is a special state characterized by lowered heart rate, decreased rate of breathing, lowered blood pressure, slower brain waves, and an overall reduction of the speed of metabolism. Benson (1975, 1984), who studied the healing benefits of this state, notes that the changes produced by the relaxation response counteract the harmful effects and uncomfortable feelings of stress. Furthermore, in this peaceful condition, the individual's mental patterns change and "worry cycles" are broken. Anxiety and fearful thoughts are disrupted by relaxation.

Having discussed the benefits of deep breathing and the problems associated with shallow breathing, let's consider some techniques for correcting improper breathing habits and patterns. The breathing techniques were drawn from several sources, including bioenergetics, yoga, and exercise physiology.

Reich (1961, 1972), who used the term *bioenergetics* to describe the flow of life force within the body, noticed that when patients hold back a thought or feeling he or she also holds their breath. As patients are instructed to open up their breathing, thoughts and feelings often pour out. Observing this in numerous cases, Reich began to focus on breathing as the key to unlocking a patient's resistance to facing uncomfortable thoughts and feelings. Lowen (1975, 1990), a student of Reich, describes some of the breathing instructions used in bioenergetic therapy. In two of these exercises, the voice is used to help deepen breathing.

EXERCISE: EXHALATION PRACTICE FOR DEEP BREATHING

> In a sitting position, preferably on a hard chair, make a continuous "ah" sound in your normal voice as you exhale, and measure the length of time with a second hand of a watch or clock. Practice this exercise regularly, trying to extend the time you can sustain the sound.
>
> Although this exercise is not dangerous, you may feel out of breath, and your body may react by breathing intensely to replenish the oxygen in your blood. Such intense breathing mobilizes the tight chest muscles, allowing them to relax. In the process, you may feel an urge to cry, which you should allow yourself to do because crying is a natural mechanism for tension release.
>
> You can also perform this exercise by counting aloud in a steady rhythm as you exhale. Focus on sustaining the expiration. By breathing out more fully, you will learn to breathe in more deeply. [Adapted from Lowen, 1990, pp. 46–47]

Another bioenergetic breathing exercise is used to accentuate the vacuum reflex involved in sucking in air. This reflex is most noticeable just before a person sneezes, when the body sucks in air with such force that it feels like a vacuum cleaner.

EXERCISE: VACUUM BREATHING REFLEX

> Using a sitting position, breathe normally for one minute to become relaxed. Now, as you breathe out, make a groaning sound for the length of a complete exhalation. On the inhalation try to make the same sound. It may be difficult at first, but it can be accomplished with a little practice. Do you sense the air being sucked into your body? [Adapted from Lowen, 1990, pp. 48–49]

Yoga offers a set of breathing exercises that are well-suited for anxiety recovery purposes. The exercises are known as *pranayama*—control of *prana* or life force. According to yoga philosophy, prana is the universal energy that animates all matter. Prana appears to be the same energy discussed by Reich as bioenergy, and the same energy discovered in subatomic physics to be the organizing force behind matter. Pranayama exercises are practiced not only for increasing energy but also for their importance in learning to control the mind. By controlling breathing as well as disciplining the mind, yoga breathing exercises are especially beneficial to the process of overcoming anxiety and fear.

The following pranayama exercises can be practiced by anyone without danger. Through them, lung capacity can be increased, allowing deeper, slower breathing. The mind is calmed, while energy and vitality are increased. Concentration is also likely to improve with the practice of these breathing exercises.

EXERCISE: YOGA DEEP BREATHING PRACTICE

Stand firmly in a calm, quiet, and airy place. Exhale though your nostrils, keeping the head, neck, and trunk erect. Try to keep the body as still as possible except for the motion of the stomach and chest muscles involved in deep breathing. Apply the "root lock" by contracting the sphincter muscles of the rectum and pulling them inwards and upwards. Exhale smoothly and quietly without exertion through the nostrils. After exhaling, do not pause, but start inhaling deeply through the nostrils. Do this about ten times for one session each day.

EXERCISE: RELAXATION WITH BREATHING

Lie down on your back with a soft pillow under your head. Cover your eyes with a piece of cloth, and begin breathing slowly and deeply. Let your mind travel slowly through your body from head to toes, and breathe relaxation into each set of muscles. Do this systematically, starting with the forehead, then moving to the facial muscles, neck, shoulders, arms and hands, back, chest, legs, and so on until you reach your toes. Then, for a moment, breathe relaxation into the entire body—into every muscle and cell simultaneously. Concentrate on an even and deep flow of breath, forming a new habit of deep, slow breathing.

Do not take more than about ten minutes, for too much relaxation leads to loss of control over the muscles. Also, avoid falling asleep during the relaxation exercise.

You may add another phase to this exercise by tensing your entire body, followed by gradually relaxing each muscle group from head to toes. Concentrate on an even and deep breathing rhythm.

EXERCISE: CHANNEL PURIFICATION

> Sit in a calm, quiet, and airy place, assuming a steady but not rigid posture. Keep the head, neck, and trunk straight. Bring your right hand up to your nose, folding the index and middle fingers so that the right thumb and right ring finger can be used to close the nostrils, one at a time. Exhale completely through the left nostril, while the right nostril is kept closed with the right thumb. The exhalation should be slow, controlled, and smooth. At the end of the exhalation, close the left nostril with the ring finger, open the right nostril and inhale slowly and completely. Inhalation and exhalation should be of equal duration. Repeat this cycle of exhalation with the left nostril and inhalation with the right nostril, two more times. Then switch and perform three cycles of exhalation through the right nostril with inhalation through the left nostril. With time, gradually lengthen the duration of inhalation and exhalation.

For those who wish to pursue some more advanced yoga breathing exercises, I recommend a yoga class, as well as study of a good book on the subject. Two of my favorite yoga books are Lidell's (1983) *The Sivananda Companion to Yoga*, and Satchitananda's (1995) *Integral Yoga Hatha*.

Another approach to deep breathing is physical exercise. In my opinion, anxiety recovery is unlikely to be successful without some form of regular exercise. My own anxiety recovery process would not have been possible without the benefits of physical exercise. There are three types of exercise that helped immensely: aerobic exercise, yoga, and strength training.

It is common knowledge that aerobic exercise promotes health by conditioning the heart, lungs, and vascular system. Aerobic exercise consists of a minimum of twenty minutes of sustained, rhythmic exercise, with heart rate between 60 and 90 percent of maximum, depending on fitness. You can use a simple method for estimating your maximum heart rate by subtracting your age from the number 220. For example, a 40-year-old would have a maximum heart rate of 180. Exercise is referred to as cardiovascular, or aerobic, if it is continuous. Stop-and-go exercises, such as tennis, downhill skiing, golf, basketball, baseball, or football, are not considered to be aerobic, although that does not mean they have no health benefits. Some excellent examples of aerobic exercise are running, bicycling, cross-country skiing, aerobics, jumping rope, and vigorous walking, as well as the use of stair-climbing, rowing, and other exercise machines. Contrary to prevailing beliefs, new studies indicate that vigorous aerobic exercise has greater health benefits than moderate exercise. On the other hand, moderate exercise is better than no exercise. The health benefits of exercise include lower blood pressure, release of muscle tension, improved circulation, improved digestion and metabolism, and stronger immune system. In addition, unlike the cardiovascular system, the lymphatic system—essential for elimination of toxins from the body—has no pump, and exercise is the best mechanism for operating this system.

Tension is stored in the body's muscles. The nervous system controls muscles through signals that cause them to contract or release. Tension, one of the most common anxiety symptoms, is a prolonged state of muscle contraction or tightness, which can lead to pain. Exercise is beneficial to anxiety reduction by releasing muscle tension. By toning the muscular system, exercise helps to regulate the body's tension level. Thus, "staying loose," an emotional state, actually describes a relaxed muscular system. The heart itself is a muscle, and exercise is beneficial to the cardiovascular system through its conditioning effect on this vital organ. Heart palpitations and racing heart—common in anxiety reactions—are less likely to produce the "second fear" in people whose hearts are accustomed to stimulation from exercise.

Exercise also has important psychological benefits. Exercise stimulates the body's production of endorphins, the feel-good brain chemicals that improve mood, self-esteem, and feelings of well-being. Breathing is stimulated by vigorous exercise, which supercharges the blood with oxygen, improving alertness, vitality, mental clarity, and memory. By discharging tension, exercise results not only in physical relaxation but also feelings of peacefulness. During exercise, people's attention is turned away from stressful circumstances—yet another psychological benefit. All these psychological benefits are vital to the anxiety recovery process.

Whatever your age or fitness level, implementing a regular exercise program is essential for overcoming anxiety and managing the stress that triggers it. There may be many reasons or excuses to avoid exercising, including fear of anxiety arousal in some cases, but these must be addressed if you are to succeed in anxiety recovery. "I don't have time," "I'm too out of shape," "I'm too old," and

"Exercise is boring" are some common explanations for avoiding an exercise program. For those who "don't have time," consider a recent study showing that men could gain an average of two years of life by expending 2,000 calories a week on aerobic exercise. Perhaps it is more a question of priorities than a shortage of time. For those who are "too out of shape," start gently, or consult your physician for advice. Your fitness level will determine the intensity of exercise: monitor your pulse and stay within 60 percent of maximum to begin with—a level that might be reached by a simple walk around the block. For those who claim they are "too old," think about the many marathon runners who did not even begin to exercise until their 50s or 60s. And for those who feel that exercise is "boring," have you really experimented with a variety of exercise options?

Yoga, an ancient spiritual and health practice originating in India, seems more gentle than aerobic exercise, but it is a powerful practice with many health benefits. The yoga system has eight different branches of practice, the most familiar of which is hatha yoga, the physical branch. In hatha yoga, a series of *asanas,* or postures, are performed with steadiness and concentration. The practice of yoga lowers heart rate and respiration, resulting in a calming effect on the nervous system. Yoga postures also affect the endocrine glands—one of the body's regulatory systems that acts through the secretion of hormones. Yoga is, essentially, a form of self-regulation, in which the emotions, the body, and the mind are brought under control. By improving the healthy functioning of the heart, lungs, nervous, and endocrine systems, as well as by calming the mind and controlling the emotions, yoga offers an invaluable advantage in anxiety recovery.

Breathing skills are at the heart of yoga. In yoga, breathing performs three vital functions: it revitalizes the body, steadies the emotions, and produces clarity of mind. In revitalizing the body, breathing not only increases the oxygen supply to every cell in the body, but it is the mechanism through which *prana*—life force—is absorbed. Breathing, like eating, interconnects the individual with outside elements needed to sustain life.

One of yoga's teachings is that spiritual reality is an eternal, unchanging state, different from the ever-changing nature of the physical world. Man's true nature is in this spiritual realm, and identification with the physical world can bring only temporary satisfaction. However, through yoga, which concentrates on the physical body, we can achieve the inner peace that connects us to the spiritual world. Indeed, the word *yoga* means "union"—to be united with higher reality.

Each yoga posture has specific health benefits. The Plow posture, for example, corrects spine deviations, eliminates fatigue, cures headaches, and rejuvenates the digestive organs, sexual glands, and kidneys. The Corpse pose has been shown to lower blood pressure. And the Headstand, an inverted posture, provides a rich supply of arterial blood to the brain, cranial nerves, pituitary gland, and pineal gland, calming the nerves. The Headstand is also known for its ability to alleviate digestive distress and varicose veins. As a whole, yoga has been found to have a positive effect on many aspects of health. In one study, reported in Lidell (1983), yoga was found to increase lung capacity for deeper breathing, reduce body weight and girth, improve stress resistance, lower cholesterol, and stabilize blood sugar.

As indicated earlier, I found yoga to be indispensable to my recovery from a life of fear and anxiety. Yoga taught me how to relax through fear and anxiety, as well as pain. Yoga is one of the ways I connect intimately with myself, keeping tuned to subtle messages from my body. Yoga helped me befriend my body, which now speaks to me regularly about my degree of balance as I navigate through the responsibilities of a busy daily life. Through yoga, I discovered a deep inner peace as I worked the tension out of my body. Even after some twenty-five years of practice, I could not stay in control without yoga. Although I can spend several hours doing yoga, not a day goes by without at least a few asanas to straighten out my posture and relieve tension and stress. A few minutes before I start my day and before I go to bed is the minimum. When I feel the need during the day, I sometimes take a break—just a moment in between appointments—to release accumulated physical tension or stress overload. A short time-out with some deep breathing or an asana helps to restore my energy. When I ignore the call and push myself over the limit, I lose concentration and develop stress symptoms. If I go even further beyond my limits, I feel overwhelmed and, if my blood sugar is low from ignoring hunger, I begin to tremble with tension and anxiety.

One of the appealing features of yoga practice is that it requires no special equipment and it can be practiced virtually anywhere. However, it is advisable to obtain proper instructions, preferably by a teacher who can observe and correct your postures. It is beyond the scope of this book to provide proper instruction in yoga. Therefore, I recommend that you read a book on yoga and consider taking a class at your local recreation center, YMCA, health club, or other community venue. Libraries will have books to consult and bookstores often have sections on yoga. Also try health food stores for information on classes and for copies of *Yoga Journal*, a monthly magazine devoted to yoga.

In the meantime, it is safe to begin practicing a simple sequence of yoga postures. I have, therefore, included some beginner yoga instructions below. For further development, and to derive the full benefit of yoga, these instructions should be supplemented with the resources mentioned above.

BEGINNER YOGA INSTRUCTIONS

Begin with the Corpse pose. Lie on your back on the floor, with your feet slightly apart and your arms out from your sides. Allow gravity to gently pull your back flat onto the floor, while at the same time allowing the earth to support you. Let go of tension by breathing relaxation into all parts of your body. Place your palms over your eyes, and press gently as you give your eyes a rest. Let your mind calm down by releasing thoughts as you exhale. Rest in peace.

Next, assume a meditative posture, sitting comfortably with your head, neck, and back erect. This is a good posture for practicing the deep breathing exercises described earlier. You can also do some gentle neck rolls and shoulder hunches to relieve tension and stress in these areas. By keeping your eyes closed, you can gain some additional rest and relaxation for your eye muscles. Since eye movements tend to correlate with mental activity, you can calm your mind by resting your eyes.

> A sequence of yoga asanas usually progresses from a sitting posture to leg raises, which are performed from a lying position, with back on the floor. Raise your legs up together, as well as one at a time. Also try pulling your knees up towards your chest. Perform all movements slowly, and do not strain. This is followed by the more advanced asanas, such as the Headstand and Shoulderstand, for which supervision is advised. However, you can try the Plow, which is an extension of leg raises: bring your legs back over your head towards the floor behind your head. This is one of my favorite asanas because it corrects my posture and relieves tension in my neck and back. The Plow is also a good introduction to the inverted postures, where the head is lower than the trunk of the body. The flow of blood into the head is refreshing and improves mental clarity. Be sure to rise slowly, preferably after returning to the Corpse position.

Some of the techniques described so far were instrumental in Harriet's anxiety recovery. Harriet, who was mentioned in Chapter 7, is a competent teacher and mother of three children. When Harriet initially came for help, she was experiencing fifteen to twenty panic attacks a day, and felt completely out of control. Daily Xanax medication was not sufficient to control her anxiety disorder. Driving was her phobic situation, and she was brought in tears to her first appointment by her husband because she was unable to drive alone. On her pre-program evaluation form at the outset of treatment, Harriet lamented, "Presently, this condition is making it difficult to focus on daily activities. I am nervous about driving nearly all the time, so I am uncomfortable and scared I'm going crazy."

During the CHAANGE program, Harriet practiced relaxation daily, following the recommended procedures. In addition, she took a yoga class and learned to enhance her breathing, which I believe accelerated the benefits of her relaxation training. At the end of the sixteen-week program, Harriet wrote: "I am finding myself using the relaxation techniques when I start to feel anxious—deep breathing seems second nature."

One other form of exercise—strength training—contributed immeasurably to my anxiety recovery. Strength training—the use of weights or resistance devices to strengthen muscles in the body—is also known as weight lifting or body building. However, strength training should not be confused with the grotesque muscles seen on the covers of body-building magazines, where steroid drugs are obviously involved. Rather, strength training uses weights or resistance to strengthen and develop the muscles that are typically underused by most people. The benefits of strength training include increasing muscle tone, strength, and endurance, improving posture and range of motion, enhancing athletic performance, allowing greater ease in carrying and lifting, reduction of muscle tension following training sessions, and preventing injuries to the body. However, the psychological benefits of strength training are equally important. In my case, self-confidence, a more intimate knowledge of and relationship with my body, personal power, and greater joy in living resulted from this activity.

I know of nothing in the literature on anxiety treatment that recommends strength training to help overcome an anxiety disorder. Nevertheless, I include it because of its role in my own recovery process.

What surprised me most was the feeling of emotional strength, personal power, and fearlessness that came with weight lifting. This was unexpected because my reason for experimenting with strength training was to build up my lean, runner-shaped body (strong legs with small torso). Within a few short months after beginning a program of strength training, I experienced a change in my attitude, along with noticeable physical improvements in muscle size. I felt stronger and more powerful as a person, and I became more assertive in my interactions with other people. My self-confidence improved as I felt more solid and balanced. The experience verified the mind–body relationship in a deeply personal way.

A typical strength training session consists of warming up by stretching and ideally some aerobic activity. Serious weight lifters may alternate strength training days with CV (cardiovascular) workouts. After warming up, a sequence of exercises is performed, consisting of controlled movements with each muscle group, using weights or other forms of resistance. The amount of weight used is determined by the amount required to perform eight to twelve repetitions, the number recommended by the American Academy of Sports Medicine. A set is the number of repetitions until muscle fatigue. After a brief rest, the set may be repeated a second or third time to get the maximum benefit. Generally speaking, there should be a minimum of 48 hours for recovery between strength training sessions, which means that one should not work the same muscles on two consecutive days. A comprehensive guide to the exercises used to develop each muscle group is Pearl and Moran's (1986) *Getting Stronger*, which includes instructions for both men and women.

The body adapts to stress by improving its ability to handle stress. The immune system, for example, is temporarily suppressed during physical exercise, but in the recovery process it is strengthened. This is essentially what happens to the muscles in strength training. Although muscles are fatigued and stressed by working against resistance, they adapt by increasing their strength and power.

When a muscle is stressed by working against resistance, the muscle cells actually break down. However, in the process of recovering from stress overload, the cells rebuild and hypertrophy—enlarge—as they mobilize to handle more stress. In this way, strength training improves our ability to handle physical stress. Strength training also activates the respiratory system, which deepens breathing in order to supply additional oxygen. Deep breathing is vital to relaxation. Furthermore, muscle tension is released during a strength training session, which also contributes significantly to anxiety reduction.

In summary, developing a natural deep breathing pattern is a vital step in overcoming anxiety and maintaining a life that is free from fear. Deep breathing is a key to the relaxation response, which is essential for anxiety reduction. Aerobic exercise and yoga are also anxiety recovery methods, having tension-releasing benefits as well as ways to expand lung capacity and deepen breathing. In addition, there are physical and psychological benefits to strength training. All of these practices are part of my own ability to live without anxiety, and I recommend them with hopes that you, too, will learn to breathe through the barrier of anxiety and dance without fear.

11

What-if?

Fear is the darkroom where negatives are developed.
Paul Foxman

As an amateur photographer, I learned how to see the world through a camera lens. A camera does not see what the human eye sees. A camera is more selective, and what it sees depends on many factors, such as lens choice and aperture setting. To take good photographs, it is necessary to think like a camera, because the final picture is determined by what the camera sees.

You are what you think, as far as fear and anxiety are concerned, and to recover you must change the way you think. Fear and anxiety, indeed all feelings, are produced by our thoughts. Depression, for example, is produced by negative thoughts, and anxiety is produced by stressful and fearful thoughts. One of the steps in overcoming anxiety, therefore, is to examine your thinking habits and patterns, and change those that create stress and anxiety. Like taking good photographs, anxiety recovery requires a new way of thinking.

In almost twenty years since Pelletier (1977) documented the role of the mind in stress and illness, research on the mind–body connection has made some remarkable discoveries. We now know that the brain and body communicate, using chemical messengers that connect to receptors on the surface membranes of our cells. The chemical messengers are mobile protein molecules called neuropeptides or neurotransmitters. Our thoughts, moods, and attitudes have a significant impact on which neurotransmitters are sent and how they are received. Pert (cited in Moyers 1994), discovered the presence of neurotransmitter receptor sites throughout the body, and calls these messengers "the biochemical units of emotion" because their activity is directly dependent on our states of mind. Neurotransmitters translate every thought, whether conscious or unconscious, as well as feelings into physiological changes, and they are found not just in the brain but in the immune and endocrine systems, heart, lungs, intestines—everywhere. Based on these discoveries, Pert says that we are a "single, integrated mind–body entity," and the messenger molecules are part of a "psychosomatic communication network" in which the mind is literally spread throughout the entire body.

By affecting the type and destination of neurotransmitters, our thoughts and attitudes can influence our health. The mind can heal because the brain and immune system are in constant dialogue via nerve fibers going from the brain to virtually every immune system organ. In other words, the brain is in direct contact with the immune system cells. The effectiveness of the immune system is influenced by how we react to the stress of everyday life, and how we perceive ourselves in relation to outside events.

What's more, viruses use the same receptor sites in cells as do neurotransmitters, and the two types of molecules appear to compete for cell contact. Therefore, the more neurotransmitters in the vicinity of cell receptors, the less likely that viruses will make cell contact. "What this means is that our emotional state will affect whether we'll get sick from the same loading dose of a virus," says Pert (Moyers 1994, p. 190).

The importance of thoughts and emotions in the onset of viral diseases is underscored by the fact that most microbes infecting humans are already in our bodies and instigate a disease only when other stresses lower our immunity. Mason (1975) notes that it is common for many pathogenic microorganisms to be harbored within our bodies without producing disease or illness. What determines whether infection will progress into illness or not depends on what Mason calls "host resistance machinery." This includes the power of thoughts and attitudes.

Stress, like germs, is often considered a cause of disease. However, new psychoneuroimmunology research indicates that it is not stress itself that causes symptoms but our reaction to or perception of stress that determines what effect it will have. For example, in a study by Maddi and Kobasa (1984), two hundred business executives at Illinois Bell Telephone Company during the AT&T divestiture were tracked to see who became sick and who did not. The healthy executives saw change as inevitable and as an opportunity for growth rather than a threat to security. Instead of seeing change and problems as insurmountable, the healthy individuals used a coping strategy involving three elements: optimistic appraisal (viewing problems pragmatically and with less pessimism), taking action to change the problem, and minimizing the effect of problems by exercise, relaxation training, or other health-promoting activities. The executives with these resources had less than a 10 percent chance of a severe illness. In contrast, for the high-stress managers who lacked these resources the probability of severe illness was greater than 90 percent.

Positive attitude can influence healing from life-threatening disease. Siegel (1986) finds from observing cancer survivors that certain attitudes determine who dies from and who survives life-threatening diseases. Siegel reports that while grief, despair, and discouragement influence the onset and course of an illness, positive attitudes—love, faith, confidence, and peace of mind—can significantly influence recovery.

The power of belief and expectation to influence health is also reflected by the fact that drugs newly released on the market are initially more effective. The fanfare with which a new drug is marketed stimulates enthusiasm among physicians, which is transmitted to patients, shaping the drug's effects positively. However, when other factors enter the picture, including actual patient response and reports of side effects, the doctor–patient community develops a more skeptical stance, ultimately decreasing the drug's effectiveness.

The placebo effect has long been known as an example of the power of belief and expectation. The placebo effect is a reaction to benign substances having no known effects. In one study cited by Cousins (1979), a group of medical students were told that they would be personally testing the effectiveness of two drugs, a stimulant and a depressant. They were informed as to the expected effects, but were not told that both drugs were actually placebos. More than half the students exhibited physical reactions to the placebos, including lower pulse, decreased arterial pressure, and even adverse side effects such as dizziness, abdominal distress, and watery eyes. In a another study cited by Cousins, a double-blind experiment was conducted to test a new drug designed to activate the endocrine system and thus enhance health and longevity. A total of 150 people over age 60 were divided into three equal groups. The first group received nothing; the second group received a placebo; the third was given regular treatment with the new drug. Year by year, all three groups were carefully observed with respect to illness and mortality. The statistics for the first group conformed to community averages. The second group, on the placebo, showed a marked improvement in health and a measurably lower death rate than the first group. The third group, on the drug, showed about the same improvement over the placebo group as the placebo group showed over the first.

Although most of the mind–body research has been conducted in relation to disease, alterations in body chemistry also occur when we have positive thoughts and feelings. Positive thoughts and feelings—love, compassion, peace, courage, faith, and hope—change the composition of neurotransmitters and stimulate the immune system. Dossey (1993) reviews a ten-year collection of literature and research on the subject. In one study, 393 coronary care patients in San Francisco were divided into two groups—one group was prayed for and one was not. At the end of the ten-month study, the "prayed-for" group was five times less likely than the other group to require antibiotics, three times less likely to develop a condition where the lungs fill with fluid, and none of the prayed-for group required an artificial airway in the throat, while 12 in the "non-prayed-for" group did. In another study, 32 people were asked to use mental imagery and visualization to protect red blood cells in test tubes from dissolving. During 15-minute concentration periods in separate rooms from the test tubes, the subjects were able to slow down the rate of cell dissolution to a degree unexplainable by chance. Similarly, another study showed that through positive thoughts 60 subjects were able to stimulate the growth of bacteria in cultures. The same group could also do the opposite: using negative thoughts they could impede the growth of bacteria in cultures. The mind's power can reach across space, as demonstrated in a study showing that subjects could inhibit the growth of fungus cultures through concentrated thoughts from as far away as 15 miles. Based on these and other studies, Dossey concludes that positive thoughts, including prayer, have tremendous healing powers.

Our thoughts can even influence machines. One study cited by Dossey showed that human mind power was able to change the output of a random event generator, steering its output from randomness towards a pattern of numbers. One interesting finding was that couples who are deeply attached emotionally had a greater effect on the machine than others, suggesting that empathy and emotional closeness allow the emergence of a stronger power to shape physical events in the world.

A number of other writers discuss the role of positive thinking. Peale (1952), for example, explores "prayer power" and reports numerous cases of individuals who were able to solve difficult life problems using this power. Cousins (1979) describes his own recovery from congestive heart failure using positive thinking and changes in lifestyle. The methods followed by Cousins included positive thinking, diet changes, meditation, and exercise—similar to the techniques I recommend for anxiety recovery. In an inspirational bestseller, Gawain (1978) shows how positive affirmations can be used to create health and happiness. These writers have translated into practical skills what research is now verifying about the power of the mind, and these skills are applicable to anxiety recovery.

The mind is primarily responsible for creating anxiety. As discussed previously, the anxiety sufferer often introduces a second fear into the body's reaction to stress. The second fear, or fear of body reactions, is an error in thinking that creates more body reactions, which create more fear. A cycle of anxiety is set in motion by the mind's interpretation of the body's reactions to stress, which increases the intensity of the body reactions. In addition to this pattern, the anxiety sufferer usually has other thinking patterns that create stress and false danger signals. One essential step in overcoming an anxiety disorder, then, is to change the cognitive messages that are sent to the brain's survival center. This is accomplished by changing what and how we think.

I have identified five thought patterns that create or contribute to anxiety. As we consider each of these thinking errors, our purpose will be to recognize and learn how to correct them. In general, the idea is to replace erroneous thinking with more positive thought patterns. This is accomplished by substituting and practicing more productive thought patterns, until new habits are established.

The first and most common pattern of thinking errors is "what-if" thoughts. What-ifs are anticipatory thoughts about what might happen in the near or distant future. What-ifs are a form of worrying, and they are invariably negative. Rarely do people think, "What if I do well in the interview?" or "What if the lab results show no problems?" Instead, the typical what-if thought is a negative, irrational, and fear-producing anticipation, such as "What if I make a bad impression or say something foolish in the interview?" or "What if the lab results show a life-threatening illness?"

The negative and irrational aspects of what-if thinking are illustrated delightfully by Silverstein (1981), in a book of poems for children:

WHATIFS

Last night, while I lay thinking here,

Some Whatifs crawled inside my ear

And pranced and partied all night long

And sang their same old Whatif song:

Whatif I'm dumb in school?

Whatif they've closed the swimming pool?

Whatif I get beat up?

Whatif there's poison in my cup?

Whatif I start to cry?

Whatif I get sick and die?

Whatif I flunk that test?

Whatif green hair grows on my chest?

Whatif nobody likes me?

Whatif a bolt of lightning strikes me?

Whatif I don't grow taller?

Whatif my head starts getting smaller?

Whatif the fish won't bite?

Whatif the wind tears up my kite?

Whatif they start a war?

Whatif my parents get divorced?

Whatif the bus is late?

Whatif my teeth don't grow in straight?

Whatif I tear my pants?

Whatif I never learn to dance?

Everything seems swell, and then

The nighttime Whatifs strike again! [p. 90]

The first step in modifying the what-if habit is to realize that worrying about the future has absolutely no positive effect on what will happen. If anything, worrying may actually increase the probability of negative events, due to focusing energy on them. What-if thinking reflects your need for control and predictability, as well as your fear of not being able to handle the unexpected. Second, recognize that although you can plan for the future you cannot predict it with certainty. By focusing so much on what might happen in the future, you cannot live in the present. It is prudent to plan for the future, but you can only live in the present. Ultimately, the goal is to develop confidence and faith in your ability to handle whatever might happen, so that you do not have to waste energy worrying in advance.

The next step is to replace your what-ifs with *so-whats*. Instead of thinking "What if I say something foolish in the interview and lose the job?" you could say, "So what if I say something foolish in the interview, I can always correct myself. If I lose the job because of one mistake, it may not be the right job for me. Besides, it won't be the worst thing in the world if I don't get the job." Changing what-ifs to so-whats is a technique from the CHAANGE program, designed to remove the scare from anticipatory thoughts. Even if you can't let go of the fear, practice changing every what-if thought to a so-what, since words become powerful if you repeat them. Furthermore, you will slowly come to believe what you say to yourself, and the likelihood for positive thoughts to influence reality will increase.

Another frequent thought pattern in anxiety disorders is *should* thoughts. Shoulds are internal commands, associated with an image of good behavior, which often exist in the form of should lists. Shoulds contribute to anxiety through the stress they create. Having many shoulds creates pressure to do certain things or perform certain rituals, because they *should* be done. When you are not actually performing a should, you may be still be preoccupied with it—planning on doing it or regretting that you have not already done it. The effect of shoulds is influenced by your personality and values—duty, strong work ethic, responsibility, and so on. Pleasure is not usually associated with these self-imposed obligations, although temporary satisfaction may come from completing a should. Shoulds are often impossible to fulfill completely, creating disappointment and frustration.

In one of my anxiety therapy groups, I asked everyone to make a list of his or her shoulds. Their responses illustrate some common patterns, but in an interesting way point out that shoulds are also a highly individual matter. What may serve as a should for one person may actually be a shouldn't for someone else. Here is one person's list of shoulds:

I should read the newspaper more often to keep up with world news.
I should exercise more and eat better.
I should call my sister more often to keep in touch.
I should always look presentable.

Another member's list contained some opposite shoulds, which nevertheless had the same results in terms of stress and frustration. Her list included:

I shouldn't waste so much time reading the newspaper, so I can get more work done.
I shouldn't spend so much time and money on the phone with my sister in California.
I should be myself more and be less concerned with what other people think.

In my anxiety therapy groups we sometimes joke that people with anxiety "should on themselves too much." As with all thinking errors, the first step in changing your shoulds is to identify them and increase your awareness of when they occur. It would help to make a list of your should thoughts. Next, make an appropriate substitution for each should thought. The CHAANGE program suggests that each should be replaced with, "It would be preferable if. . . ." Another appropriate substitution would be, "I could choose to. . . ." Both techniques are designed to eliminate the stress and negative feelings produced by so many shoulds. An example of a replaced should would be, "I could choose to spend less time (or more time, as the case may be) reading the newspaper." For practice, you can go over your should list and write down the replacement thoughts. Thereafter, mentally substitute the replacement thought every time you recognize a should. With practice, you can free yourself from shoulds and take a giant step forward in dancing without anxiety or fear.

The next pattern to address is *perfectionistic thinking*, or simply perfectionism. As discussed elsewhere, this is a common pattern among anxiety sufferers, who attempt to meet impossibly high standards in all activities. Perfectionism, like many should thoughts, creates enormous stress. Perfectionism also leads to constant dissatisfaction and disappointment with anything less than perfect performance. In addition, low self-esteem and other negative feelings are associated with failing to be perfect. Perfection is related to a need to be in control, which is invariably frustrated by the real world. Furthermore, perfectionism makes it impossible to relax or take pleasure in accomplishments that do not meet the unreasonably high standards.

In *The Republic*, Plato insisted that the real world was an imperfect reflection of ideals that cannot exist in physical form. Roger and McWilliams (1991) challenge us to consider whether we would even want life to be perfect. Here, in teasing what-ifs, are the questions they would have us address:

What if life were perfect?
What if you lived in a perfect world of perfect people and perfect possessions, with everyone and everything doing the perfect thing at the perfect time?
What if you had everything you wanted, and only what you wanted, exactly as you wanted, precisely when you wanted it?
What if, after luxuriating in this perfect world for the perfect length of time, you started feeling uneasy about the predictability of perfection?
What if, after a perfect length of additional time, you began thinking, "There seems to be a lack of risk, adventure and fun in perfection. 'Having it my way' all the time is starting to get dull."
What if, after yet another perfect length of time, you decided, "Perfection is a perfect bore."

What if, at that point in your perfect world, you noticed for the first time a button marked, "Surprise."

What if you walked over, considered all that might be contained in the concept of "surprise," decided, "Anything's better than perfect boredom," took a deep breath, pushed the button. . . . [p. 1]

Perfectionism can be a worthy goal but all too often it is a compulsive habit that controls people, causing frustration and disappointment. I have a strong tendency towards perfectionism, and I take pride in high quality work. However, since perfection is impossible to attain in all situations, I learned instead to strive for *excellence.* Excellence is achieved when I do my best given the time constraints and conditions—which are often less than perfect—with which I have to work. I can feel good about whatever I do if I do my best under given circumstances, which include the need to balance my many responsibilities and commitments.

Another step in taking control of perfectionism is to give yourself permission to be human. Being human means living in the real world, with multiple responsibilities and commitments, as well as operating within many constraints over which you have no control. It is important to establish reasonable limits on what can be accomplished in a given amount of time. Being human also means making mistakes and learning from them. Allow yourself to be less than perfect, so you can learn, grow, and change.

Another step in becoming more reasonable with yourself is to focus on the *process* of doing, rather than the *outcome* of doing. Are you enjoying the process of life, or are you too focused on achieving perfection and punishing yourself for your imperfect performance? At the end of your life, will you feel good about how you lived, or will you measure the value of your life in terms of how perfect it was?

Negative thinking, the next pattern to be addressed, contributes significantly to the dark feelings of depression, helplessness, and powerlessness. These feelings add to the cycle of anxiety by making the condition seem impossible to overcome. For most anxiety sufferers, who already feel unable to control their fear, negative thinking creates more fear, as well as more depression. Negative thinking can also cause anxiety. As discussed earlier, negative thinking produces a type of neurotransmitter that sends signals of danger and despair throughout the body. Frequent negative thinking activates the fight/flight mechanism, but inhibits the energy needed to drive it. The car is revved up but can't go because there is no air in the tires. Negative thinking says you are a victim, with no control or choice about it. In negative thinking there is less possibility for happiness, health, fulfillment, or recovery. Negative thinking seduces you into giving up and giving in. The body is much more vulnerable to stress, and less able to recover from its effects, when there is a high concentration of negative thoughts.

Negative thinking comes in many forms. Projecting bad events into the future, comparing yourself to others and not measuring up, being judgmental, always assuming the worst, seeing only the down side of things, having hostile or hateful thoughts, and not believing in yourself are some of the many forms of negative thinking. One anxiety patient, an intelligent and creative artist with two adolescent children, became aware of her negative thoughts and wrote them down as part of her recovery process. These were some of her negative thoughts:

> I'm a bad mother because my daughter is bored this summer.
> When my boss goes on her leave of absence I hope I don't have too many responsibilities or stress, otherwise I'll go crazy or my anxiety will spike out of control.
> I have to get all this work done today or else it will all pile up and I will never get it done.
> Things are going too smoothly.
> My friend's mother has a heart problem—maybe I have one, too.
> I'm never going to be able to do all these things—it's too hard coming back from vacation.
> I'm overwhelmed—the anxiety will surely get out of control this week.
> Because we are having trouble with my teenage son, it must be my fault.

Imagine the messages sent by these negative thoughts to the heart, immune system, and other organs in this individual.

The way to correct negative thinking is deceptively simple: replace negative thoughts with positive thoughts. As you become aware of specific negative thoughts, convert them to positive alternatives. In addition, develop a habit of thinking positively by practicing affirmations and intentionally focusing on positive, uplifting thoughts. Be aware that negative thinking is usually a habit, and thus likely to be resistant to change. Therefore, a consistent effort will be necessary to establish new habits of positive thinking. I sometimes point out to my patients that since they already act as if negative thoughts are true, they may as well practice acting as if positive thoughts are true.

In replacing negative with positive thoughts, try converting each negative thought into its opposite. For the woman who found herself saying, "I'm overwhelmed, I'll never get all this work done," the opposite thought would be, "I'll do the best I can, and in time the work will get done." Here are some other examples:

TABLE 11–1: NEGATIVE TO POSITIVE THOUGHTS

Negative	Positive
I woke up feeling tired. I'm going to have a miserable day.	I woke up feeling tired, but I'll pace myself and my energy will return. This could be a great day.
I wish I had as much money as he seems to have. Then I'd be happier.	Happiness does not come from having more money. I will focus on enjoying the process of living in the present, rather than waiting for something to happen before I am happy.
If something does not come easily, it means I'll never be good at it.	Most learning involves trial and error, as well as mistakes. This is the feedback mechanism that helps learning. I could be good at something if I want to practice.

Another approach to positive thinking is to practice affirmations daily. An affirmation is a self-statement having three ingredients: it uses "*I*," it contains an *action verb*, and it is *positive*. Some examples are: "I enjoy being free of worry, fear and anxiety," "I like knowing I have a choice about the way I live," "I am enjoying the process of changing and growing," and, "I feel good about myself, and I enjoy each and every day."

The theory behind the power of positive affirmations is that when you make a statement you do not initially believe to be true, the discrepancy creates an internal tension. That tension is difficult to reconcile or live with, so there will be an impulse to reject either the affirmation or the underlying negative belief. If the positive affirmation is repeated frequently, say fifty times every day, subtle adjustments will begin to make the affirmation a reality.

One final pattern in many anxiety cases is *black-and-white thinking*. This habit consists of judging things as either good or bad, right or wrong. Black-and-white thinking is an all-or-nothing approach to life, offering only two categories in which to put all experiences. Black-and-white thinking also reflects discomfort with uncertainty and open-ended situations. At the same time, black-and-white thinking is based on the survival instinct's need to know what is safe and what is not—an overactive need in the anxious person. Black-and-white thinking is limiting because it ignores the multiple shades of meaning and possibilities in life. Here are some examples of black-and-white thinking:

If I don't understand something, it means I'm stupid or it's too complicated.

If I make a mistake, it means I'm no good.
If I don't like one aspect of something, I can't like any of it.
If I start feeling anxious, it means a full-blown panic attack is coming and I'll be out of control.
If someone hurts my feelings, I can't like that person anymore.

Some years ago, I published a study of black-and-white thinking, which at the time I called "low tolerance for ambiguity" (Foxman 1976). I was interested in what personality traits go along with a black-and-white style of thinking. Using psychological tests, 36 subjects were classified as relatively high or low in self-esteem with equal numbers of males and females in each group. All subjects then performed on a test of tolerance for ambiguity. I found that regardless of gender the high self-esteem group showed a higher tolerance for ambiguity than the low self-esteem group. When confronted with an unstructured task, where no rules or guidelines were given and where there were no right or wrong answers, the high self-esteem group was free to play with multiple possibilities. There were no signs of anxiety in high self-esteem subjects under these conditions. In contrast, the low self-esteem group was uncomfortable with the unstructured situation and judged their own responses negatively. These findings suggest that people with positive mental health are more tolerant of ambiguity and less likely to engage in black-and-white thinking, a concept I explored in a subsequent publication (Foxman 1980).

To eliminate black-and-white thinking, begin by accepting that in being human you cannot know everything.

Refrain from judging things as good or bad, and practice not putting everything into a category. Learn to let things be. Relaxation and meditation will help because these practices involve a *letting* rather than *doing* attitude, allowing things to be as they are. In addition, recognize that there is usually more than one way to do something, and more than one way to interpret the meaning of things. Distinguish between facts and opinions, and keep in mind that most of what people say is a matter of belief and opinion. No one can be wrong in his or her opinion, so give yourself and others the right to hold differing points of view. It would also be helpful to allow other people to be different, and refrain from imposing your standards or values on them. Finally, rejoice in the many possibilities life offers, as well as in your choice of how to live your life. This includes the possibility of dancing without anxiety, and fulfilling your purpose in life. Towards these goals, I offer this affirmation for anxiety recovery.

POSITIVE AFFIRMATION FOR ANXIETY RECOVERY

> I will not worry in advance about what might happen. I will live each day, take care of myself, and take things as they come. I will plan for the future but live in the present. I know that anxiety is a normal part of life and that it is not life-threatening. I will have faith in myself and trust that I can handle whatever may happen. And I will remind myself that whatever happens was meant to be.

12

Facing Your Fear

> *To recover, you must know how to face, accept, and go through anxiety until it no longer matters. This is the only way to permanent cure.*
>
> Claire Weekes

Virtually every anxiety sufferer has specific situations that are avoided or that produce symptoms of discomfort or anxiety. Whatever they are—being in crowds, being alone, stress, relaxing, public speaking, driving, bridges, airplanes, elevators, darkness, exercise, meetings, conflict, strong feelings—all must be experienced and handled successfully in order to overcome the anxiety associated with them. Facing fear is the way to convert a phobic situation from an ordeal to "no big deal." All of the information contained in this book is designed to help you accomplish this one essential step. Without facing the fear, all the insights, understanding, and information in the world will not be enough to recover from anxiety. You must face and directly experience your anxiety in a new way in order to overcome it—to dance fearlessly.

Feared or avoided situations are called *phobic* situations. We worry about, anticipate, and even dread their occurrence. Phobic situations can evoke a fear response just by thinking about them. When frightening anxiety occurs in a particular situation, a mental link forms between the situation and the feeling. Thereafter, that same situation takes on a new meaning: it becomes "dangerous" because in it the anxiety may happen again.

This conditioning process is illustrated by James, a sensitive and perfectionistic man who worked in a government agency. James had an extremely distressing experience while presenting at a departmental meeting. In his agency, the staff rotated the running of weekly meetings, and took turns updating each other on the latest government regulations and policy changes. On one particular occasion, while he was presenting, James was overcome with paralyzing anxiety and his mind went blank. Self-conscious and embarrassed, he excused himself from the meeting room. From that moment on, James dreaded meetings, and when he was scheduled to present, he spent days in agonizing anticipatory anxiety. His worrying and negative imagery about meetings activated a fight/flight reaction, which began to generalize to other social situations. James contacted me for help because his anticipatory anxiety was out of control, interfering with his sleep, appetite, and effectiveness on the job.

Weekes (1978) develops the idea of *sensitization* as an explanation for the intensity of anxiety experienced by some people. As noted earlier, any situation triggering a fear reaction can become phobic—a feared situation. In a phobic situation, a link is established between the physical sensations of anxiety and the situation in which it occurs. Weekes suggests, however, that because the nervous sensations (pounding heart, weakness, churning stomach, etc.) are so intense, they themselves become frightening and trigger more anxiety. A vicious cycle then develops in which the person sensitizes to his or her physical reactions—develops more fear of the fear reaction—intensifying the anxiety whenever a phobic situation is encountered. In time, the sensitized person can become more concerned about the physical reaction to the phobic situation than to the situation itself. Sensitization makes even normal sensations of anxiety seem frightening.

Weekes points out that the person with an anxiety disorder typically experiences two fears. The first fear is what we all feel in response to danger. It is a normal reaction to a stressful or traumatic situation, and it ends when the stress or danger subsides. Due to their personalities, however, some people tend to react strongly to the first fear, experiencing it as life-threatening, and often add a second fear—fear of the first fear. In Weekes' words,

> the sensitized person's first fear is so electric, so out of proportion to the danger causing it, he usually recoils from it and at the same time adds a second flash—fear of the first fear. He is usually more concerned with the feeling of panic than with the original danger. And because sensitization prolongs the first flash, the second may seem to join it and the two fears are experienced as one (p. 363).

Anxiety is usually precipitated by stress. Stress activates the fight/flight response, which is the body's mechanism of defense. This is the first fear, a normal reaction of the body to sudden or prolonged stress. Preoccupation with the intensity of this reaction, and the uncomfortable symptoms involved in it, produces an additional emotional response, the second fear. The second fear is recognizable not only by a heightened fear reaction, but by the "what-if" thinking that usually accompanies it: "What if this is a heart attack? What if this is the beginning of a major panic attack? What if something terrible is wrong with me? Could this be a life-threatening illness? What if I can't control it, what will happen next?" What-if thinking is part of the second fear.

We have little control over the first, normal reaction to stress or trauma. The first fear is part of our survival reaction—the fight/flight response to danger—something we would not want to eliminate even if we could. However, it is possible to eliminate the second fear. This important step is accomplished in part by changing our inner dialogue about the initial body reactions. We can begin to change our inner dialogue about the fight/flight reaction by reassuring ourselves that it is merely an adrenaline reaction, that it is not life-threatening, that it will subside in time, and that we can handle it. Substituting such thoughts and thinking positively help to modify the second fear, interrupt the anxiety cycle, and make it possible to face feared situations.

Most people instinctively protect themselves from feared situations by avoiding them if possible. Turning away from the first signs of anxiety can bring some relief, and therefore avoiding phobic situations is effective in preventing the first fear. However, there are several problems with this way of coping with anxiety. First, some situations are unavoidable, such as the weekly staff meetings that James dreaded. Other situations, such as car travel for some commuters, grocery shopping, being alone, or social situations, are also difficult to avoid because they are built in to daily life for most people. On the other hand, infrequently occurring situations, such as air travel or taking vacations far from home, can be avoided without significant restriction of daily life. Notwithstanding the price of life restriction, the biggest problem with avoidance is that it does not address the underlying fear of fear. So long as you remain fearful of your reaction to any phobic situations, you are not free and you are unable to dance without fear.

Naturally, no one would feel comfortable facing his or her fears without preparation and new skills. Even when equipped with new skills, there is often a hesitation to face a feared situation. This hesitation is poignantly illustrated by Paula, an attractive, youthful-looking woman with five young children. In spite of an engaging smile and bright brown eyes, Paula was passive and uncomfortable around other people, particularly those in positions of "authority," such as her children's teachers, school principal, doctors, and even store clerks. Paula knew that she was intimidated by most people, and that she avoided social situations. We identified her underlying fear of rejection, that common fear shared by almost every anxiety sufferer. Although Paula was instructed in assertiveness skills and knew what she needed to do to overcome her fear of rejection, she continued to avoid the moment of truth when speaking up was the right thing to do. Typically, Paula would recognize the times when speaking up was necessary and appropriate, but she would inevitably back down, missing the opportunity to grow and to overcome her fear of rejection. Her self-esteem suffered deeply, but her fear of facing the fear seemed insurmountable.

I encouraged Paula to participate in group therapy, which she did with initial reluctance and high anxiety. By meeting and becoming comfortable with other people who understood her fears, Paula began to interact verbally with others and express her feelings. In time, she began to report experiences in which she spoke up to others. One instance was a meeting with one of her children's teachers, who Paula felt was not meeting the child's needs as a student, and who was not responding to Paula's phone calls. Another success took place when Paula, who had a nursing background, was asked to serve as a support person for a woman friend who was having a hospital childbirth. In that instance, Paula had a positive experience speaking as a representative for her friend to the nursing and medical staff at the hospital. By joining the therapy group, Paula faced her fear of dealing with people and gradually developed assertive communication skills and self-confidence in social situations.

Another case illustrates how fear of anxiety can persist well beyond the point where actual anxiety symptoms subside. Elaine, a vivacious and verbally expressive woman, came to one of her therapy appointments approximately two months after starting the CHAANGE program and declared, "Dr. Foxman, I haven't had a panic attack now in about six weeks and I'm worried about it." When I inquired about this, Elaine explained that she did not trust the fact that her anxiety symptoms had subsided. "I almost feel that I am getting away with something, as if I'm supposed to have a certain amount of anxiety, and that I'm due for a really big one," she reasoned. In addition, Elaine revealed that she was afraid of feeling anxious, and that she had a high level of anticipatory anxiety—fear of the fear that might happen. I pointed out to Elaine that although she had made progress, she was not anxiety-free because she had not yet faced her biggest phobic situation. In her case, being alone was the biggest fear. She would need to face and experience her fear in order to realize that she could handle it. It was evident that while Elaine's avoidance of this phobic situation kept anxiety at a distance, she had not completed her recovery. As long as she remained fearful of an anxiety reaction, Elaine could not be free.

Many people cope with their anxiety with a determined effort to "not give in." The need for control is often so strong that the person forces himself or herself to go through the phobic situations, feeling that "running away" would mean weakness or failure. In one case, a determined man who renounced weakness said at the outset of treatment, "I'm going to fight this thing! I'm going to beat it!" Unfortunately, fighting it only prolongs the anxiety.

Weekes (1978) distinguishes between fighting and facing fear, and offers a four-step desensitization process that we use in the CHAANGE program. The first step, *facing*, refers to avoiding avoidance. That is, facing a fear requires a willingness to meet the fear on its own turf, and resisting the temptation to distract oneself or put it out of mind. Instead of running away, using distraction, or trying to forget about it, facing a fear literally means standing squarely in the face of it.

The second step, *accepting*, is the opposite of fighting against fear. Accepting a fear is an attitude of allowing it to occur. In accepting anxiety, you surrender and receive it as an opportunity to make progress. This is followed by *float-*

ing, which goes beyond acceptance by experiencing the fear without resisting or bracing to endure it. Floating through fear is riding it out like an ocean wave, openly working with it. As Weekes puts it, "floating resembles accepting but implies moving forward through the sensations and feelings without offering tense resistance, as one would when floating on gently undulating water" (p. 362). This, of course, requires an ability to relax in the face of fear, which is possible only as a result of practicing relaxation skills.

Finally, the fourth step is *letting time pass*, which has two meanings. Letting time pass means leaving the past behind and facing fear with a new attitude and expectations. Instead of focusing on how long it will take to overcome anxiety, or how long it has been since you have suffered with it, facing fear using new skills can be viewed as a practice opportunity. Letting time pass also concerns the issue of impatience—a need to see immediate results in order to believe in the possibility of overcoming anxiety. It is important to trust that an anxiety episode will pass in time. Indeed, if you knew for sure that an anxiety episode would last a predetermined length of time, it would be much less threatening and easier to face.

To summarize, you can practice facing fear using these steps:

FOUR-STEP PROCESS FOR FACING FEAR

1. Facing
2. Accepting
3. Floating
4. Letting time pass

Using the four-step process, you can experience fear as a mind–body wave that approaches, passes through, and leaves. Looking back, all anxiety sufferers, especially those who experience panic attacks, know that an episode of severe anxiety always passes, but the fear of it taking over does not allow an open, accepting attitude towards it. There is a tendency to fear that anxiety will not end, that it will completely take over. In my work with people who suffer from anxiety, I note three categories of such fear: fear of going crazy, fear of losing control in public, and fear of dying. These associated fears magnify anxiety, as Weekes suggests. The only way to overcome these associated fears is to face and go through the anxiety experience, where true recovery lies.

In my own anxiety recovery process, I knew the difference between avoiding and facing my phobic situations. I knew when I was avoiding, and although it brought temporary relief, I also knew that I was only postponing the moment of truth when facing my fear would be necessary for recovery. My most troubling phobic situation was being alone. I worked hard to avoid it by planning social contact whenever I was not at my office. My anxiety level would go up whenever I had no plan for the unstructured time in my schedule. Travel alone far from home was even more frightening, and I always made sure a companion would accompany me. As I gradually faced these phobic situations, and learned to relax through them, I was able to overcome the fear. One specific experience stands out as a significant step in facing my deepest fear. I accepted an opportunity to further my professional training by relocating for two years from San Francisco to Nashville. I had to separate from my friends and go alone. Tennessee was completely unfamiliar to me, and I did not know anyone there before I relocated. Although extremely apprehensive, I had a higher purpose for facing this challenge, which turned out to be one of the most helpful and positive experiences in my anxiety recovery. Not only did I survive, but I thrived socially and professionally. I developed many friendships and received a lot of support for my work.

Although I took a giant step forward in dealing with my fears, I continued to fear being alone and I avoided it as much as possible. Upon completion of my training I took another significant step towards overcoming this phobia. In this case, I responded to an inner calling to do some traveling by myself. My desire to travel had incubated for a long time. My interest was growing stronger, and images emerged of handling the challenge positively. An inner voice called to me and I finally accepted the invitation by setting out on what became a one year journey of personal triumph over my biggest fear. Traveling alone in a camper throughout North America, I faced every conceivable aspect of being alone. Through this experience, I found peace and strength within myself.

In our hearts, we know when we are avoiding and when we are facing our fears. In the end, we must come face to face with our fears to develop confidence in our ability to handle them. This is the only way to fully recover from an anxiety disorder.

So far, we have discussed anxiety in terms of two kinds of fear: fear of phobic situations, and fear of fear itself. We also noted that it is necessary to face the fear—to experience it directly—in order to overcome it. In directly experiencing the fear, the sensitization process is reversed. Facing the fear helps to separate the fear reaction from the phobic situation—from the body's normal alarm reaction to stress or trauma. Facing the fear is a necessary part of learning a new reaction to these situations and replacing the fear reaction. The new learning involved in facing fear is known as *desensitization*.

There are several desensitization approaches, all of which begin with learning to relax. Relaxation, as discussed in Chapter 8, is a foundation skill for desensitization. Unfortunately, relaxing runs directly against the survival instinct, which is to react quickly with a fight/flight response upon exposure to any situation perceived as threatening. This survival reaction is automatic in situations associated with anxiety, trauma, or stress. To prepare for facing your fear, then, you must first practice relaxation skills so that you will be able to use them effectively in the phobic situation. By combining relaxation with a phobic situation, a new pattern is formed, which dramatically alters your attitude towards the situation and your reaction to it.

One method is called *systematic desensitization*. The basic idea is to first combine relaxation with thinking about, or imagining, the phobic situation. In the CHAANGE program, we ask people to make a list of situations that are uncomfortable or anxiety-arousing. We then ask that the list of situations be numbered from least to most distressing. A person's most feared situation will have the highest number. Beginning with the least feared situation, create a mental movie of yourself entering and going through the situation. Use as much detail as possible, creating a sequence of images. Then, after eliciting the relaxation response, visualize yourself going through the situation step by step until you can complete the entire sequence for each situation on the list. At first, you may find yourself reacting anxiously to the imagined situation, and be unable to remain relaxed. Stop there, take a break, and return to relaxation practice. After relaxing again, start the visualization from the beginning. Usually, people find that they can visualize a little further into the situation each time they repeat the visualization. Repeat the process until you can complete an entire phobic situation while remaining relaxed and calm. At that point, it is time to enter the situation—to face the fear in real life.

In real life, it is best to enter a feared situation gradually. Using a sequence similar to the imagined situation, start with small steps and build on them until you can experience the full situation. Let's take fear of driving as an example. A person who experienced a panic attack in a car, or a traumatic automobile accident, may develop a fear of driving, and may become tense and anxious at the thought of being in a car. Furthermore, other circumstances resembling the conditions surrounding the trauma may evoke significant anxiety. The first step in facing this situation is to practice relaxation without driving or being in a car. Then, practice relaxation while imagining or visualizing getting into a car, checking out the controls, starting the car, driving around the block, driving in traffic, and so on. Once this can be done mentally, these steps can be repeated in real life. Many patients have overcome their fear of driving, and many other types of phobic situations, using this procedure. Here is a summary of the steps involved in systematic desensitization:

SYSTEMATIC DESENSITIZATION PROCESS

Make a list of phobic situations.
Number the list from least to most troubling.
Elicit your relaxation response.
Starting with the least troubling situation, visualize yourself going through it while remaining relaxed and open.
Stop the process whenever you feel uptight, and go back to relaxation.
Start again from the beginning of the phobic situation and practice until you can relax throughout the complete visualization.
At that point, begin to face the situation in real life using relaxation and positive thinking.
View this gradual process as an opportunity to overcome anxiety, and do not be discouraged by any fear reactions.

The same procedure can apply to virtually any fear. Public speaking, parties and social events, being alone, shopping, traveling, crowded places, interpersonal conflict—all can be approached through the process of combining relaxation with gradually facing the situation. However, it is important to not move too quickly or directly into desensitization. Setbacks are more likely to occur if too big a step is taken or if the relaxation skills have not been practiced sufficiently. In addition, an educational phase is necessary to relieve a person from confusion about anxiety and to help overcome fear of the body's fight/flight reaction.

A setback is a return to a prior level of fear, often accompanied by feeling discouraged and hopeless. Many anxiety sufferers are already skeptical about recovery, because of the duration and intensity of their suffering. They want desperately to overcome the condition, but do not want to be let down or surprised by an unexpected anxiety episode. There is also a natural tendency to remain guarded, to not trust relaxation and openness. These concerns make it difficult to face the fear. The idea of facing, accepting, remaining open, and allowing anxiety to pass through runs directly against the survival instinct. Therefore, if too big a challenge is invited and the fear is overwhelming, a setback occurs and all the defense mechanisms are reinforced. As a result of a setback, anxiety sufferers feel that any progress made is lost, or that their skepticism is justified. Like a game of Parcheesi, a setback feels like going back to the start box.

In the process of facing their fear, some people may find it helpful to distract themselves, rather than concentrate on relaxing or floating through the experience, as Weekes advises. This can be effective if it is done in the spirit of facing and accepting the fear, and as a temporary measure to cope with it. Distraction does not contribute to recovery if it is used to deny the fear, or to run away from it. Focusing on other things or activities, while allowing the fear to pass through, can contribute to the successful handling of a phobic situation. Here are some simple distraction techniques that can be used in this way:

DISTRACTION TECHNIQUES

Counting backwards from 100 by 3s or 7s

Counting objects such as letters on signs, cars of a specific make or color

Repeating a reassuring affirmation, such as, "These feelings are not life-threatening and I can handle them" or "It's only a matter of time before these feelings subside and I can make it until then"
Saying the words to a song or poem
Making a list (wish list, gift list, grocery list)
Writing down your thoughts
Visualizing a place you like and describing the scene in detail
Focusing on the details of things around you
Making physical contact with things around you (touching a tree, piece of furniture, item of clothing; manipulating the buttons on an electronic device; rubbing a smooth rock or other object between your fingers or in your hand)

Anxiety recovery can be defined as having the skills and confidence to handle anxiety or fear to the point where it no longer matters. Facing the fear is the way to practice that skill and develop such confidence. When it no longer matters, there is no need to worry about it or waste energy anticipating it. When it no longer matters, the chances of experiencing sudden or overwhelming anxiety become negligible. When it no longer matters, you can dance without fear.

13

Feeling Safe with Feelings

A new heart I will give you, a new spirit put within you. I will remove the heart of stone from your flesh, and give you a heart that feels.
C. Stern (ed.), *Gates of Repentance*

Most anxiety sufferers are uncomfortable with strong feelings and avoid them whenever possible. Fear and anxiety, of course, involve strong feelings, but they are by no means the only feelings that make people uncomfortable. Anger, hurt, guilt, ambivalence, and even excitement are "unsafe" for many. Such intense feelings produce anxiety, which further reinforces the secondary fear response. This chapter will explore the relationship between anxiety and feelings, and offer ways to deal safely with feelings.

As discussed previously, most adult anxiety sufferers were reared in families with unhealthy patterns of dealing with feelings. The most common pattern is emotional repression, in which feelings are blocked before they are expressed. Feelings can also be avoided through denial, intellectualization, and other defense mechanisms. When feelings are blocked off, the physical arousal or "charge" associated with them freezes in the body as muscle tension. This can become a pattern, called *body armor* by Reich (1961, 1972), which further blocks a person's ability to feel.

The fight/flight reaction can fixate on certain feelings, based on negative experiences associated with those feelings. A good example is anger, a feeling that is often expressed as out-of-control behavior. Anyone who has been victimized by violence or intimidated by someone else's rage will tend to react to anger with fear. In this case, the fear response fixates on the anger stimulus. Fear can also develop in response to our own anger, if we have ever lost control or felt that we might behave destructively. By this conditioning process, anger triggers fear.

Fear is part of the fight/flight response to danger. When that danger consists of intense feelings, our survival instinct will activate the fight/flight response in reaction to those feelings. Shallow breathing, elevated heart rate, muscle tension, and other fight/flight mechanisms can thus be activated by feelings. Naturally, the survival instinct will attempt to avoid "dangerous" feelings by use of defense mechanisms. However, if a feeling is sufficiently intense, it may penetrate the defenses, leading to heightened fear and anxiety.

In many cases, by learning to defend against their feelings, children are actually developing coping skills for emotional survival within their families. The ability to block off feelings can be adaptive, protecting children from negative consequences for expressing their feelings. For example, children who might otherwise cry when upset can, by holding it in, protect themselves from such negative feedback as "Don't be a crybaby!" or "Crying won't solve anything." Or where anger might meet with punishment, holding it in can be a safeguard.

Dysfunctional emotional patterns in families range from *repressive*, where feelings are not permitted, to *abusive*, where intense feelings are expressed destructively. On either end of this continuum, the likely result is emotional inhibition in the children, especially in those who are sensitive or fearful. As a result, most children from emotionally dysfunctional families do not learn how to express feelings appropriately. They do not develop a vocabulary for their feelings, and they may not learn to use words for identifying what they feel. In some cases children may know how they feel, but they do not know how to express their feelings. They may therefore hold their feelings in as a form of self-preservation. Subsequently, when they leave the dysfunctional family as adolescents or young adults, they will be unprepared for interacting effectively with other people.

Since children learn primarily by imitation, their emotional styles tend to reflect the emotional styles modeled by their parents. Parents who are uncomfortable with feelings create an environment in which feelings are not a natural part of daily interaction. For the children, feelings will not be safe, and skills in communicating feelings will not be acquired. As with many other abilities, the development of emotional skills is affected most by early life experiences. As a result of rearing in emotionally dysfunctional families, the majority of anxiety sufferers—and most other people who seek psychological counseling—need help dealing with feelings.

Generally speaking, boys are at a greater disadvantage in developing emotional communication skills due to the mistaken idea—widely held throughout the world—that emotional expressiveness is a sign of weakness in men. The idea that "real men don't cry" exemplifies this myth. Girls, on the other hand, are reinforced for expressing feelings, and girls' play style often involves sharing feelings, compared to the more competitive play style observed in boys. These differences can become a significant source of conflict in adult relationships, where men and women may find that their communication suffers as a result of gender differences in emotional style. The male emotional style, for example, is often described as *controlled,* with greater reliance on logic than feelings. In contrast, the female emotional style is often described as *expressive,* with greater reliance on feelings and intuition than logic.

What should we learn about feelings early in life? First, that feelings are natural, normal, and safe. What is unsafe is the *behavior* associated with some feelings. For example, the feeling of anger is, in itself, safe. But violence, aggression, or other out-of-control behavior is not safe. One of the first lessons to be learned about feelings is that we have choices about how we *express* our feelings, and that there are both appropriate and inappropriate ways of doing this. Anxiety surrounds feelings when we do not learn to distinguish between feelings and behavior, and when skills for handling feelings are not learned. Since confusion between feelings and behavior seems to be greatest with anger, a separate discussion in the next chapter is devoted to this particular feeling.

Second, that the source of most feelings is our own thoughts. Cognitive psychologists believe that all feelings are launched by our thoughts and perceptions. Depression, for example, is the result of negative or depressing thoughts, and, as we discussed in Chapter 11, anxiety is often produced by what-ifs, shoulds, worrying, and other thoughts. From this viewpoint, therapy for emotional disorders consists of changing the underlying thought patterns that launch our feelings.

Rational-emotive therapy was developed by Ellis (1994) and based on the idea that thinking precedes feeling. In this therapy approach, changing irrational beliefs to rational beliefs changes the way a person feels. For example, the irrational belief, "I must have love and approval from everyone in order to be happy," leads to fear of rejection and criticism. Such a belief also leads to fear of expressing feelings that might upset others, as well as passive behavior and a tendency to agree to do things when you do not want to. The underlying irrational belief, however, can be changed: "I would like to be loved by everyone but I don't need this to be happy. It is not reasonable to expect everyone to like me, or to please everyone all the time. There will be times when people won't love me, just as I don't love everyone I meet. Even if someone doesn't love me, I know other people who do love me." Another common irrational belief is, "I must be good at everything I do. I cannot make any mistakes." This belief is the basis of perfectionistic behavior and it leads to stress, frustration, and feelings of low self-esteem. Once these irrational beliefs are replaced by rational beliefs, the corresponding behavior and feelings tend to change.

Although thoughts may be responsible for our feelings, the reverse is also true: our feelings can influence our thinking. Once a feeling is launched, we tend to focus on thoughts that are linked to that feeling. When we feel depressed, for example, we are likely to remember things that caused us to feel depressed in the past. Indeed, when feeling depressed, our thoughts about the past, present, and future may all be filtered by the lens of depression. Likewise when we feel anxious, we tend to "awfulize" and "catastrophize"—to worry and anticipate bad things, such as losing control, going crazy, having a heart attack, and so on. This is called "state-dependent thinking," meaning that our thinking can be influenced by our emotional state.

Feelings involve both mind and body. Physically, feelings are controlled by both the brain's limbic system and autonomic nervous system (which controls the hormones responsible for the physical aspects of feelings). In many cases, the body's reactions to strong feelings—increased heart rate, perspiration, shallow/rapid breathing, trembling, and so on—are identical to the fight/flight response, but the mind determines *how* we will react to these body reactions. Without the mind's ability to distinguish between the fight/flight response and strong feelings, all feelings would probably trigger fear and anxiety in sensitive people.

Our ability to identify feelings—to know what we feel—is another important skill. This requires a vocabulary for feelings—the words to be used in identifying feelings and verbally communicating them to others. Young children begin with only two words to identify feelings: "good" and "bad." But there are dozens of feelings, and feelings often arise in mixtures and combinations. For example, you can feel angry, hurt, and sorry at the same time. Another combination that can be confusing is love and hate, felt at the same time towards the same person.

Feelings are often energizing, due to increased adrenaline levels at times of emotional arousal. When we are in touch with our feelings and can express them, we feel more energetic. In some cases, the adrenaline "rush" associated with strong feelings can be mistaken for anxiety. On the other hand, when we are out of touch with our feelings, or cannot express them, we may experience numbness, depression, and fatigue.

It is also important to understand the "feeling curve." Feelings follow a natural course involving a waxing phase, a peak, and a waning phase. The pattern can be compared to ocean waves that approach, reach a crescendo, and then wash away from shore. Happiness, sadness, anger, grief, and fear all follow this basic pattern. If we understand this, we will be more effective in handling feelings. There will be more options in handling a feeling if, for example, it is recognized in its early, waxing stage. Once a feeling reaches a peak in intensity, it is more difficult to control because rational thinking is outweighed by strong emotional arousal. Nevertheless, it is always possible to control one's behavior, even when feelings seem to take over.

Elium and Elium (1992) take this concept even further. They describe the feeling curve as having a "point of no return." When feelings build up beyond this threshold of emotional intensity, we enter a "non-thinking zone," in which rational thinking is impossible. In this zone, the discussion of feelings and decision-making is not advised. "Just feel," Elium and Elium recommend. After a feeling peaks and emotional equilibrium is restored, we can think clearly again. In this "clear-thinking zone," communicating feelings and problem solving are more likely to be successful.

An automatic link can form between a specific feeling and a specific behavior. Anger and explosiveness, hurt and withdrawal, fear and avoidance, depression and overeating are some examples. Through the conditioning process described earlier, these links are established as automatic or unconscious habits. It is, therefore, important to distinguish between feelings and behavior in order to break the link between them.

There are no right and wrong feelings. A feeling is an emotional reaction to something, usually thoughts or perceptions. While the underlying thoughts and perceptions may be distorted, it is not quite accurate to say that the corresponding feelings are wrong. Indeed, it could be said that feelings are always right in relation to their triggering thoughts or perceptions, however distorted those thoughts or perceptions may be. In communicating feelings, the most productive attitude is to allow each person to have his or her feelings, and focus instead on the thoughts, perceptions, and assumptions underlying the feelings. It is also important to recognize that everyone has a right to feelings, just as everyone has a right to opinions.

In helping people develop skills for dealing with feelings, the CHAANGE program provides a Bill of Rights and Responsibilities. This is a list of rights we each have as a human being, with our corresponding responsibilities for allowing others to have the same rights. The bill of rights and responsibilities provides a framework for communicating feelings within relationships—between customer and store clerk, employee and supervisor, friend and friend, parent and child, husband and wife. As you read through the following bill of rights and responsibilities, ask yourself, "Which rights are acceptable to me, and which are not?"

BILL OF RIGHTS AND RESPONSIBILITIES

1. The right to be treated with respect (recognizing your responsibility to treat the other with respect)
2. The right to have and to express your own feelings and opinions (recognizing your responsibility to allow the other to express feelings and opinions)
3. The right to be listened to and taken seriously (recognizing your responsibility to listen to and take others seriously)
4. The right to set your own priorities and to choose your own opportunities (recognizing your responsibility to allow others to set their own priorities and opportunities)
5. The right to say no without feeling guilty (recognizing your responsibility to allow the other to say no)
6. The right to ask for what you want (recognizing your responsibility to allow others the right to refuse)
7. The right to get what you pay for (recognizing your responsibility to allow others to get what they pay for)
8. The right to ask for information from anyone (recognizing your responsibility to allow the other the right not to give that information)

9. The right to make mistakes (recognizing your responsibility to accept the consequences of those mistakes)
10. The right to choose not to assert yourself (recognizing your responsibility to allow the other not to assert also)

A useful distinction can be drawn between *expressing* feelings and *communicating* feelings. Expressing feelings usually means raw release of built-up emotional energy. This could be called venting, which serves an energy-discharge function. However, in a relationship it is more productive to communicate feelings, which means to discuss feelings as a way to resolve them. In communicating feelings, one does not act out the feelings, but rather talks—with self-control—about them. As already pointed out, discussing feelings is not productive during the non-thinking zone of the feeling curve. It is sometimes necessary to first release the emotional charge associated with a feeling in order to reach a point of clear thinking and ability to discuss your feelings. This may require a physical-release activity, such as exercise, or simply doing something while a feeling completes its cycle. Once self-control is reestablished, emotional safety and productive communication are possible. Only then can the other person hear or empathize with your feelings without defensiveness or concern about safety. On the other hand, this does not mean becoming intellectual or losing touch with your feelings. Later in this chapter, some guidelines are offered for healthy communication about feelings.

Having been taught that feelings are "dangerous," anxiety-prone people tend to block or suppress feelings in order to avoid them and feel safe. Since this is an unnatural pattern, we can expect some symptoms to develop when feelings are frequently held in or suppressed. What are the symptoms of emotional suppression?

Recall that anxiety stems from the interaction of sensitivity, personality, and stress. In some cases, unexpressed feelings—which build up internal pressure—can be the stress ingredient that triggers anxiety. Generally speaking, when the anxiety is a vague, undefinable uneasiness, it is probably the result of unexpressed feelings.

Depression is another sign of unexpressed feelings, as Peck (1978) suggests. In *The Road Less Traveled*, Peck defines unexpressed feelings as "stuck feelings." Depression can result from holding in sadness, grief, and even anger. Taking this idea further, psychoanalytic theory suggests that when anger is held in it can turn against the self. If you find yourself being self-critical along with feeling depressed, anger turned inward may be the underlying source.

Psychosomatic symptoms are physical symptoms that are caused or influenced by psychological pressures, such as pent-up feelings. Headaches, ulcers, high blood pressure, and asthma are some common psychosomatic symptoms associated with unexpressed feelings. Since feelings are a form of energy, that energy will accumulate if it is not released. Like a pressure cooker, unexpressed feelings accumulate within the body, creating a powerful internal pressure that can destroy health.

Muscle tension is yet another symptom of unexpressed feelings. As discussed elsewhere, blocked feelings create the form of muscle tension known as *body armor*. There is some evidence that blocked feelings are associated with tension in specific muscle groups. Anger and frustration, for example, are associated with tension in the neck and shoulders. Grief and sadness are often held in by tightening the chest and eye muscles. Fear is commonly held in by tension in the stomach and diaphragm muscles, which, in turn, restricts breathing. Blocked sexual feelings are often indicated by muscle tension in the pelvic region. These correlations may not be precise, but the idea that bottled-up feelings are associated with muscle tension is widely accepted, and you can verify this from personal experience.

Once a pattern of muscular armor is established as a result of holding feelings in, the tension itself makes it difficult to be in touch with feelings. Therefore, while some therapeutic approaches advocate tuning into feelings, this will be difficult in cases with extensive muscular armor. Relaxation training and softening of the muscular system—through massage, stretching, and so on—may be necessary in order to invoke feelings. In addition, shifting out of your mind and into your body will help.

What are some methods for tuning in to feelings and dealing effectively with them? You have already taken the first step by considering the preceding ideas about feelings, and understanding the consequences of holding feelings in. The next step is to get in touch with and feel safe with your feelings. Our goal is to overcome fear of feelings, including fear of fear.

It is important to develop a "feelings vocabulary." A feelings vocabulary, as the term suggests, is a repertoire of words to use in identifying and communicating what you feel. Below is a list of feelings (Table 13–1) and a simple exercise that you can use to enhance your feelings vocabulary. Review the list a few times, and then begin to record your feelings. You can go through the list at the end of each day, and check those feelings you experienced during that day. The list of feelings has columns for recording feelings for ten days. After completing the exercise, try to name your feelings as you experience them. You may copy the blank list to repeat this exercise as necessary.

EXERCISE: FEELINGS VOCABULARY

At the end of each day review the following list of feelings. Check each feeling you experienced during that day. Do this daily for ten days. Repeat as necessary. The goal is to develop a vocabulary for identifying and expressing feelings.

As you become aware of feelings during the day, name them to yourself or check them on the list. The list of feelings is in alphabetical order to help you find the right words. There are a few blank rows at the bottom of the list for you to add your own feeling words.

When you are equipped with a richer vocabulary for feelings, the next step consists of tuning in to the physical aspect of your feelings. When we use expressions such as "pain in the neck," "heartbroken," "scared stiff," "so mad I could cry," and "gut-level feeling," we acknowledge that feelings are often located in our body. Therefore, by tuning in to your body, you are more likely to identify and experience your feelings. Gendlin (1978) offers an "experiential focusing" technique to accomplish this. Incorporating Gendlin's guidelines, here are four steps for tuning in to your feelings:

TABLE 13–1: FEELINGS VOCABULARY

	Days									
Feelings	**01**	**02**	**03**	**04**	**05**	**06**	**07**	**08**	**09**	**10**
Alienated										
Ambivalent										
Angry										
Annoyed										
Anxious										
Apathetic										
Ashamed										
Bored										
Concerned										
Confident										
Confused/puzzled										
Curious										
Depressed										
Disappointed										
Discouraged										
Disgusted										
Ecstatic										
Embarrassed										
Enthusiastic										
Envious										
Excited										
Frightened										
Frustrated										
Fulfilled										
Guilty										
Happy										
Helpless										
Hopeful										
Hostile										
Humiliated										
Hurt										
Impatient										

TABLE 13–1: FEELINGS VOCABULARY *(continued)*

	Days									
Feelings	01	02	03	04	05	06	07	08	09	10
Inspired										
Interested										
Joyful										
Lonely										
Loved										
Miserable										
Negative										
Nervous										
Optimistic										
Overwhelmed										
Peaceful										
Pessimistic										
Positive										
Proud										
Rejected										
Relieved										
Remorseful										
Restless										
Sad										
Satisfied										
Scared/fearful										
Shy										
Stubborn										
Surprised/shocked										
Suspicious										
Tired										
Withdrawn										

TUNING IN TO YOUR FEELINGS

1. Relax. Spend five or ten minutes in meditation, yoga, visualization, or a muscle relaxation procedure. This will help you focus on your body.
2. Ask yourself, "What am I feeling right now?"
3. Attune to the place in your body where you feel emotional sensations. Use your feelings vocabulary as you scan your body for the location of feelings, and name them as they become apparent.
4. Wait and listen. Be a patient observer and, without judging, allow your senses to pick up on your feeling's place in your body. When you get a general sense of what you are feeling, ask the following questions to further identify your feelings: Where in my body is this feeling? What is the shape of this feeling? What is the size of this feeling? If this feeling had a color, what would it be?

Fear of feelings will lessen if you can simply *be* with your feelings, and suspend any judgments or negative thoughts about them. Thoughts such as "I shouldn't feel this way," "He'll be upset with me if I tell him how I feel," and "I won't be able to handle my feelings," are all based on false assumptions, and they can be replaced. Replace them with the truth about feelings: you have a right to your feelings, feelings are not inherently dangerous, feelings and behavior are two different things, you have a choice about how you express your feelings, feelings always pass at the end of the feeling curve, and you can learn how to communicate feelings effectively.

It will also be helpful to cultivate an accepting and nonjudgmental attitude towards your feelings, much the same way as you would treat thoughts arising in meditation. In discussing the spiritual advantages of a painful childhood, Muller (1992) offers some meditations to create a "place of safety" for feelings. In exploring fear, for example, Muller advises us to relax, and as we allow fear to arise, ask,

> Where is the sensation strongest? In the chest, the muscles, the belly? What additional images arise along with the fear? Watch where the fear stays longest, watch as it begins to recede. Simply investigate this fear, making peace with the sensations that arise. If we resist the urge to protect ourselves and move gently into the experience of fear, what other sensations or impulses arise? (p. 36).

By letting fear exist simply as images in the mind and sensations in the body, we can feel safe with fear and let it pass without the usual disturbance and secondary reactions. This attitude is similar to Weekes' (1978) approach to anxiety, discussed in Chapter 12, in which she advises us to face, accept, float through, and let time pass.

We have already discussed the important distinction between feelings and behavior. Keeping this distinction in mind will prove helpful in cultivating emotional safety, and in accepting feelings without judgment or fear. Knowing that you can simply be with your feelings, without responding to any impulses to act them out or behave in a programmed way, will help lower your fear. In this sense, being with your feelings is a quiet and private process that allows you to move through emotional sensations without taking action. If action is necessary and appropriate, it is best done with self-control.

Feelings sometimes do require action. In some cases, it is necessary to discharge the energy or tension associated with a feeling. If this cannot be done through nonjudgmental meditation, other release mechanisms may prove useful. These include talking about your feelings with someone you trust, writing your feelings in a diary or journal, or writing a letter (that does not necessarily need to be mailed). With anger, there are some additional methods for releasing the emotional charge (see Chapter 14). These are all methods for letting feelings out—for discharging emotional energy—rather than communicating feelings directly to specific people. By far the most difficult action is to verbally communicate your feelings to other people, especially to those who may have behaved in ways that aroused hurt, anger, or other negative feelings. These are people with whom you may have some unresolved issues.

I personally had great difficulty with assertive communication. I feared that if I communicated my feelings to other people, they would become angry or upset with me. I intellectualized my feelings, and avoided assertive communication by telling myself that conflict was negative and the world needed more peace. Like most anxiety sufferers, I struggled with a fear of rejection, which led me to please other people and avoid conflict. I was, in all honesty, often passive and compliant, even when it was not in my best interest. I was frequently unable to be honest about my feelings. In addition, I feared my own feelings when they were intense, and assumed I would be unable to control them. Anger, sadness, and guilt were particularly difficult for me to handle.

I was able to overcome this problem, but not without great effort and practice. One of the most helpful tools was found in Seagrave and Covington (1987). Founders of the CHAANGE program, Seagrave and Covington offer a simple three-step formula for expressing feelings assertively. I have added a fourth step, which makes the technique more complete and successful, at least for me.

"How do you tell the carpet cleaner that he didn't clean your carpet? How do you tell your guilt-giving mother-in-law that you won't be having guests for Thanksgiving dinner? How do you say 'no' to car-pooling for a friend? How do you ask your supervisor for a raise?" (p. 178). With these questions, Seagrave and Covington highlight the type of situations where assertive communication is appropriate. They suggest the following steps for effective communication in situations where conflict or rejection is anticipated.

STEPS FOR ASSERTIVE COMMUNICATION

Step One: Use an empathy statement.
Step Two: State what you want.
Step Three: Suggest an outcome to the other person.
Step Four: Seek an agreement.

Step One is a way to open up communication and reduce the probability of defensiveness on the part of the listener. With an empathy statement, such as, "I know you are very busy but I need to speak with you about something important," you show the other person that you understand his position and that you are sensitive to his needs and feelings. An empathy statement is a signal that you are "safe" to talk to—that you are in control of yourself.

Step Two, stating your feelings or needs, is what most people do without first establishing safe ground for assertive communication, and without the subsequent steps that help insure success. Expressing your feelings without the complete package is rarely successful, and seldom leads to change. When you state your feelings or needs, be sure to use "I statements" rather than "you statements." For example, you would say, "I felt hurt when you said. . . ," rather than, "You hurt me when you said. . . ." Another example would be, "I am disappointed in the way this product works, and I want to return it for a refund."

Step Three is frequently overlooked by people when they state their feelings. Without a clear idea about what you want as the outcome of the communication, you are unlikely to get it. It is always helpful to first ask yourself, "What do I want to happen as a result of this communication. What is purpose of this communication?"

Finally, results are more likely to be favorable when you include Step Four, asking for an agreement. By simply asking, "Are you in agreement?" your effectiveness will increase, because people are more likely to follow through if they make an agreement. An agreement is a commitment. If someone makes an agreement with you but fails to follow through with it, you then have a more solid basis for your next assertive communication. In that case, you can remind the person that an agreement was made, and communicate your feelings—such as disappointment or frustration—about his or her lack of follow-through. Of course, as already mentioned, it is important to have a clear idea of what you want to happen as a result of the next assertive communication.

A great deal of fear and anxiety could be prevented if we learned that feelings are safe, that feelings and behavior are two different things, that feelings are a form of energy that needs to be released, that feelings follow a natural and predictable course, and that it is healthy to communicate feelings. It would also help reduce fear and anxiety if we practiced the skills necessary for identifying, expressing, communicating, and otherwise dealing with feelings. These ideas and skills are best learned in childhood, when we are forming our emotional and social patterns. However, it is never too late to acquire the information and skills to change our feelings about feelings. And with respect to the most feared of feelings—fear itself—it is certainly possible to make peace. Hopefully, by practicing what you have learned about feelings, you will find, as Muller says about fear, "perhaps there is no danger at all, merely a shift in sensations" (p. 36).

14

Anger and Fear

> *Perverted anger is a major force producing and sustaining anxiety.*
>
> Theodore Rubin, *The Angry Book*

In general, feelings are anxiety-arousing for many people, but anger is the most troubling emotion because it is often associated with out-of-control behavior. The emotion of anger triggers fear of the behaviors that are associated with it. What might happen if you or someone else became angry?

Fear of anger can be evoked through memories of violence, abuse, or out-of-control behavior that occurred in the past under the influence of anger. If you were the target or victim of someone's out-of-control anger, you would naturally develop fear of this emotion. Even *you* may have lost control when you were angry, and scared yourself. Just witnessing anger from a distance—a fight between other people or an angry scene in a movie—could be enough to trigger anxiety.

Anger is also anxiety-arousing because in the body it is similar to the fight/flight reaction. Increased heart rate and blood pressure, irregular breathing, muscular tension, and general arousal due to increased adrenaline are some obvious similarities. In addition, fear of losing control is common with both anger and fear. The overlap between anger and fear in their physical and emotional aspects may make it difficult to distinguish between the two.

Lee (1990) identifies four mechanisms we use to avoid anger. A "stuffing and storing" pattern is one mechanism, in which angry feelings are suppressed and stored out of awareness. Stuffing and storing anger is similar to the operation of a pressure cooker. When anger is not expressed on a timely basis, it goes into storage but adds some internal pressure to the cooker. The emotional pressure builds over a period of time as more angry feelings are stuffed and stored, and at a certain point it overpowers the safety release valve. Then, even minor frustration can result in an *explosive release* of anger that is out of control and disproportionate to the situation triggering it. Alternatively, there may be more of a gradual *implosion* of emotional pressure, resulting in physical symptoms, such as indigestion, ulcers, high blood pressure, and chronic fatigue. In addition, emotional symptoms, such as irritability, mood swings, depression, and anxiety may also develop as a result of stored anger. We must prevent a build-up of anger to avoid such symptoms.

Stored anger appears to increase the risk for heart disease. Shekelle and colleagues (1983) studied 1,877 men and found that those who scored high on a hostility scale were one-and-a-half times more likely to have a heart attack than men who had lower hostility scores. Barefoot, Dahlstrom, and Williams (1983) did a follow-up study of 255 physicians who took a battery of psychological tests while they were medical students. Twenty-five years later, those with lower hostility scores had one-sixth the incidence of coronary heart disease of those who scored higher on hostility. Williams and colleagues (1980) tested 424 patients who were referred for coronary angiography. Forty-eight percent of patients with low hostility scores were found to have coronary atherosclerosis, but 70 percent of patients with higher hostility scores had significant atherosclerosis. These findings suggest that chronic anger—which Rubin (1969) refers to as an anger "slush fund"—can damage your heart and arteries.

Passive-aggressive behavior is another mechanism through which anger is avoided. Passive-aggressive behavior is an indirect and disguised expression of anger, whereby a person unconsciously expresses anger. Coming late for meetings, "forgetting" things, and procrastinating are some forms of passive-aggressive behavior. Typically, the person is unaware of both the anger and the passive-aggressive behavior, and therefore does not take responsibility for them.

Lee observes another anger defense mechanism, which he calls "New Age transcendence." This refers to a belief that anger is a negative emotion that should not be expressed—that we can choose to transcend. Lee points out that while some people try to transcend their anger, they are merely denying it. This avoidance mechanism is usually unsuccessful because there is no release of emotional tension and the anger is still present.

Reaction formation is another defense mechanism that we use to avoid anger. This mechanism involves a display of behavior that is opposite to anger, such as friendliness or being "nice" towards someone with whom we are angry. Like passive-aggressive behavior, reaction formation is a way to disguise anger, in an effort to avoid dealing with it.

Stuffing and storing, passive-aggressive behavior, and reaction formation are some of the ways we avoid our *own anger.* There are some additional mechanisms we use to avoid *anger in other people*. We may attempt to prevent others from becoming angry through pleasing and compliant behavior, designed to keep us on good terms with others and prevent conflict. This comes easily to those with the "anxiety personality," who are overly sensitive to rejection and disapproval. We also avoid anger in others by physically withdrawing from situations where they may be angry. Although this may protect us in the short run, it does not effectively deal with anger in a relationship. As a last resort, when physical avoidance is not an option, we may shut down emotionally or go numb. In this case, we become unresponsive and distant to avoid dealing with anger.

People with anxiety personality traits create their own anger and resentment. The tendency to take on the responsibilities of others and do more than your share, the need to please others by saying "yes" when you feel "no," difficulty setting reasonable limits, a tendency to be easily influenced by others, and lack of assertiveness may all lead the anxious person to become resentful. When feelings of anger and resentment arise they are usually stuffed and stored, or avoided through other mechanisms, which creates more emotional pressure and anxiety.

We do have a choice about how we deal with anger, but we must first acknowledge our angry feelings. This can be accomplished with the Feelings Vocabulary and Tuning into Feelings exercises described in Chapter 13. After identifying our anger, we can begin to transform this emotion into more positive energy.

With anger, more than any other emotion, it is important to separate the negative aspects of anger-driven behavior from the underlying feeling. Anger is a *feeling*. Violence, destructiveness, verbal abuse, withdrawal, and aggression are *behaviors*. There is no necessary connection between the two. However, based on past experiences in which anger may have been expressed destructively, the most appropriate option for expressing anger is the one least likely to be used by most people—verbal discussion of anger with the person towards whom the feelings are directed.

The biggest obstacle to appropriate verbal expression of angry feelings is the *physical tension* generated by it. Anger is typically associated with intense neuromuscular activation, which gives anger a highly charged quality. This muscular tension is often responsible for the sudden and explosive release of anger in the form of violence and aggressive behavior. In order to be in control of angry feelings, and to engage in appropriate verbal discussion, one must first release this physical tension.

There are a number of methods for discharging the physical tension associated with anger. Vigorous exercise, hitting a pillow or mattress, progressive muscle relaxation, and other tension release activities all help to lower the charge and explosive potential of anger. Sometimes just taking time out and focusing on another activity may allow muscle tension to subside. Here is a safe, simple, and effective way to discharge the physical tension associated with anger:

EXERCISE: TENSION RELEASE FOR ANGER CONTROL

> In private, take a hand towel and fold it in half lengthwise and then fold a second time. After that, fold the towel in half the other way. Twist the towel between your two hands and hold. Now, close your eyes and think about the situation which has aroused your anger. Allow yourself to imagine vividly the situation or person toward whom your anger is directed. As you mentally focus on the anger, begin to twist the towel with everything you have. As you wring the towel, repeat out loud, "I'm angry, I'm angry, I'm angry."
>
> Do this ten or twelve times, each time allowing the intensity of the feeling and the energy put into the towel wringing to increase. You have succeeded in discharging your physical tension if your body feels limp—like cooked spaghetti. You will then be more in control and able to discuss your anger appropriately.

The purpose of discharging angry tension is to make way for more constructive behavior. Discharging angry tension in exercises such as the one above should be a private, safe, and constructive activity. We must be mindful that venting anger towards others is destructive. As Tavris (1982) warns, venting anger towards others can increase rather than decrease anger.

Once you have discharged the physical tension, anger is safer to feel and discuss. Try to stay with the feelings associated with anger and begin to consider what you want to do with them. Most likely, you will need to talk with someone towards whom the feelings are directed. You may still fear the anger based on many years of conditioning, but remember that anger is simply a feeling and not necessarily linked to any particular behavior. You can decide what to do with the feelings.

You could, of course, stuff and store your angry feelings but that option will only backfire with one symptom or another. It is best to learn how to discuss your feelings of anger and resentment. Do this the same way you would want others to discuss their angry feelings with you: with sensitivity, self-control, safety, and respect. To do this you must be in control of yourself and feel *safe*. Here is a method for creating personal safety when discussing anger with another person in a tense or charged situation:

EXERCISE: INVISIBLE SAFETY SHIELD

To help you feel safe, draw an imaginary boundary or safety zone around yourself. Consider yourself physically and emotionally safe as long as the other person does not intrude into your safety zone. Draw the boundary line wherever you need—the line may differ from person to person. Under some circumstances where safety is a significant issue, you may want to tell the other person where your boundaries lie and what you need in order to feel safe when discussing your feelings. Normally, it may be sufficient to privately define your safety zone and determine in advance what steps you would take if you feel threatened. Your safety zone is behind this invisible shield of protection. As you speak from inside this safety shield, practice relaxing and feeling safe in the presence of angry feelings.

Once you establish a safety shield, you can express angry feelings appropriately using the assertiveness skills described in Chapter 13. Remember to focus on your own feelings, without criticizing, blaming, or demoralizing the other person. Start with empathy and make "I" statements. After expressing your feelings, offer a solution or ask for what you need. For example, you may need an apology, or perhaps a commitment by the other person to change a particular behavior pattern. Always keep in mind that anger is not dangerous unless there is loss of control or it is expressed destructively. You want to experience your anger while regulating the physical tension associated with it. You want to learn to verbally express your angry feelings in a constructive mode with a positive outcome.

What about your slush fund of angry feelings? These are the feelings that have accumulated over a period of many years through stuffing and storing. You may have a slush fund of past anger even after you learn how to deal effectively with anger in the present. It would be healthy to bring yourself up to date by cashing out your slush fund of anger. Here is a method from the CHAANGE program that has helped many people cash out their old slush fund of anger:

EXERCISE: CASHING OUT YOUR ANGER SLUSH FUND

Begin by making a list of each thing about which you feel angry. Be as specific as possible. Identify names, places, and dates for each item.

Go back over your list and make choices about which angry feelings you want to let go. Base your choices on your understanding of how energy is wasted in maintaining your slush fund, and on what you feel ready to release. Think about the effect of stored anger, but be honest with yourself about which feelings you can truly let go. On your list, cross out the angry feelings that you choose to release. You may be surprised at how the list can dwindle.

For each remaining item on your list, begin to work it through: do something physically releasing, such as playing tennis, golf, hitting a pillow or mattress, or throwing rocks into a lake. With each "hit," name the specific person or event in your mind. Do this until the anger disappears.

Occasionally, there is old anger in your slush fund that seems resistant or impossible to release. Such difficult-to-release anger may be related to a painful trauma or abuse, which you may not be ready or able to let go. For such situations, there is a powerful method offered by Hay (1987). Based on the belief that letting go of anger requires *forgiveness,* Hay suggests an exercise designed to help you forgive. The exercise involves visualization of the person toward whom you are angry. You are asked to picture the person as a young child who feels vulnerable, insecure, and in need of reassurance. When you view the other person this way, you may be more able to forgive. Again, however, there are some situations in which you may simply not be able to let go. It is at this point where Hay advises, with caution, a *revenge visualization.*

The revenge visualization may be necessary to satisfy a desire to retaliate, to hurt someone who may have hurt you. If you can do this in the privacy of your own imagination, you may be able to safely discharge the negative wish and free yourself to forgive. Here is the essence of Hay's recommendation for this purpose:

EXERCISE: REVENGE VISUALIZATION

Close your eyes and relax. Begin to think about the person whom you are unable to forgive. What would you like to do to this person? What does this person need to receive your forgiveness? Visualize that happening now. Get into the details and continue until the person has suffered enough for you to feel finished.

When you feel ready to forgive, let go forever. Usually at his point you feel lighter and freer. Do this exercise only once for each person with whom you need special help to forgive. Do not indulge in revengeful thoughts because they will have a negative effect on you. As a last resort, this method can help you reach closure on anger and forgiveness.

May you dissolve the dark clouds of anger and resentment using the ideas and methods offered here. May your load be lightened, and your fear of anger overcome. May you enrich your life with a full spectrum of feelings. May you be true to yourself at all times and achieve your personal best. If someone wrongs you, may you use your skills to give appropriate feedback and resolve your anger.

15

Sex and Anxiety

> *. . . undischarged sexual excitation is the central mechanism of anxiety. . . . The prospects of cure and the success of the cure are directly dependent upon the possibility of establishing the capacity for full genital gratification.*
>
> Wilhelm Reich

Sexual issues can both cause anxiety and result from anxiety. Sexual abuse, for example, the most traumatic disruption to psychosexual development, can create fears of sexual intimacy, problems with trust, and anxiety about sexual pleasure. However, even when anxiety occurs for other reasons, having nothing directly to do with sexuality, it can disrupt sexual drive and pleasure. And yet, sexuality—particularly orgasm—can be a healing power in anxiety recovery, as it is one of nature's mechanisms for releasing tension and stress.

Sexual energy is a form of life energy. Hippocrates, the first known physician, practiced medicine based on the concept of a life energy. For Hippocrates, recovery from illness was the work of nature, involving the healing power of life's own energy forces. Later, Paracelsus, personal physician to Erasmus, practiced according to the same concept and referred to life energy as "vital force."

Early scientists found that life energy has a natural rhythm and flow. In 1791, Galvani proposed—and we now know this to be true—that life energy flows through our bodies by a process of expansion and contraction, the same expansions and contractions found in all somatic structures, including the pulsations of the cardiovascular, digestive, and muscular systems. The flow of life energy seems to be a universal pattern in nature, reflected in the way energy moves through plants and trees, as well as in the ebb and flow of the oceans.

The flow of life energy in each of us needs to be regulated in order to maintain biological equilibrium, and nature provides a number of means for accomplishing this. Relaxation, rest, and sleep, for example, are necessary for recovery from energy expenditure. Food, which provides fuel for energy, also contributes to the recovery phase, and helps the body to stock up for future energy output. Exercise, on the other hand, is important for releasing pent-up life energy. Changes in breathing are another mechanism for regulating energy, as the body adjusts oxygen supply to meet energy requirements. All of these mechanisms are addressed in this book as part of regulating anxiety.

Sex is another one of nature's mechanisms for regulating energy, and it is the most pleasurable. Like exercise, sex

has a tension-releasing function. As we will see, sex is a way to renew the body's energy, by virtue of the deep peace and relaxation it produces. The mind, which is temporarily "lost" in complete sexual release, is also refreshed by sex.

Sexual drive, like other life energy patterns, flows in pulsations that build up to a state of sexual tension. Periodically, as the state of sexual tension accumulates, there is a natural need for release or discharge. Sexual tension and release are nature's way of maintaining a state of biological balance or equilibrium. Although the time period involved in this cycle seems to vary from person to person—there are no rules about what is normal—most people do experience a periodic need for sexual release. An insufficient discharge of sexual energy—a block in its natural flow—leaves a person in a state of accumulated tension, which is responsible for many emotional symptoms. Indeed, anxiety resulting from an accumulation of excess sexual energy and enervation of the body is one of the signs of sexual frustration.

Reich (1961), a student of Freud, took an interest in sexuality in an attempt to understand psychological disorders. Reich believed that sexual repression was the basis of anxiety. He said, "It became more and more clear that the overloading of the vasovegetative system with undischarged sexual excitation is the central mechanism of anxiety, and, hence, of neurosis" (p. 119). While Freud believed that anxiety about sexual impulses causes sexual repression, Reich emphasized that sexual repression causes anxiety.

Reich believed that blocks in the flow of feelings and sexuality develop in children to avoid punishment or rejection by parents. To cope in a family where feelings and sexual expression are suppressed, muscular rigidities form in the child to block the flow of feelings. Furthermore, Reich noted a relationship between the ability to flow emotionally and the discharge of feeling during sex. People who are bound with muscular blocks—*body armor* as he called it—are unable to discharge fully in a total orgasm. In addition, those who are raised with a negative attitude towards sex—or towards feelings in general—tend to develop what is known in psychoanalysis as "pleasure anxiety," which is anchored in chronic muscle tension. These observations and concepts led Reich to a theory about sexual orgasm and its relationship to anxiety, as well as illness and health in a broader sense.

Sexual orgasm is the key to counteracting anxiety and to a healthy emotional life, according to Reich. His formula seems almost too simple, but certainly reasonable: tension → bioelectric charge → bioelectric discharge → relaxation. At the time Reich studied the orgasm, it had already been discovered by Galvani that, mechanically, the human body was a bioelectric organism. We can, in fact, measure the electricity in muscles with a simple device called an electromyelogram (EMG), which is used today in biofeedback and relaxation training. Reich's idea was that when tension builds up in the body, an electric charge—a *stasis* as he called it—also builds up. An accumulation of excess charge overloads the autonomic nervous system, causing anxiety.

This idea is compatible with the anxiety model discussed throughout this book, namely that anxiety is caused by an irrational fear reaction to strong physical activation in sensitized people. Reich went further, however, by saying that anxiety is energized by frustrated sexual drive. In addition, Reich noted that sexuality and anxiety have opposite effects. Sexual pleasure is relaxing and expansive, while anxiety contracts us, causing tension and pulling us inward.

Reich boldly suggested that three to four thousand orgasms in a lifetime—approximately once per week assuming an active sexual life of fifty to sixty years—are necessary to maintain biological and psychological equilibrium. Orgasms at this rate would counteract a build-up of tension and frustration, as well as the tendency for repressed feelings to harden into muscular armor. Orgasmic release is not limited to the pelvis, although the genitals are located there. Orgasm releases feelings and tension throughout the body, and therefore it was considered by Reich to be a therapeutic answer to many emotional disorders. In addition, even when feelings become blocked in childhood as a coping response in an emotionally repressed family, regular sexual orgasms in adulthood can help release those blocks and return a person to a feeling life.

On the other hand, the same fears that might be triggered by feelings could interfere with attaining orgasm. In fact, sexual arousal is a strong emotional state, as well as a time of intense physical activation. Elevated heart rate, rapid breathing, increased body temperature, heightened muscle tension, and sweating—the physical aspects of sexual arousal—are virtually identical to the fight/flight reaction that is triggered by any situation involving danger. But danger can include strong feelings in people who are unfamiliar with or afraid of them. Since sexual arousal—necessary for orgasm—involves intense feeling, it may be feared by those who are anxious about feelings. Furthermore, even without fear of feelings, sexual arousal may be anxiety-arousing for those who are uncomfortable with body activation, because of its kinship with anxiety symptoms.

This was indeed the case with Sara, a young woman with panic disorder who presented a problem with sex during one of her psychotherapy sessions. Sara, a single mother in her early thirties, contacted me for help with panic disorder with agoraphobia. I noted that she had a tendency to wear form-fitting clothes with a notable flair—bright colors, lace, exaggerated styles—and she walked and behaved in a coy, seductive manner. Sara had been sexually abused as a girl by an uncle. She had a live-in boyfriend, and two young preschool children from a previous relationship. In one of her therapy sessions Sara said, "This is embarrassing, but I was having sexual relations with my boyfriend and as I became aroused and my breathing became erratic, I had a panic attack. Why did it happen, when I didn't want it to?"

In addressing Sara's question, I pointed out that sexual arousal has many qualities in common with anxiety. Sexual arousal involves activation of the vascular, respiratory, glandular, and other organ systems, and physically resembles the fight/flight reaction in anxiety. Although sexual arousal is normally associated with pleasure, in Sara's case there were at least two obvious complications. One was her anxiety disorder, in which panic attacks and severe anxiety were associated with body arousal. She was, at that point in therapy, still fearful of fear. She was afraid of physical arousal because it was so similar to the frightening symptoms of severe anxiety. Erratic breathing seemed to be a trigger for Sara's panic anxiety. It is also likely that gasping breaths during sexual arousal activated memories of the hyperventilation she experienced during previous anxiety episodes.

In addition, Sara was a victim of childhood sexual abuse, which meant that some anxiety was associated with sexuality. While it did not occur consistently, Sara had problems with trust and relaxation during sexual activity with her partner. She reported that she had to be in the mood for sex, which in her case included feeling in control of any sexual interaction. Since orgasm, and the progressive excitation leading up to it, involves a surrendering to powerful feelings, as well as a loss of normal consciousness and control, Sara could not easily give in.

Sara's body language also revealed her issues with sexuality. On the surface, she appeared to be sexually potent and free. This was expressed in her exaggerated hip movements as she walked, her tight clothes, and her seductive mannerisms. However, her seductive behavior belied her sexual anxiety and insecurity. Inside, as a victim of sexual abuse, Sara was uncomfortable with her sexuality. Assuming that sex was the basis of any man's interest in her, Sara emphasized her sexuality to attract attention and bolster her self-esteem. But she needed to be in control of men, and she played with them in a teasing way. Developmentally, her playfulness seemed to correspond to the age at which she was sexually exploited. In this way, Sara was acting out some of the issues emanating from her history as a victim of sexual abuse, including her anxiety about sex, and her need to be in control was a way of handling the anxiety.

Most, if not all, sexual problems involve anxiety. Two kinds of anxiety have been identified in sexual disorders: pleasure anxiety and performance anxiety. In the past, all male sexual disorders were called *impotence* and all female sexual disorders were called *frigidity*. Based on the work of Masters and Johnson (1970), Kaplan (1974), and others, it is now recognized that many sexual problems involve problems with feelings, such as inhibited desire, anxiety about pleasure or performance, and pain (not due to a medical condition). Premature ejaculation, for example, reflects anxiety about sustaining pleasure. Inorgasmia is viewed as an inhibition of the orgasm reflex due to fear of orgasm. Anxiety seems to be the basis of many sexual problems, and in most cases a sexual problem produces anxiety. Accordingly, therapy for most sexual disorders includes anxiety reduction as part of the solution.

Reich (1961) offers a number of techniques for releasing muscular armor—for opening blocks to the flow of life energy within the body. Viewing the body as having a number of segments that can become armored, Reich advises selective tension-release exercises. For releasing tension in the head and face, for example, he recommends repeatedly opening the eyes wide, and making frowns and grimaces with the face. For the oral segment, consisting of mouth and jaw, Reich suggests yelling, sucking, biting, and crying exercises. Reich also notes that it is more difficult to release armor in lower body segments without first freeing up the higher segments. This is important because sexual release involves primarily the pelvic region, the lowest body segment in Reich's scheme of emotional blocks. Therapy to free up the sexual response, therefore, requires a multi-modal approach to soften the armor throughout the body. A variety of techniques is necessary, such as desensitization to fear of physical activation, changing attitudes towards sexuality, and helping people become more comfortable with feelings. These happen to be some of the components of effective anxiety treatment, discussed at various points elsewhere in this book.

A block in the natural flow of sexual energy creates a state of rigidity, tension, and frustration. This will typically manifest in the body as an armored pelvis—a contracted pelvic region with little feeling. Once this pattern forms, sexual gratification becomes even more difficult, and a vicious cycle develops in which tension and frustration intensify even further. To counteract this, Lowen (1975, 1990), one of Reich's students and patients, developed a series of therapeutic exercises to help release pelvic armor and improve sexual functioning.

Lowen notes that in masturbation and sexual intercourse the pelvis thrusts or rocks back and forth as part of the mechanism for sexual feeling and orgasmic release. He also observed that all fears affect the pelvis, causing a contraction of muscles in the pelvic floor and, when fear is chronic, a general tension in the pelvic region. Accordingly, his recommendations for bringing more feeling into the pelvic region, and for improving sexual functioning, consist of exercises that relax the pelvis. In a normal state, the pelvis moves freely back and forth with the natural movement of the body, in harmony with breathing. During exhalation, the pelvis moves forward, and during inhalation the pelvis moves backward. These rocking movements are subtle during normal breathing while sitting or standing. As breathing intensifies during sexual arousal, pelvic rocking also intensifies, and at the height of excitement and climax they become rapid and powerful. However, anxiety immobilizes the pelvis, which becomes fixed in either a forward or backward position, restraining its movement during sex. In this case, feeling during sex is cut off, and full orgasmic release is prevented.

Lowen (1990) prescribes several exercises for checking the pelvic position and for releasing pelvic tension in order to improve sexual functioning. In one exercise, you stand before a mirror and observe your back by looking over your shoulder. Move your pelvis forward and backward and note any feelings associated with each position. Note your habitual pelvic position. Then breathe deeply and slowly into a loosely held pelvis, trying to feel a respiratory wave go deep into the structure. Some people feel anxiety in the movement of the pelvis as they breathe into it.

Lowen adds that for people with significant tension, pelvic movement is restricted. However, for the person who is relatively free of tension, the orgasm reflex—that involuntary pelvic movement associated with orgasm—will manifest while lying on a bed and breathing. You can check this for yourself by lying on your back on a bed with your knees raised and your feet in contact with the bed. Your pelvis will move spontaneously—up with inbreath and backward with outbreath—if there is no muscular tension blocking the respiratory waves as they pass through the body. If you do not observe this pattern, it is likely that your pelvic mobility is restricted by muscle tension.

To help relax the pelvis and bring more feeling into sex, you can practice the following exercise. While standing with your feet about eight inches apart and knees bent slightly forward, try to push down on the pelvis while breathing deeply into the abdomen. At the same time, try to open the anus as if you would let some gas out. Then, try to pull up the anus and pelvic floor by squeezing the buttocks. Repeat this exercise frequently in order to learn

the difference between tension and relaxation in the pelvis, and to increase its relaxed state. The reward will be an increase in sexual feeling.

Sexual activity is not the only mechanism for pelvic movement and associated pleasure. Dancing, which involves rhythmic movement of the pelvis, is also pleasurable for many people. It is no accident that the popularity of rock-and-roll music—which rocks and rolls the pelvis—coincided with the so-called sexual revolution in the 1960s and 1970s. Elvis Presley—"Elvis the Pelvis"—the Beatles, Bo Diddley, Chubby Checker, and other early rock-and-roll musicians launched an era of music that is often associated with sexual expression, as well as a defiance of "uptight" values and behavior. Michael Jackson, Madonna, Mick Jagger, and Tina Turner, to name just a few examples, carried on this tradition of sexuality in music, which seems to have incredible appeal worldwide. Such music is not just for listening; it is something felt in the hips, which spontaneously want to rock—to thrust rhythmically as in sexual intercourse. Dancing to music is an opportunity for sexual expression in a world that, in many ways, is sexually and emotionally repressed.

Yoga is another approach to developing and maintaining a flexible body, and there are a number of postures that address the pelvic region. Specifically, the Plow, Bridge, Fish, Cobra, and Bow postures all mobilize the hips and pelvic region. Yoga is discussed in Chapter 10, which contains suggestions and resources for learning how to perform these postures. As discussed in that chapter, yoga is a form of physical and mental self-regulation that has an important place in anxiety recovery. By decreasing body tension, yoga can help release muscular armor and mobilize

feelings, which can help improve sexual functioning. Like other practices, especially those involving physical activity such as exercise and strength training, yoga can also improve body image and therefore sexuality. In fact, any practice that improves health, self-esteem, and body image is likely to have a positive effect on a person's sexuality.

In psychoanalytic theory, anxiety results from the conflict between impulses seeking gratification and fear of rejection or negative feedback—the reality consequences of immediate gratification. Strong anger pressing for immediate expression, for example, is likely to result in out-of-control behavior and negative consequences. Likewise, the sexual drive must be channeled into appropriate behavior, such as courtship and emotional intimacy, in order to be gratified in an interpersonal context. A balance must be found between immediate, unregulated gratification of the sexual drive on one hand, and blocking of sexual expression on the other hand. Anxiety is associated with both extremes. The risks associated with direct sexual expression are cause for anxiety, yet the build-up of tension resulting from a sexual drive that is not expressed—blocked due to fear of consequences—also produces anxiety. When there is no release, the symptoms of a frustrated sexual drive include anxiety.

As an energy system, we process energy on an input and output basis. Anxiety diverts energy from other activities, and uses it to maintain body arousal during the fight/flight response. Reich (1961) used the term "sex-economy," emphasizing that sexual energy is part of a system continually adjusting itself to maintain balance. Increases in heart rate, breathing, and metabolism—the physical arousal in anxiety—use energy at a high rate.

Worry and anticipatory anxiety also drain energy that would otherwise be available for other activities. Most anxiety sufferers report feeling more tired and drained as a result of their anxiety disorder, and sexual interest and drive also suffer. In addition, the secondary aspects of anxiety, such as depression, low self-esteem, and negative body image, contribute to a loss of sexual energy. On the other hand, excess sexual energy is often sublimated into other activities, as Freud (1935) suggested; that is, sexual energy that is not released through orgasm can be transformed into fuel for other activities, such as work.

Anxiety also results from premature exposure to sexual impulses, especially when they are intense or involve abuse. A child witnessing sexual intercourse between parents, for example, may perceive the activity as aggressive behavior, and may become anxious and confused. Violence is also overwhelming to children, causing fear and anxiety. These are traumatic experiences for children, whose development is likely to be affected as a result of such trauma. Of course, sexual abuse of a child, which sometimes involves violence, is highly damaging. In my own case, early exposure to violence contributed to my anxiety disorder, as discussed in Chapter 1. Feelings of vulnerability and fear were already in place as part of my personality before I was sexually abused. The combination of violence and sexual abuse only intensified my anxiety.

Sexual abuse can be violent, as in rape, but it can also be subtle, as in seductive behavior between a parent and child. When parents are unfulfilled in their sexual relationship with each other, one or both may turn to their children for affection, admiration, and sexual excitement. In addition, children usually pass through an oedipal stage of developmental at age 4 or 5. During this period, children may be sexually attracted to the opposite sex parent, who may respond inappropriately. Furthermore, as children enter puberty and develop as sexual beings, parents may have difficulty controlling their sexual interest. Sometimes, overt sexual contact between a parent and child takes place. Indeed, most sexual abuse occurs within families. Or a seductive intimacy may develop, in which the child is exposed to the parent's sexuality. This may take the form of immodest behavior or an inappropriate interest in the child's sexual development. Stimulated by the parent's sexual attention, the child may feel "special," but at the same time feel anxious about the possibility of incest or of jealousy from the other parent. To cope, the child may cut off sexual feelings and develop other symptoms of anxiety.

Our society also sexually stimulates children. Children are exposed to the media, particularly advertisements, which sexualize virtually everything, from cars to laundry soap, in the name of marketing. Television programs directed towards children and general audiences are often interspersed with sexualized commercials directed towards adults, but even child-oriented commercials may have sexual connotations. There are also teen magazines, loaded with sexually stimulating material. Some parents take pride in the sexual sophistication of their children, as if it prepares them for adult life, but instead it robs them of innocence and creates anxiety in the process. There is a difference between sexual sophistication and sexual aliveness. As discussed in the chapter on anxiety in children, any demands or stimulation to which children are subjected before they have the intellectual, emotional, or social skills to handle it are likely to create anxiety.

Whether subtle or explicit, sexual abuse invariably affects the personality and general development of children, as well as their sexual functioning as adults. Sexual abuse can result in a conflict between the desire for sex and the emotional pain it may evoke. To cope with such pleasure anxiety, victims of sexual abuse may cut off sexual feelings altogether, or they may develop strong needs for control in sexual relations. Trust, which is normally required for healthy sexual intimacy, can also become an overriding issue. In some cases, victims of sexual abuse may reenact the traumatic experience with new partners, in an effort to work through the emotional pain and achieve a more comfortable outcome. The effect of sexual abuse can also be housed in the body itself—in muscular rigidity of the pelvis or other affected regions (muscles appear to have memory and they can store the feelings involved in trauma). In addition, feelings of insecurity and inadequacy about body image are likely to develop in victims of sexual abuse. Furthermore, sexual abuse often triggers a post-traumatic stress reaction, the anxiety disorder that involves intense fearfulness and avoidance of anything resembling the abuse situation, nightmares and flashbacks, difficulty relaxing, numbing of general responsiveness, and difficulty feeling love and other emotions. These anxiety symptoms can interfere with a healthy sexual life.

In the case of a woman named Rachel, a history of sexual abuse resulted in a multitude of symptoms, including depression, severe anxiety, and repression of traumatic memories. When she first presented herself for help, Rachel was dealing with the loss of her parents, who both died within the same year. She began therapy with one of my colleagues, with a primary concern about depression.

However, the loss of her parents added to an already high level of stress, and a panic anxiety disorder was triggered. Rachel was then referred to me for specialized help.

Rachel, a nurse and mother of two children, was overloaded with stress from a recent relocation. Her family moved into a temporary housing situation while waiting for their old house to sell. She was in a new job and community, busy adjusting to new circumstances. The loss of her parents overloaded Rachel with more change and adjustments, and she became symptomatic. Her panic attacks were intense, and she became fearful of doing things on her own. Her job was in jeopardy due to conflict with a supervisor toward whom Rachel was angry but fearful. Her concentration and attention deteriorated, and she was moody, irritable, and angry at work.

Rachel participated in the CHAANGE anxiety recovery program and had a successful experience. Her progress, including discontinuing the medication she was taking at the outset, is discussed and summarized in the chapter on successful recovery stories. She terminated treatment feeling in control after approximately seven months of therapy. Not once during her treatment for anxiety did Rachel mention sexual abuse or reveal any signs of it, although many other issues were addressed.

However, several months after Rachel completed her anxiety treatment, she contacted me in distress about some dreams she was having. Over the next few weeks, she had a series of dreams and memories about her older brother sexually abusing her. She recalled, one by one, the specifics of each incident, until she put the entire picture together. Several additional months of psychotherapy helped her through this process, which included dealing with anger and other intense emotional reactions to her memories, and sorting out the impact of the abuse history on various aspects of her personality, sexuality, and social functioning.

Rachel's family background experiences, including the sexual abuse, contributed to her anxiety disorder, and illustrate how most anxiety disorders develop, as discussed in Chapters 3 and 4. All the ingredients were in place for Rachel's anxiety disorder, which surged to the surface as an adult during a period of high stress. The sexual abuse occurred in a family with many of the characteristics associated with the anxiety personality: emotional repression ("My parents never told me they loved me"), rigidity, poor communication ("We never talked about our feelings; I felt I couldn't tell my mother about the abuse"), a family secret, many rules, praise based primarily on accomplishments, and so on. As a result, Rachel developed many of the anxiety personality traits: fear of conflict and anger, difficulty relaxing, a need to be in control, difficulty with assertiveness, perfectionism, a strong need to please others, and high achievement needs. When these background factors and personality traits met with high stress in adulthood, Rachel's anxiety symptoms emerged. The many emotional issues she had—fear of authority figures, trust problems, lack of assertiveness, fear of feelings (especially anger), and avoidance of conflict were attributable to her family background, including the sexual abuse, and these set the stage for her subsequent anxiety disorder.

Actually, Rachel developed two different anxiety disorders. The first was the panic anxiety disorder that appeared at the height of her stress, after her parents died. The second was a post-traumatic stress disorder that developed in reaction to Rachel's memories about the abuse.

What was so interesting about Rachel's case was the fact that she could not face her sexual abuse history—or even remember it—until she acquired some emotional skills and achieved a degree of anxiety recovery. Prior to her anxiety recovery, the traumatic memory repression served as a defense mechanism to protect her from feelings she could not handle. In other words, Rachel could deal directly with the sexual abuse only after she had developed the skills that would permit her to handle the pain. In her case, the anxiety disorder was an opportunity to receive help and, ultimately, to face a significant source of her fears and emotional difficulties.

Fortunately, Rachel was married to a sensitive, understanding, and patient man. There was enough security and trust in the marriage that Rachel was able to have a reasonably satisfying sexual relationship, although she was only comfortable with sex if she was in control of when and how. Her husband supported her recovery efforts, which made a big difference in the effectiveness of her therapy.

In a healthy sex life, there is no anxiety about sexual excitement, intimate contact, and release of control during orgasm. Normal sex involves a complete convulsive discharge in the embrace of a love partner, with a momentary loss of consciousness. Control is joyfully surrendered, as the trance of sexual excitement takes over. Although the genitals are sensitized by an infusion of blood, the whole body participates. The intensity of sexual feelings and build-up of a powerful energy toward explosive release is pleasurable, not frightening. Likewise, no anxiety is associated with the sense of boundary loss and merging of two bodies into one. The ego loss in sex is called by the French *le petit mort*—the little death—and the renewal following complete sexual release is like a rebirth. After a strong orgasmic release, there is a feeling of deep peacefulness, and a healing sleep may follow. In a sexually healthy and alive person, all this takes place spontaneously, without conflict, ambivalence, or anxiety.

Consciousness is altered by complete sexual gratification. As sexual excitement increases, the everyday concerns of the mind fade into the background and drop off. In surrendering to the trance of sexual arousal, the mind—with its worries and anxious thoughts—is left behind. Unfortunately, this is why some people do not think clearly during sex and fail to take appropriate safety and birth control precautions. In addition, the sense of separateness dissolves, as the sexually gratified person merges with the sexual partner. As the boundaries of individuality become more permeable, the sexually fulfilled person opens to a kinship with all life.

But the full benefits of a healthy sex life are not available to people whose sexuality has been damaged. In men, sexual feeling may not be fully cut off but held in a rigid pelvis, which limits the phase of involuntary movements required for full orgasmic release. Although genital excitement may be strong, for many men it will end in premature ejaculation because a rigid pelvis cannot hold the sexual charge until it can embrace the whole body. In women, anxiety about body image and sexual attractiveness or feelings of inadequacy, guilt, or anger can inhibit sexual responsiveness. When the male partner is not able to sustain sexual excitement, or is insensitive to the stimulation requirements of the female partner, arousal does not reach the level required for a strong orgasm. Deprived of adequate stimulation by her partner, the woman may not approach ecstasy or the full benefits of orgasmic discharge.

Masters and Johnson (1966) report that men and women differ biologically in their sexual response, a fact that must be understood and taken into consideration to have a fulfilling sexual relationship. The male sexual response consists of a single cycle of excitation, during which tension and associated pleasure build up to a point of "ejaculatory inevitability," followed by orgasmic release. Recovery from orgasmic release in men is a relatively short period, but during this period interest in further stimulation drops sharply. The female sexual response also consists of an excitation phase, but it is typically of longer duration, which means that more time is usually required for women to reach the point of orgasm. In women, the point of orgasmic release may be a single moment or multiple moments, and the recovery phase is slower than in men, resulting in a more gradual loss of interest in sexual stimulation.

Without understanding the differences between male and female sexual patterns, the potential for couples to experience sexual frustration is very high. Men who assume that their female partners have the same sexual response as their own are likely to climax too soon, resulting in loss of interest in their partner's sexual fulfillment. Women who do not understand the differences between the male and female sexual response may think there is something wrong with themselves sexually if they do not experience orgasm at the same time as their male partner. If we add to this any differences in sexual backgrounds in a couple, as well as differences in emotional and communication style between men and women, the likelihood of conflict—and anxiety—about sexuality increases. These difficulties can occur in otherwise sexually healthy people, but complications and frustration are even more likely whenever sexual issues or other emotional problems are brought to bed.

How often do Americans have sex? Michael (1995) reports the results of a survey in which 3,500 Americans, ranging in age from 18 to 59, were selected through rigorous polling methods. *Sex in America: A Definitive Survey*, indicates that Americans fall into three groups. One-third have sex twice a week, one-third a few times a month, and one-third a few times a year. It appears that only one-third of Americans have sex at least once a week, as Reich advised. This is not the complete story, however, since having sex does not mean having orgasms. In another recent study by Janus and Janus (1993), only 15 percent of women and 65 percent of men always had an orgasm during sex. The numbers improve if "often" is added to "always." In this case, 61 percent of women and 93 percent of men always or often have orgasms during lovemaking. On the other hand, only 44 percent of women and 56 percent of men feel they are functioning at their biological maximum. Frequency of orgasmic release is the issue here. If Reich was right about the need for frequent orgasmic release in order to maintain healthy biological equilibrium, a large number of American adults, perhaps two-thirds, do not meet this criteria.

The *Sex in America* study provides a detailed analysis of sexual patterns, some of which are likely to shatter old myths. For example, married couples have the most sex and are the most likely to have orgasms when they do. Nearly 40 percent of married people say they have sex twice a week, compared to 25 percent for singles. Another myth is that people are more likely to masturbate if they do not have a sex partner. However, the study indicates that the people who masturbate most often are the ones who have the most sex with a partner.

Within an emotionally strong relationship, a healthy and active sex life can make a difference in anxiety regulation. Orgasmic release maintains healthy biological equilibrium by counteracting the effects of stress, particularly tension and the fight/flight reaction, which are the primary triggers for anxiety. Orgasm also counteracts the muscular armor that develops in those who were raised in emotionally repressive families or who were abused in any way. Frequent sexual release can replace such armor with a capacity for feeling. Sexual release also induces relaxation, which is essential for preventing anxiety. In all these ways, sex can be one of the most important, and pleasurable, aspects of anxiety recovery.

16

Setting Limits on Stress

Once a man bought an ox to help him plow. The ox worked hard for six days, but on Saturday, it would not go out into the fields. The man sent for the person who had sold him the ox. The former owner apologized and explained, "Saturday is my Sabbath. The ox is accustomed to resting on this day." The new owner decided that if an ox could understand the Sabbath, he should learn more about it himself. This he did, and one day he became a great rabbi.

Sabbath Day Legend

In the story of creation, God took a day off, after six days of work, to behold the fruits of His labor. Virtually all wisdom traditions and religions have a Sabbath day, a regularly occurring day of rest and reflection. Even God rested on the seventh day. Why?

Work involves physical and mental effort. We can function at high levels of effort for limited time periods, but we require periodic recovery to restore our energy. Without regular recovery from even the normal stress of everyday life, we will be at risk for stress-related symptoms. For the anxiety-prone personality, stress overload leads to an anxiety condition.

Endurance competitions such as triathlons and marathons demonstrate the extraordinary human capacity for handling stress. Effort reaches extreme peaks during these events, but this is only possible with proper training and regular recovery to restore the athlete's energy and to prepare for the next challenge. Without adequate recovery an athlete would experience physical and emotional burnout, leading to a decline in performance. The same requirement applies to all of us in our daily lives. We need to recover on a regular basis from the stress of life in order to function effectively, without physical and emotional breakdown.

Imagine relaxation as your natural state of equilibrium. Imagine feeling rested, refreshed, and ready for whatever may happen, the way you would want to feel at the beginning of each day. Your outlook is positive and your body is energized, yet you are at peace and feel in control of yourself. Think of this as your relaxation baseline, or home base. Throughout each day, however, you find yourself being drawn away from this inner peace as you deal with tasks and responsibilities.

The effects of stress accumulate when you do not recover on a regular basis. The signals of stress overload first appear as mild symptoms, such as irritability, headaches, dizziness, lost or increased appetite, sleep difficulty, back pain, difficulty concentrating, and fatigue. If you are in tune with yourself, and skilled at stress recovery techniques, you can counteract these signals and return to your relaxation home base.

A symptom can be viewed as the body's attempt at a cure. That is, every symptom is a signal of stress in a system trying continually to maintain healthy equilibrium. If we can recognize the stress overload messages brought by our symptoms, and respond accordingly, we can prevent more serious breakdowns or crises. Anxiety is such a crisis, and it is triggered by stress overload in people who are predisposed to the condition as a result of their personality traits. In order to prevent stress overload, we must be able to recognize the early warning signals. We must also have a repertoire of self-healing and stress recovery skills.

Incomplete stress recovery weakens our immune systems, making us vulnerable to disease. Prolonged stress appears to be involved in heart disease, diabetes, arthritis, gastrointestinal disorders, chronic fatigue syndrome, and other physical disorders. Stress is also a key ingredient in emotional conditions, such as depression and eating disorders as well as anxiety. Children, like adults, can develop symptoms and illnesses due to stress.

Disease means *dis-ease*, or *not at ease*. When we are not at ease, we are away from home base—from relaxed equilibrium. In an effort to restore that equilibrium, the body employs a number of emergency mechanisms. For example, stress hormones, such as glucocortisol and acetacholomines, are produced to raise the body's ability to store glucose from carbohydrates. This raises blood sugar level, providing more energy for the body to use in dealing with stress.

Such emergency responses are helpful in the short run but harmful in the long run. When stress is prolonged, the same hormones that increase blood sugar level will inhibit insulin action, *lowering* the body's ability to store glucose from carbohydrates. As a result, energy dwindles during prolonged stress. But there are more serious health consequences. During uncontrolled stress, carbohydrate metabolism is replaced by greater fat production to supply needed energy. Also, because our energy requirements are so high during prolonged stress, we crave and eat more fats—as much as 30 percent more than normal. The accumulation of fats in the body increases the risk for heart disease. In addition, lower insulin production during prolonged stress increases the risk of diabetes. Prolonged, uncontrolled stress compromises the immune system and health as the body's resources are used to cope with stress.

Selye (1956) identifies three stages in the effect of stress on the body. In the first stage, which he calls the *alarm* stage, the fight/flight reaction is triggered to confront the stress. Stress hormones activate the body and provide energy to be used in fighting or fleeing from stressors. The second stage, called the *resistance* stage by Selye, involves repair and damage control. Rest and relaxation are crucial to the resistance stage. If the stress continues, stage three, the *exhaustion* stage, sets in. Resistance is already weak so the early warning symptoms intensify into more severe disease. By stage three, the immune system is unable to produce lymphocytes and natural killer cells, and we become vulnerable to invading foreign substances.

Regular and complete stress recovery is illustrated in Figure 16–1. The diagram of regular stress recovery shows how we return to relaxed equilibrium as a result of practicing stress recovery techniques on a regular basis. On the other hand, when stress recovery is inconsistent or incomplete, we do not return to our natural relaxation baseline. In that case, stress accumulates and we become more vulnerable to its negative effects. A diagram of incomplete stress recovery is shown in Figure 16–2.

FIGURE 16–1: REGULAR AND COMPLETE STRESS RECOVERY

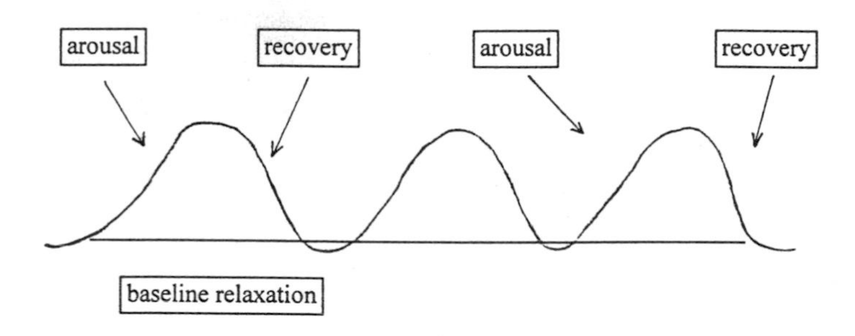

FIGURE 16–2: INCOMPLETE STRESS RECOVERY

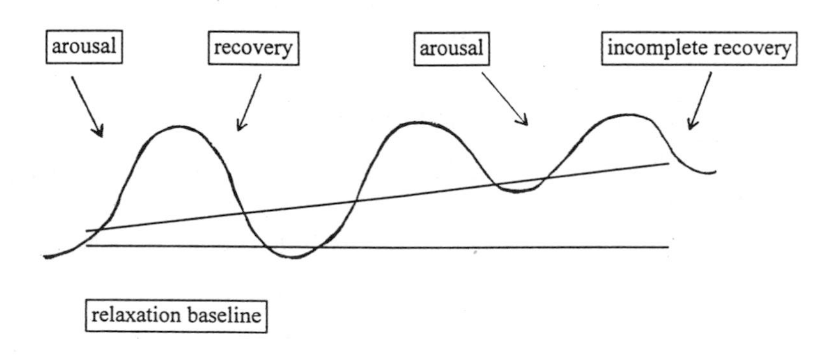

Stress is a natural part of life and therefore it cannot be entirely avoided. Selye suggests that some stress is actually necessary for physical and emotional growth. Even positive events can be stressful, as Holmes and Masuda (1967, 1972) demonstrate. Holmes and Masuda developed the Social Readjustment Rating Scale, consisting of life events rated for their stress impact. Events that are generally considered to be positive, such as marriage, pregnancy, job promotion, and even a vacation, can be stressful due to the adjustments and effort they require. Of course, negative stress, such as divorce, death of a family member, problems in a relationship, or financial crisis, has a direct impact on coping ability. But stress is not the problem. The problem is lack of stress recovery.

How do you get back to relaxed equilibrium—to home base—if you have reached stress overload? There are three steps in reducing the effects of high stress. The first step is to recognize the symptoms of stress. A summary of the common symptoms is shown in Table 16–1 below.

TABLE 16–1: RECOGNIZING THE SYMPTOMS OF STRESS

increased heart rate	grinding teeth/clenching jaw
cold/sweaty hands	headaches
stuttering	anxiety (panic attacks, worry, avoiding)
restlessness	loss of or increased appetite
irritability/moodiness	back or muscle pain
muscle tension	dizziness
fatigue	weakness
nervousness/trembling	sleep difficulty

The second step is to identify the stressors in your life. The Social Readjustment Rating Scale, also known as the Life Stress Scale, was developed by Holmes and Masuda (1967) as a way to calculate stress level. This self-rating scale asks you to circle the items that happened to you within the past year, and add up the total number of stress units. The Life Stress Scale is show in Table 16–2. Pelletier (1977) reports that the full impact of high stress is often delayed by up to one year. Keep this in mind as you calculate your stress level. To get an estimate of your present stress level, include the stressors that occurred within the past one to two years.

Having recognized the effects of stress and identified the stressors in your life, the third step is to implement a stress recovery plan. Many of the anxiety recovery exercises in this book and in the CHAANGE program are stress recovery methods. Exercise, dealing assertively with people, yoga, meditation, enjoyable recreation, and relaxation are all important components in recovery from stress and anxiety. Ideally, we need a repertoire of skills and activities for maintaining our relaxation baseline. Let's look at some additional stress recovery approaches.

One way to regulate stress is to simplify your life. St. James (1994) offers some concrete and creative suggestions for doing this, including ways to simplify your household, wardrobe, financial system, and social life. Managing your time more efficiently and just taking better care of yourself in the areas of nutrition, rest, and exercise are also important. Table 16–3 highlights a variety of stress reduction methods to consider.

Perhaps it is now evident why many wisdom traditions incorporate periodic rest days. A weekly Sabbath day helps

TABLE 16–2: LIFE STRESS SCALE

This widely reprinted self-test lists 43 stressful life events and the value of each in "stress units." To use the Life Stress Scale, check off events that have happened in your life within the last 12–24 months, then add up the total number of stress units. Use the blank lines between items to add your own events, assigning the appropriate number of points by comparing them to the events ranked on the chart. A score of 150 gives you a 50 percent chance of developing an illness. A score of 300 or more gives you a 90 percent chance. This scale provides an estimate only, and other factors may affect your chances of developing an illness. A stress recovery program will significantly reduce your vulnerability.

Life Event	Value	Your Score
☐ Death of spouse	100	___
☐ Divorce	73	___
☐ ______		___
☐ Marital separation	65	___
☐ Jail term	63	___
☐ ______		___
☐ Death of close family member	63	___
☐ Personal injury or illness	53	___
☐ ______		___
☐ Marriage	50	___
☐ Fired from work	47	___
☐ ______		___
☐ Marital reconciliation	45	___
☐ Retirement	45	___
☐ ______		___
☐ Change in health of family member	44	___
☐ Pregnancy	40	___
☐ ______		___
☐ Sex difficulties	39	___
☐ Gain of new family member	39	___
☐ ______		___
☐ Business readjustment	39	___
☐ Change in financial state	38	___
☐ ______		___
☐ Death of a close friend	37	___
☐ Change to different line of work	36	___
☐ ______		___
☐ Change in number of arguments with spouse	35	___
☐ Mortgage over $10,000	31	___
☐ ______		___
☐ Foreclosure of mortgage or loan	30	___
☐ Change in responsibilities at work	29	___
☐ ______		___
☐ Son or daughter leaving home	29	___
☐ Trouble with in-laws	29	___
☐ ______		___
☐ Outstanding personal achievement	28	___
☐ Wife begins or stops work	26	___
☐ ______		___
☐ Begin or end school	26	___
☐ Change in living conditions	25	___
☐ ______		___
☐ Revision of personal habits	24	___
☐ Trouble with boss	23	___
☐ ______		___
☐ Change in work hours or conditions	20	___
☐ Change in residence	20	___
☐ ______		___
☐ Change in schools	20	___
☐ Change in recreation	19	___
☐ ______		___
☐ Change in church activities	19	___
☐ Change in social activities	18	___
☐ ______		___
☐ Mortgage or loan less than $10,000	17	___
☐ Change in sleeping habits	16	___
☐ ______		___
☐ Change in number of family get-togethers	15	___
☐ Change in eating habits	15	___
☐ ______		___
☐ Vacation	13	___
☐ Christmas	12	___
☐ ______		___
☐ Minor violations of the law	11	___
YOUR TOTAL		___

TABLE 16–3: SETTING LIMITS ON STRESS

eat a healthy diet	exercise regularly
simplify your life	set short-term and long-term goals
manage your time	use humor and make time for play/fun
accept what you can't change	set reasonable limits
say no without feeling guilty	practice relaxation techniques
share your thoughts/feelings with someone you trust	recognize that alcohol and drugs do not solve life's problems
make time for daily rest and relaxation	learn and practice meditation
avoid the morning rush by preparing the night before	seek professional help with difficult problems such as marital distress, chronic anxiety, anger, depression
conserve your energy	

release a week's worth of accumulated stress, or at least the stress that is not discharged daily through adequate sleep, proper diet and nutrition, exercise, and other forms of stress recovery. In addition, many traditions observe special holidays, such as Lent, Rosh Hashanah, and Yom Kippur, during which rest, meditation, reflection, time with family, and even fasting is advised. Some secular holidays such as Labor Day, Memorial Day, Veterans Day, and other commemorative holidays consist of days off from work and school. These special days seem to be excellent opportunities for stress recovery, reflection, and returning to your relaxation baseline. Taking advantage of these opportunities can help you regain perspective, reestablish priorities, and recharge your body.

In keeping with the idea of taking time out for stress recovery, I have developed two exercises, Recovery Day and Catch-Up Day, which are described below.

EXERCISE: RECOVERY DAY

Now that you understand the importance and need for periodic stress recovery, plan a special day off that you will devote to cleansing yourself from accumulated stress. On this day you will not drive a car, travel, go to work, or have any other agendas. This will be a quiet day, the kind of day you would take for yourself if you were sick and had to stay home. It would be good if you could be alone on this special recovery day.

On this day do everything slowly, deliberately, consciously. Practice all the recovery skills in your repertoire, such as relaxation, meditation, yoga or stretching, eating properly, and generally taking good care of yourself. Experiment with some new methods. Try a period or even an entire day of silence: do not talk or communicate with others in person, by telephone, or electronically. Read some inspiring text and savor an uplifting thought, repeating it to yourself. Become quiet inside and conserve energy, doing only those activities that are directed towards healing yourself from stress.

Plan several days each year for stress recovery and symptom prevention. You can modify this exercise by periodically taking a half day for this purpose.

EXERCISE: CATCH-UP DAY

More stress is added to your life when you feel like you are falling behind in tasks and responsibilities. This exercise is designed to help you feel more in control and less stressed.

Devote a day to catching up with yourself by doing only unfinished projects. These may include returning mail-order items, paying bills, sewing or clothes repair, cleaning out a closet, or completing anything that you have begun but not finished. Do not begin any new projects.

Imagine that with each completed item you are eliminating a barrier between you and your inner state of peace. As you move through such a day, think about how much better you would feel if you undertook fewer responsibilities. Resolve to take better care of yourself by setting more reasonable limits.

The anxiety personality tends to make too many commitments and approaches life in a compulsive, perfectionistic way. We also tend to focus on the needs of others, often at the expense of our own health. As a result, taking time for yourself to recover from stress may seem selfish or produce feelings of guilt. As a sensitive person you might also wonder how you can focus on your own needs in the midst of all the suffering around you. Should you feel selfish or guilty?

This dilemma is often faced by sensitive people seeking to balance personal needs with responsibilities and commitments to family, friends, work, and community. My answer is simply this: if you do not take care of yourself you will eventually have nothing left to give. You will burn out and have no energy to care for others, to do good work, or to improve the human condition. If you have an anxiety disorder, you are already paying the price for high stress. You need regular stress recovery in order to prevent your own symptoms from interfering with your ability to give to others.

EXERCISE: HEALING YOURSELF WITHOUT GUILT

This exercise is designed to help you take care of yourself so you can take care of others. The general idea is to balance the scales of giving to others and replenishing yourself so that you can continue to give.

Begin by making a list of all activities that have in the past brought you a sense of renewal. You may also expand the list to include any activities that have in the past or might in the future bring you joy, pleasure, or satisfaction. For activities that have worked for you in the past, note the last time you experienced each. This will give you some idea of the extent to which you give to yourself.

Having made the list, you now have a sense of what you can give to yourself. Decide which activities and experiences you want to increase in your life, and begin to nurture yourself for the sake of humanity.

17

Play Therapy for Adults

The first rule of the game is that it's not a game.
Alan Watts

Life is a serious matter when you are anxious or fearful, as it must be when the fight/flight response is activated. But as we know, the fear in anxiety disorders is irrational: it is not a matter of life and death, and survival is not at stake. In anxiety, we perceive our lives to be threatened by phobic situations, those personally dreaded situations in which anxiety occurred and might occur again. In worrying, negative thinking, anticipatory anxiety, avoiding, and other manifestations of anxiety we are poised to protect ourselves—to fight or flee. We hesitate to let down our guard when we suffer from an anxiety disorder. Life becomes grim, a struggle, a tense existence. It's no fun, and it seems there is no energy or time for play.

In virtually every case of anxiety I have seen, there is a lack of joy in living. Spontaneity, fun, and play are lost as the anxiety sufferer's energy is diverted towards emotional survival or coping with stress. Without proper help, the anxiety sufferer may not understand why he or she is anxious or what can be done to overcome the condition. There is often a feeling of losing control or being a victim of anxiety. Use of medication may reinforce such feelings. Hope may be lost. Faith is challenged and may give way. Life with an anxiety condition can become serious, negative, gloomy, and depressing.

These feelings are often expressed by patients when they first present themselves for anxiety treatment. Kelly, for example, was an attractive but grim woman who came to a free anxiety-screening clinic I hosted on National Anxiety Screening Day. She was a dedicated budget coordinator at a manufacturing company, but was a workaholic who put in an unreasonable amount of time and energy on the job. She was all work and no play. However, during treatment she discovered that this was her way of coping with anxiety: she threw herself into her work to hide from her fears. Naturally, this pattern created more stress, which intensified her anxiety symptoms. I noted that Kelly had a huge, engaging smile with lots of beautiful teeth, which I rarely saw in the early phases of therapy. Kelly spoke for many anxiety sufferers on her pre-program evaluation form, when she described what life can be like with a severe anxiety disorder:

> I'm very weary of not feeling in control of myself or my life. As the years go by, I find I worry, stew, and fret over everything, good and bad. About six months ago, I started having panic attacks very early in the morning. I'm not sure if they start after I wake up or if they wake me up. However, I do know that the panic attack

> sets the pace for the rest of my day! I know that many people don't like being near me—I'm negative, gloomy and irritable. I want to learn to relax, enjoy life, and *have some fun* [emphasis by patient]. I don't want to live the rest of my life like this. Anxiety is nobody's friend. I'm not sure if the CHAANGE program can help me or not, but I'm willing to try it, even if it adds to my anxiety in the short term.

Kelly's joylessness and negativity were further reinforced by the fact that she had seen six mental-health professionals over a period of approximately fifteen years, most of whom she described as "not what I needed" and "not good experiences."

In another case, Christine had been taking medication for many years to control anxiety. She was a productive educator who had published several books, but was unable to enjoy life or feel good about her professional accomplishments. She, too, had a history of prior therapy experiences, which she described as "somewhat helpful." Christine's biggest fear was that she could not handle the general stress of life without medication, and she became fearful about discontinuing it. At the outset of treatment, Christine described her condition as follows: "I feel that I view events and tasks in terms of their stress-producing potential, rather than in terms of positive experiences. My enjoyment of life is affected by my level of anxiety. I'm not as free as I would like to be." Christine's straightforward statement about her condition could apply to virtually all anxiety sufferers. Joy and freedom are blocked by anxiety, as energy is earmarked for the grim task of coping with stress and anxiety.

Playful living may be unimaginable to those who suffer with anxiety, but losing the ability to play is actually one of the reasons why anxiety develops. Without play, anxiety personality traits take over—perfectionism, hard working with little satisfaction, difficulty setting reasonable limits, the need to please others, difficulty relaxing, and so on. Life is stressful enough, and when these traits are mixed in, anxiety is inevitable. Play, as we will see, is a therapeutic outlet that keeps life in balance and helps counteract anxiety and stress.

Why do children play, and what role does play have in adult life and anxiety recovery? Children play for the same reasons as animals play. The young in most species play in order to learn social skills, for mock combat/hunting/evasion, and to experiment with sexuality and mating before sexual development reaches maturity. Even domesticated animals, such as cats and dogs, exhibit their inborn programming to develop survival skills through play. Cats and dogs play the exciting games of stalking and hunting—holding still, waiting, pouncing, dodging, nipping—as well as rough-and-tumble mock fighting. Play is part of nature's plan for survival. Play is practice and preparation for life.

For children, play is an opportunity to develop human survival skills in a safe atmosphere where learning is allowed and mistakes are tolerated. Play serves a number of human survival purposes. For example, play is one of the primary outlets for stress and tension, not only for children but also for adults. Elkind (1981) discusses play as an "antidote to hurrying." "Hurried children" are pushed into adulthood by schools, media, and their highly stressed parents, and they are deprived of developmentally appropriate play. As a result, hurried children show symptoms of anxiety and stress. Adults with anxiety disorders also tend to be hurried, even if they were not rushed into adulthood. Their personality traits—perfectionism, need to please, difficulty setting reasonable limits, high achievement needs, and so forth—almost guarantee a hurried and stressful life.

Neill (1960) takes a similar but more radical position on the subject of play. In describing Summerhill, a school in England based on a philosophy of freedom and governed by the students themselves, Neill asserts that children are often "hothoused" into adulthood by being deprived of adequate time for play. Unfortunately, the agents responsible for the "adulteration" of children are usually their own fearful parents, concerned about their children's future—their scores on the Scholastic Achievement Test and their ability to compete for college acceptance and financial aid. But Neill says there is more to it than that, and points to the "disapproval of play" by parents who have forgotten the yearnings of their own childhood and how to play. Parental disapproval of, and even antagonism towards, play may also be based on "a vague moral idea" that being a child is not so good—a waste of time. Whatever the explanation, Neill comes to this conclusion: "One could, with some truth, claim that the evils of civilization are due to the fact that no child has ever had enough play" (p. 64).

Play is a vehicle for the development of imagination. In play, children invent reality by creating a fort out of a piece of plywood, a weapon out of a stick, a playhouse out of a cardboard box, a theater out of a pallet or platform, or cars and trucks out of blocks. Imagination, however, is not just some fanciful pastime. Imagination is the basis for creativity, problem solving, and inventiveness. Without imagination, there would be no advances in technology, and civilization would not evolve. Through play, children also attain a sense of power and control over their environment. Being in charge of their play, children can manipulate objects and project their own meaning into the world.

Piaget (1952, 1962) noted two categories of play in children. *Symbolic play* is the activity through which children experiment with the world, taking it in, part by part, and exploring its properties and significance. An empty matchbox may symbolize a miniature bed, car or truck, or boat. Put the cover on and it may be a cash register or a treasure chest. Symbolic play fosters conceptual understanding about the physical world, and thus serves a necessary survival purpose. In *imitative play*, children imitate what they observe, acting out the social behavior of adults surrounding them. A child playing mother to a baby doll typically mimics mothering behavior, and may display tenderness or hostility as the case may be. Imitation is the means by which children learn to eat with utensils, button buttons, zip zippers, as well as interact with others. As such, imitative play has enormous survival value.

Freud (1911) also identified two modes of adaptation to the world, which pertain to adults as well as children. *Primary process*—a person's private, inner world—consists of imagination, fantasy, and dreams. Primary process provides an outlet for the expression of needs and wishes, especially for socially unacceptable material such as sexual or aggressive impulses. Primary process is unrealistic in that it does not need to conform to social convention or rules. Anything goes in primary process. Like Piaget's symbolic play, primary process uses imagination to toy with the world. Art, music, writing, play, and most creative work are generated by primary process and what some would call "right brain" thinking. Primary process helps to fulfill our inner needs and maintain psychological balance. This is as much a matter of survival as learning to interact socially or develop physical skills.

Secondary process was Freud's term for reality-oriented thinking. This mode is concerned with adjustment and adaptation to outside reality—the physical and social world. Secondary process is rational, and geared towards dealing effectively with daily life, which includes the demands of school, work, family, and relationships. Secondary process is the means by which plans are made, commitments are kept, bills are paid on time, and the gas tank is kept from running dry.

Freud (1911) also developed the pleasure and reality principles. The *pleasure principle*, concerned with self-gratification, is expressed through the primary process mode. The *reality principle*, not surprisingly, is concerned with adjustment to the physical and social environment. Accordingly, health is a delicate balance between the pleasure principle, which serves inner needs without regard to others, and the reality principle, which serves one's needs in relation to others and society as a whole. Play assists in maintaining this balance because it serves personal needs—self-expression, tension release, discharge of socially unacceptable impulses—without jeopardizing the stability of community and society. Play serves as a safety valve that balances and revitalizes the individual, while preserving his or her relationship with others and the world.

The pleasure principle is embraced by Ornstein and Sobel (1989) in their work with preventive medicine. They find that the healthiest adults sometimes abandon all the rules and official advice about health, guiding their behavior instead by the pleasure principle. They may disregard proper diet, exercise, and medical checkups, but nevertheless flourish in life and cope well with stress. Even in cases of chronic disease, certain people remain hardy and robust, managing to prevail in spite of their illnesses. What is the secret? Pleasurable pursuits—sometimes grand but mostly simple—that give rise to positive moods, optimism, and happiness. The pleasure principle is nature's way of alerting us that what we enjoy can actually be good for us.

In some cases, the needs of both individuals and society are expressed through play. Consider team sports, where there may be individual players, teams, and institutions or communities identified with teams. When a game is played, it is not just the players who play, but entire institutions and communities who play along, cheering, shouting, and identifying strongly. This excitement and identification can go too far, as when a riot breaks out based on the outcome of a game. In the Olympic games, entire nations identify with their athletes, and play becomes an expression of national pride and political identity.

Beyond its survival value and documented health benefits, play has merit in and of itself. Play is recreation in the truest sense of the term, an opportunity for re-creation, for creating oneself anew. Play is a healing retreat from the stress and seriousness of life—from reality. Soothing to the mind and spirit, play is like taking off a too-tight shoe. It is a break from the work of life, and a way of enjoying the fruits of our labor.

In a sense, play is the goal of life. If you ask yourself why you work and what is the goal of life, what would you say? You probably work to support yourself and your family—to meet your basic needs for food, shelter, clothing, and so on. But how do you evaluate your success? Once you meet your basic needs and attain a level of physical comfort, you would most likely want to enjoy the process of living, and perhaps have some fun. Unfortunately for some, retirement is the only time for play, for sitting back or enjoying activities for which there was no time previously due to work and other responsibilities. Among the most tragic stories are those about people who worked hard but died before they had a chance to enjoy the fruits of their labor, and such stories are even more poignant when the death, say of a heart attack, was *caused* by the stress of work. We are also saddened about death in children, whose opportunity to experience the joy and potential of life is lost. Looking back at the end of your life, what do *you* want to feel? My guess is you would want to feel that your life was fulfilling, that you succeeded in reaching your personal goals, and that you found time to play and enjoy living. What we yearn for most is not more work, but more play.

Is play selfish? Is there time for play, when so much needs to be done? Many anxiety sufferers, accustomed to stress, negative thinking, and preoccupation with anticipating and dealing with anxiety, may not have energy for or interest in play. Others with anxiety personality traits, such as concern about what others think, difficulty relaxing, perfectionism, and high achievement needs, may view play as self-indulgent or irresponsible. And the sensitivity of some anxious people, who are acutely aware of and identify strongly with the suffering of others, may lead them to ask, "How can I play amidst human suffering? Is it moral, or even possible, to ignore those in need while I play?"

Play is not selfish. Play is necessary to revitalize yourself in order to return with renewed energy and commitment to the world of responsibility and work, including caring for others and working for social justice. Mother Teresa, considered by many to be an example of pious selflessness, says, "She gives most who gives with joy. . . . The best way to show our gratitude to God and the people is to accept everything with joy. A joyful heart is the normal result of a heart burning with love" (cited in Muller 1992, p. 130). In other words, when we are fulfilled and joyful, we are more likely to transmit love of life and hope to others. In play, we celebrate life and rejoice in life's unlimited potential for renewal of body, mind, and spirit. In this vein, Thich Nhat Hanh, a Vietnamese Buddhist monk whose writings have won the hearts of many, teaches, "If you are happy, all of us will profit from it. All living beings will profit from it. Happiness is available . . . please help yourself" (cited in Muller 1992, p. 130).

We generally make allowances for children to play, even if we do not appreciate the survival purpose of children's play. We simply assume it is normal for children to play, although many parents are anxious for their children to get serious about life in order to be successful as adults. However, as adults, we do not make the same allowances. Play is often viewed as a waste of time, a begrudged diversion from the real purpose of life—survival. But the real purpose of life is a matter of definition, varying from culture to culture. As a Westerner who lived in Japan and popularized Buddhism in America, Watts (1983a) viewed some cultures as more playful than others. Watts considered China and the former Soviet Union, for example, to be "earnest" societies that generally exclude play and frivolity. Dedicated to survival, the style of life in these countries is drab " . . . because they think that the point of life is to go on living, and so long as you get by, no matter how horrible the food is, how drab the dress, you are getting by. . . . This is completely missing the point" (p. 32).

In contrast, Buddha taught that life should be lived with joy, and his disciples are said to have been exceptionally jubilant. In Buddhism, play is a spiritual quality—the essence of spiritual life. Buddhism is built on the concepts of nonattachment, living lightly, and keeping balance. Play is the key to not being caught in the melodrama of life. For health and joy, avoid extremes and seek the "middle way," Buddhism advises. Muller (1992), drawing on Buddhism in exploring the spiritual advantages of a painful childhood, suggests, "Play is a natural by-product of nonattachment; we are less afraid about how things will turn out. Play is the joyful attitude of the children of God. When we are spontaneous and happy, we are dancing with the divine light in all things" (p. 130).

Here we begin to recognize the important benefits of play in anxiety recovery. Play is a form of nonattachment—of letting go, one of the most essential anxiety-reduction skills. In fear and anxiety, we tend to hold on to irrational thoughts, worries, and anticipations. Letting go of such thoughts can be accomplished through play, which favors primary process rather than secondary process concerns of coping with the outside world. We play for its own sake—for fun—rather than to control what might happen. In order to play, in fact, we must let go of outcome and be unattached to what will happen. Anxious people have habits and personality traits that create stress and engender anxiety, to which they must become less attached. Play is spontaneous and concerned only with the present moment; it is almost always in the here and now. As such, play is a good antidote to the future focus of worry and anxiety. Play is also relaxing, if not during then at least as a result. This too is essential for anxiety recovery.

There are many forms of play. Children's play, of course, varies with age and encompasses an infinitely wide range of activities from peek-a-boo and hide-and-go-seek to sophisticated games of strategy such as checkers and chess. Solo games, artwork, sports, hobbies, and more also qualify as play. With adults, the range of play is just as wide, and includes recreational activities, crafts, exercise, dancing—anything that involves joy, pleasure, or satisfaction. My favorite forms of play consist of skiing, bicycling, boating (including water-skiing), hiking, being with nature, photography, landscape gardening, exercise, socializing with friends, writing, woodworking, listening to music, and sitting quietly. All of these activities bring me joy, pleasure, or satisfaction. I try to live life as a whole playfully, as a dance to enjoy but also from which to learn and be enriched. One of my goals in life is to eliminate the distinction between work and play, but until I succeed I'll seek a healthy balance between the two.

The reality and pleasure principles correspond to the division between work and play. Both are necessary for survival, and in healthy living the two are kept in balance. What happens when the balance between work and play is lost? Too much work and too little play disrupt the stress and recovery cycle. While the human body can handle enormous stress on a short-term basis, recovery from stress is necessary to rebuild and replenish the resources depleted during stress. As discussed elsewhere, high or prolonged stress not only depletes energy resources, but keeps the body in an action-oriented mode involving a high pitch to all organ systems. The first signs of stress overload occur as mild symptoms that signal a need for time out—for rest, relaxation, or play. Ignored, these signals become louder, in the form of more intense body reactions. Finally, organ systems break down and disease processes are initiated. At any stage in the sequence, anxiety can be triggered in sensitive people who react strongly, or with fear, to their body reactions.

Play, however, relieves the survival focus and allows for natural stress recovery processes to take place. In this sense, play is therapeutic, serving a healing or regenerative function. Play can be healing when it is soft, involving quiet rest and relaxation. Play can also be healing when it is hard, involving tension release and discharge of pent-up frustration or feelings.

Play helps you remember who you really are. For many people, life is like performing in a play without knowing how to take a break or get offstage. In this theater of life, people perform their roles and follow their scripts with such conviction and sincerity that they forget it's a play. Their behaviors, thoughts, and feelings can be so well rehearsed that they become established as habits, which are acted out automatically and without self-awareness. Masks and costumes are mistaken for true identities. In the theater of life, people may relate to you in terms of your web of social roles: as an employee, a parent, a bank account number, a consumer of goods and services, or a tax-paying citizen. But privately, in the quiet moments of the night, you become aware of your personal essence and identity. Then it's gone again, lost before dawn and another day of performing. Yet there is hope for finding yourself.

Playing is the way to get offstage. In playing, you throw off your mask and costume and abandon your social roles in the make-no-sense act of having fun. Play gives little credence to reality. The pleasure principle rules in play, as a smile breaks through your face. In play, you remember your childhood, if you had one to begin with. If not, then play is the way to find it. There is a child trapped in each of us, longing to play, to be spontaneous and irresponsible—to be free.

Friends can help us play. When you play with friends, a new agreement is reached, that life on stage is too serious. Indeed, play helps you look back on yourself, putting things in their proper perspective. Playing with your friends creates community—a social support system, one of the most important ingredients in health.

When I play, I fancy that I am free. I let go in skiing, diving off the boat into the lake, walking through the woods, singing a song, dancing to music. Time stops, it is now only, and the past and future become irrelevant. I may have to plan for play time, but when it's here, it's all there is for the moment. And when I am playing I think, "This is it!" When I play, I am dancing with life.

Is there room for play in your life? Try the following exercise to assess the fun factor in your case, and to help direct your attention to how you can increase it.

EXERCISE: PLAYFUL LIVING

> Sit down and relax with your eyes closed. Take a few minutes to breathe deeply and elicit the relaxation response. Scan your body from head to toes and release any tension as you exhale.

Now begin to review the happiest moments in your life. Visualize enjoying yourself, having fun, experiencing pleasure, feeling satisfied. Take mental notes on these images, in preparation for the next part of the exercise.

Open your eyes and make a list of all the things that come to mind. This is your activity list for playful living.

Next, go over the list and note in the margin the last two or three times you engaged in each activity. This will give you some idea of how often you play.

If you want to increase your joy of living, you now realize what has already worked for you. You can add any new or unfamiliar activities you think might be fun. Decide which activities you want to increase in your life, and make a personal commitment to allow more playfulness into your life.

18

What About Drugs?

. . . medicines do not "cure" anybody, per se.
Medications in the Treatment of Panic
Disorder and Panic Disorder with
Agoraphobia: A Consumer's Guide

Drugs are by far the most common treatment for anxiety disorders, but drug therapy alone is the least effective form of help. How can the least effective form of help be the most frequently used?

The vast majority of people who seek professional help for problems with anxiety first go to their medical doctor or hospital emergency room. This is understandable considering the physical nature of anxiety symptoms. Heart palpitations, chest pains, difficulty breathing, nausea, weakness, trembling, numbness, hot and cold flashes, muscle pain are all physical symptoms that send anxious people to their doctors. Most anxiety sufferers misinterpret their physical symptoms and fear they are experiencing a catastrophic physical illness—a heart attack, a life-threatening disease, a serious organ malfunction. Medical doctors, of course, have a biological perspective and are trained to treat the physical basis of disease. Naturally, they use the diagnostic tools of their trade, as well as the healing strategy with which they are most familiar—drugs.

But there is more to it than that. When physicians are confronted with the symptoms of an anxiety disorder, they may not diagnose the underlying disorder. What is most apparent are the arousal symptoms—the fight/flight response—produced by the underlying anxiety condition. Beneath the unusually intense or frequent body symptoms are the psychological components of anxiety: personality traits that produce stress, thought patterns that falsely trigger the fight/flight reaction, learned fear of body symptoms, anticipatory dread, and so forth. Whether anxiety is essentially a biological or a psychological condition is very much a matter of debate, but in a practical setting, such as a doctor's office, the physician will search for a medical basis for the condition.

Although the symptoms of anxiety are certainly real, there is rarely a medical basis for them. While an anxiety patient usually presents with a host of body symptoms, there is no actual physical problem or abnormality in the body or its organ systems. Heart palpitations in anxiety do not reflect heart disease, breathing difficulty does not reflect a lung or respiratory disease, nausea does not reflect a stomach illness or intestinal virus, and so on. From a medical viewpoint, there is often nothing to treat in anxiety disorders except the obvious fight/flight reaction, which is not an illness or disease. In addition, physicians are generally not attuned to the personality traits and conditioning process involved in the development of anxiety disorders.

The medical doctor facing an anxious patient has several options. The first is to diagnose the fight/flight reaction, and advise the patient to relax more or manage stress better. Without further guidance, however, this recommendation is difficult to implement, as any anxiety sufferer would agree. Most doctors do not have the expertise or time to provide the cognitive and behavioral therapy that is required to learn relaxation and stress management skills.

A second option is for the doctor to treat the symptoms of anxiety, which is usually done with tranquilizing drugs. This is by far the most frequent response of medical doctors when dealing with anxious patients. There are several types of drugs that are typically prescribed for anxiety symptoms, and they will be discussed later in this chapter.

Another option is for the doctor to diagnose the anxiety disorder, and refer the patient to an anxiety treatment specialist. Unfortunately, this is rarely done because it requires not only a recognition of the anxiety disorder, but also a belief in the effectiveness of psychological counseling and a willingness to refer to non-medical health care providers. Knowledge of locally available specialists in anxiety therapy would also be required. In many communities there are few, if any, anxiety treatment programs or specialists, although the numbers are likely to increase as the prevalence of severe anxiety disorders becomes more apparent and as training opportunities become available. (One such opportunity is training for mental health professionals in use of the CHAANGE program. Interested professionals should contact CHAANGE, listed in Appendix B.) When the psychologically minded physician does refer, the referral is likely to be made to a mental health professional with a general practice, without the specialized training required for effective anxiety treatment. Indeed, many anxiety sufferers who contact me as a specialist have had prior therapy—many episodes with numerous therapists in some cases—that was not successful in addressing the anxiety condition, even though the therapy may have been helpful in other respects.

Another disheartening option is when the physician does not take the anxiety patient seriously. Because there is usually no medical basis for the anxiety, and because anxiety patients may present repeatedly with unfounded concerns about their bodies, they may be viewed as annoying complainers or hypochondriacs.

Drugs are the most common treatment offered to anxiety patients because the gatekeepers of health care are physicians. However, the National Institute of Mental Health reports that drug treatment is most effective when used in combination with psychological counseling, particularly cognitive-behavioral therapy. Alone, drugs for anxiety show limited effectiveness, and they have a number of significant disadvantages, such as side effects, need for frequent adjustments, and withdrawal risks. These issues make drugs unattractive, especially when less complicated—and very effective—alternatives are available. In addition, as Munjack (1988) reports, the relapse rates for patients treated with medication alone are very high. In a consumer guide to medications in treatment of panic anxiety, Munjack reports that management of anxiety disorders with drugs usually requires months and sometimes years of maintenance treatment, and people are kept on certain drugs—up to an additional year—beyond the point where symptoms appear to be controlled.

The cost of unnecessary medical treatment for anxiety, including drugs, is astounding. Up to $30,000 in some cases is spent over a period of years on ineffective treatment and on the process of obtaining an accurate diagnosis. Inappropriate treatment may include hospital emergency room visits, costly laboratory and stress tests, outpatient office visits, inpatient hospitalizations, and long-term use of drugs. Medications can be expensive, and some individuals take them for well over a decade, sometimes with no noticeable improvement. In contrast, a study of the cost effectiveness of the CHAANGE anxiety treatment program, a structured psychological approach that does not use drugs, found a 26 percent reduction in the cost of medical care for program graduates over a one-year period after completing the program. The cost savings were even more significant because the expenses for health care in the CHAANGE study *included* the cost of the program plus sixteen therapy sessions. Effective treatment for anxiety saves money, and in this day of soaring health-care costs—a national crisis and political agenda—cost-effective treatment that really works should be of great interest. Considering the high prevalence of anxiety disorders—approximately 25 percent of the population or 65 million people at some point in their lifetime—any proven treatment program for anxiety that can save significant dollars could make more than a dent in the national budget.

In a two-billion-dollar-a-year funding package for brain research, the U.S. Congress in 1990 dubbed the '90s the "decade of the brain." Exciting advances in brain research have fueled optimism about the potential for using drugs to treat depression, anxiety, and other emotional disorders. For example, sensitivity in the limbic system, the brain's center associated with emotions, has been shown to be heightened in anxiety sufferers. And discovering how thoughts and emotions influence body reactions has led to the idea of altering biochemistry with drugs to reduce anxiety. But anxiety is not a disease or illness, and rarely is it a matter of faulty biochemistry. Changes in brain chemistry could reasonably be considered an effect just as easily as a cause of anxiety. While anxiety may be temporarily relieved by tranquilizers, that does not mean anxiety is caused by inadequate supplies of arousal-inhibiting chemicals in the body. Anxiety symptoms usually reflect good biological response capabilities—quick fight/flight reactions—that have been conditioned to fire off unnecessarily due to trauma, stress overload, or misperceptions of danger.

In my view, anxiety is caused by the interaction of biological sensitivity, family background, personality type, and stress. Anxiety is both a biological condition, because it involves the body and genetic sensitivity, as well as a psychological condition, because it involves thinking, feelings, and behavior. The fight/flight response is, of course, a biological event. In truly life-threatening situations, where the brain's survival center triggers a fight/flight reaction before thought even takes place, there is no doubt that biological mechanisms are at work. However, in anxiety there is usually no clear threat or danger, and the fight/flight reaction is triggered by a thought, image, memory, feeling, or sensory stimulus. We can even have sudden episodes of anxiety—panic attacks—triggered by *unconscious* thoughts or at night during sleep when we are not aware of our thinking. We can also accumulate the effects of stress and respond with anxiety in a delayed fashion, days or even months after the occurrence of high stress. Pelletier (1977) reports that a six- to eight-month delay between a period of high stress and the onset of symptoms is common. Pelletier also reports that personality style plays a major role in determining the type and severity of conditions that are triggered by stress. These psychological factors interact with biological mechanisms to produce anxiety. A complete and accurate understanding of anxiety disorders must include a mind–body model—the idea of an interaction between biological factors, psychological conditioning, and stress. Anything narrower is likely to lead to incomplete or ineffective treatment.

It would be reasonable to assume that anxiety sufferers have a biological sensitivity—perhaps a sensitive "smoke alarm" in the limbic area of the brain—that predisposes them to react strongly to many types of stimuli. Stress can trigger the fight/flight reaction, which then can become linked to the situation producing it. A cycle of anticipatory fear, learned avoidance or other coping habits, negative thinking, false beliefs, more body reactions leading to more fear, and so on, develops into a downward spiral of anxiety. The anxiety condition can then drive itself and be maintained by learned habits, thinking, and behavior.

It is tempting to think of eliminating anxiety with a drug capable of short-circuiting the biological-sensitivity component of anxiety. How convenient it would be to resolve anxiety by blocking the body's reactivity to the many situations that can trigger it. Indeed, one type of drug used in treating panic disorder—the beta blocker—is intended to inhibit the production of activating hormones, such as adrenaline, thereby reducing the physical symptoms associated with anxiety. The inhibiting effect of this type of drug on heart rate, blood pressure, muscle tremor, and sweating makes it a commonly prescribed drug in controlling hypertension.

However, for the vast majority of people, the disadvantages of drug therapy for anxiety outweigh the advantages. To begin with, the very idea of relying on a drug to cope runs against the grain of the anxiety-prone personality. For example, most anxiety sufferers have a strong need to feel in control. Taking drugs is objectionable because it conflicts with control needs, with not being controlled by any outside forces, including chemicals. Another characteristic is the anxiety sufferer's high sensitivity, which raises the probability of strong reactions to drug effects. For example, the side effects of imipramine (Tofranil), a commonly prescribed drug in anxiety treatment, can include dry mouth, constipation, blurred vision, weight gain, lower blood pressure, decreased sexual responsiveness, and difficulty urinating, all of which can intensify anxiety in people who react strongly to changes within the body. Even the intended effects of drugs can increase anxiety because of their biochemical impact.

Another disadvantage of drug therapy for anxiety is the laborious trials and experimentation that are often required to find a workable drug choice and dosage. Even after an acceptable drug and dosage is in place, the effect of some drugs decreases with time, requiring further adjustments. These are not only inconveniences but also another source of anxiety, as well as discouragement, for those who may already feel their case is unique or hopeless. High stress can also override the positive effects of drugs, resulting in a return of symptoms.

Another problem is the need to withdraw gradually from some drugs, in order to prevent a "rebound effect"—a sudden return of anxiety symptoms. Rebound or withdrawal symptoms are likely to increase the second fear reaction, which can set the anxiety cycle in motion once again. This is a significant problem with the benzodiazepine class of drugs, for which close medical supervision is advised during the tapering off period. The addictive quality of some drugs, such as diazepam (Valium), is also frightening to those with a high need for control. Indeed, many patients taking drugs when they initially come to my anxiety treatment program express concerns about discontinuing the medication. Will they have a relapse? Will they be able to function without the drugs?

In one memorable case, the anxiety problem itself was presented as a fear of discontinuing drugs. Christine, the educator who was discussed in Chapter 17, relied on drugs to cope with stress for many years. She was taking two drugs, one for insomnia and one for generalized anxiety. Despite her obvious competencies as a person—intelligence, social skills, drive, and resourcefulness—Christine believed she would be unable to function in life without drugs. However, she wanted desperately to discontinue her reliance on them.

Christine's history revealed that her mother had used tranquilizing drugs, which added credibility to her reliance on them. What's more, Christine had a traumatic experience several years before I met her, when she attempted to stop taking her drugs. She lasted only two weeks before she became overwhelmed with panic anxiety. Nevertheless, Christine felt that drugs were limiting her life, particularly in terms of feelings. She was afraid of feelings, and used drugs to avoid experiencing them. This was, in fact, Christine's basic problem. Having been raised in a family where feelings were suppressed and denied, she became uncomfortable with feelings. As an adolescent, she began using alcohol, followed in adulthood by prescription drugs to subdue her feelings. With this history, Christine felt that she would not be able to cope with feelings if she discontinued the drugs.

Christine focused on her fear of discontinuing drugs, which I considered to be a phobia, along with her fear of feelings. As part of her treatment plan, I recommended the CHAANGE program for its emphasis on learning new skills, such as relaxation, managing stress, changing inner dialogue, assertive communication, facing fears, and dealing with anticipatory anxiety. I also felt that improved confidence and self-esteem—common benefits of the CHAANGE program—would help.

The CHAANGE program approach proved immensely helpful in Christine's case. She acquired the skills needed to replace the drugs as a means of coping with stress and feelings. Christine was finally able to discontinue the drugs, after relying on them for some twenty years. What's more, she did not resume alcohol as a coping mechanism. Christine was prepared to function in life without drugs. In addition, her attitude became positive, her worrying diminished, and her mood and energy improved. On the post-program evaluation, Christine wrote,

> I feel more in control of my thoughts and feelings than before. I feel I have a more positive attitude in general and spend less time worrying about things, particularly those I can't change. I feel I like myself better and am not so hard on myself, and when I do have negative

> thoughts about myself I'm able to dismiss them more easily. I find I brood less. I feel more physically comfortable, less tense, and less nervous.

The last word I received from Christine was that she had made a successful professional trip to present at a conference, without drugs.

Medication is sometimes used in the treatment of anxiety in children. However, there are few well-controlled studies of the value of medications on children and adolescents with anxiety disorders. The best studies have been done on the effect of the antidepressant imipramine on school-phobic children. This drug was found to be associated with return to school and decreased separation anxiety. On the other hand, the side effects of this drug can include drowsiness and decreased frustration tolerance. There is also a risk of serious—even fatal—side effects on the cardiovascular system in children using this and similar drugs. These concerns apply to other drugs, such as benzodiazapines, whose side effects include sedation and cognitive performance deficits as well as abuse and dependency on the drug. Although the benzodiazepines have been used in adult anxiety cases, little support exists for their use with young people. Considering the fact that about 80 percent of children with anxiety disorders can benefit from therapy without medications, my opinion is that drugs should be used as a last resort, with attention to side effects and risks.

Drugs can play a vital, although limited, role in anxiety treatment. In recognizing this, psychologists and other mental health professionals refer anxiety patients to physicians or psychiatrists for drugs in certain cases, as part of a team approach to treatment. For example, I refer patients for medication when their anxiety symptoms are so distracting that their ability to focus and concentrate—to learn—is too impaired for relaxation training, cognitive therapy, or other aspects of effective psychological treatment. In such cases, drugs play an important support role in a comprehensive anxiety recovery program, and they can be discontinued when new skills allow the person to function without drugs.

In a similar vein, drugs can be helpful when a secondary depression develops from anxiety to the extent that it, too, interferes with concentration, sleep, and ability to learn. In such cases, an antidepressant drug can help to control the depression, freeing up energy to be used in an anxiety recovery process. In addition, some antidepressant medications, such as imipramine (Tofranil) and fluoxetine (Prozac) are reportedly useful in reducing panic disorder.

Drugs have some other important advantages as part of anxiety treatment. For an infrequently occurring anxiety problem, such as a flying phobia, there may be little opportunity to practice anxiety control skills. In such cases, a symptom-blocking drug can help a person to face the situation and perhaps replace the need for a more complete course of anxiety therapy. On the other hand, this approach may not be sufficient to counteract the anticipatory dread associated with the phobic situation.

This was the dilemma in Maria's case. Maria, a competent woman who worked as a supervisor at a large corporation, developed a fear of flying as a result of a turbulent flight from New York to Florida. The rough ride triggered panic anxiety in this woman, who did not have a history of anxiety problems, although she did have all the necessary prerequisites: sensitivity, anxiety personality traits, and stress. In all other areas of her life, there were no apparent problems; she interacted effectively with people and showed no anxiety symptoms. Five years later, having not been able to go on any vacations involving flying, she came for help.

Maria was motivated for overcoming the flying fear because she wanted to be able to join friends and family on vacations. She took well to relaxation training and to desensitization using imagery. However, there were no opportunities to practice flying, short of actually going on a flight, which she refused to do because of her intense anxiety. However, a combination of graduated exposure to airplanes and a short-acting drug to counteract the anxiety symptoms was successful. The cognitive and behavior therapy helped Maria deal with the anticipatory anxiety about flying, as well as provide the skills and confidence needed to handle anxiety on board if it were to occur. Working in concert with the psychological techniques, the drug helped to reduce the intensity of anxiety symptoms. Medication contributed to Maria's ability to face the phobic situation, which created the opportunity for her to desensitize to it. The biggest step in her recovery was taken when Maria completed an enjoyable vacation with friends that involved a round-trip flight from Boston to San Francisco. She used medication on the departing flight, but not on the return flight. Maria had faced her biggest fear, and formed a new attitude towards flying.

Another advantage of drugs is that they can be used in cases where people are not interested in a psychological approach to overcoming anxiety. Although the vast majority of anxiety sufferers do not want to take drugs, there are some who simply do not want to participate in psychological therapy and who are willing to rely on a drug to manage their anxiety. This was illustrated in Patricia's case.

Patricia was a bright but somewhat shy and self-conscious lawyer who functioned comfortably in one-on-one interactions with people, where her role was clearly defined. However, she had some traumatic anxiety experiences when addressing a jury. Since she knew in advance when such occasions would take place, Patricia managed to cope with her anxiety by preparing diligently and rehearsing her speech. Nevertheless, the anxiety associated with that situation, including the torturous anticipatory dread, became too intense, and Patricia came for help.

Patricia was quite clear that she wanted a drug that she could take before she was scheduled to address a jury and for infrequent occasions where she would need to "perform" before a group of people. She specified the new beta-blocker type of drug, reasoning that if she could identify the trigger for anxiety and block it with an effective drug, this would be a logical and sufficient solution to the problem. I sensed that Patricia had a strong need for control, including controlling her anxiety in the quickest way possible, and was willing to rely on a drug as she went on with her career.

In addition, Patricia was unusually resistant to a psychological approach, even though she recognized that it would be preferable in the long run to be able to control the anxiety without drugs. One revealing remark seemed to explain her unwillingness to enter a deeper recovery process. In response to a routine question I ask about marital satisfaction, Patricia said, "I don't really love my husband. Do we have to talk about that?" I then realized that Patricia had an issue—a potentially painful issue—she was not ready to face. We met for several sessions, during which I arranged for her to obtain appropriate medication. She then stopped coming to see me.

Drugs can, in some cases, be effective in reducing physical symptoms. Since the primary physical mechanism in anxiety is arousal—the fight/flight reaction—drugs that tranquilize the body can bring relief. So-called "anti-anxiety" drugs, such as the benzodiazepines (Xanax, Ativan, Librium, Klonopin, Centrax, Serax, Tranzene, and Valium), do have this calming effect. One of these drugs, Xanax, has also been found to have panic-reducing qualities. These drugs have the added advantage of acting quickly, usually within a few days, or even minutes with drugs such as Valium. In addition, the benzodiazepines are generally well-tolerated; they have fewer side effects compared to other drugs used in anxiety treatment. On the other hand, they can be habit-forming, a serious disadvantage. In the case of Xanax, another disadvantage is that it may cause drowsiness or a "medicated" feeling for some. One may feel too groggy to concentrate on new learning, a concern for those interested in an anxiety recovery process.

It should be acknowledged that some anxiety sufferers attempt to control their symptoms with nonprescription drugs, such as alcohol or marijuana. It is estimated that up to 60 percent of those with alcohol dependence are anxiety sufferers who turned to this drug as a form of self-medication. Nonprescription drugs are used by anxiety sufferers for the same reason as prescription medications—symptom relief. Unfortunately, this coping strategy is ineffective in the long run because it does not result in learning any new skills for preventing or controlling anxiety. In addition, the potential for addiction, especially with alcohol, is high, which creates an additional problem.

As mentioned earlier, antidepressants are sometimes used in anxiety treatment to counteract the depression associated with anxiety. Some antidepressants also seem to reduce anxiety symptoms, such as panic and obsessive-compulsive patterns. The advantage of antidepressants is that, once regulated and tolerated, they do not tend to create a drugged feeling and they do not significantly interfere with concentration and motivation. Another advantage is that antidepressants do not tend to promote the types of drug dependencies found with the anti-anxiety drugs discussed above. However, the disadvantage of antidepressants is that many people experience unpleasant side effects, typically during the first few days of administration but chronically in some cases. Some of the common side effects include dry mouth, blurred vision, constipation, drowsiness, dizziness, and, in some cases, increased heart rate and weight gain. If the dosage levels are managed correctly, many of these side effects are minimal and the body eventually adjusts to the drug. It is important to remember that several weeks may be needed to regulate the dosage of these drugs, during which the side effects may not improve. Although these drugs are considered safe for long-term use, it is recommended that contact be maintained with the prescribing physician to ensure optimal benefit and dosage regulation.

The monoamine oxidase inhibitors (MAOIs), another group of drugs used in anxiety treatment, have also been used to control depression. If tolerated, they may also be effective in some cases in blocking panic anxiety. Phenelzine (Nardil) seems to be the most effective MAOI for this purpose. MAOIs have also been used in treating social phobia. MAOIs are thought to increase concentration of hormones such as epinephrine, norepinephrine, and serotonin in storage sites throughout the nervous system, which, in theory, is the basis for their antidepressant action. Use of these drugs is dangerous if combined with certain foods, such as cheese, wine, and beer, or with certain over-the-counter medicines—a significant disadvantage. Also, these drugs have the highest number of unpleasant side effects, a fact which makes many physicians hesitant to prescribe them. MAOIs are not a simple type of drug to administer, and considerable patience may be required on the part of both physician and patient for this type of drug to be effective.

The beta-blockers are a class of drugs most commonly used to control hypertension. They act by making the autonomic nervous system, which controls functions like heart rate, blood pressure, muscle tension, and sweating, less reactive to stimulation. They are nonaddictive, and they do not have any sedating effects. The usefulness of beta-blockers in anxiety treatment lies in their ability to control the body's reactivity, which in turn can reduce the subjective experience of anxious feelings.

Finally, the selective serotonin reuptake inhibitor (SSRI) class of drugs is becoming popular in the treatment of panic disorder. These include fluoxetine (Prozac), sertraline (Zoloft), and paroxetine (Paxil). These drugs generally produce fewer side effects than antidepressants or MAOIs, and they do not cause physical dependency as do benzodiazepines. However, the major problem with SSRIs in treating panic disorder is their propensity to cause an initial hyperarousal reaction in which the patient becomes even more anxious and agitated than before taking the drug. This can be counteracted to some extent by starting with very low doses of the drug and increasingly slowly.

Table 18–1 provides an overview of the drugs used in anxiety treatment.

In this chapter, we have discussed the pros and cons of drugs in the treatment of anxiety. It should be apparent that although there are some important benefits, there are overwhelmingly more limitations and problems with drug therapy. In my opinion, drugs do not result in anxiety recovery, which requires cognitive and behavior change. Drugs are not a reasonable long-term solution to anxiety, because they cannot by themselves teach the necessary skills. Drugs are most effective when used as part of a more comprehensive approach to anxiety recovery. It should also be kept in mind that many people have recovered completely from anxiety disorders without drugs, using cognitive-behavior therapy. Virtually all patients who begin the CHAANGE program on medication are able to discontinue the drugs—usually within the 16-week process. Some case examples are described in Chapter 22. Most anxiety sufferers want to be free, to function freely and effectively in life without the limitations of anxiety and without reliance on drugs.

TABLE 18–1: DRUGS USED TO TREAT ANXIETY

Generic Name	Brand Name	Prescribed For	Usual Dose*	Drug Class
alprazolam	Xanax	PD, GAD, D	0.5-5	Benzodiaz.
diazepam	Valium	GAD	5-20	Benzodiaz.
clonazepam	Klonopin	PD	1-6	Benzodiaz.
lorazepam	Ativan	PD	1-10	Benzodiaz.
prazepam	Centrax	GAD	20-60	Benzodiaz.
chlordiazepoxide	Librium	GAD	60-100	Benzodiaz.**
oxazepam	Serax	GAD	30-120	Benzodiaz.
chlorazepate	Tranxene	GAD	15-60	Benzodiaz.
imipramine	Tofranil	D, PD	100-300	Tri. antidepr.
desipramine	Norpramine	D, PD	100-300	Tri. antidepr.
nortriptyline	Pamelor	D, PD	25-150	Tri. antidepr.
phenelzine	Nardil	D, PD, SP	45-90***	MAOI
tranylcypromine	Parnate	D, PD, SP	20-50	MAOI
buspirone	Buspar	GAD	30-60	Anti-anx.
propranolol	Inderal	HBP, PA	40-240	Beta-blocker
atenolol	Tenormin	HBP, SP, PA	50-100	Beta-blocker
labetalol	Normodyne	HBP, PA	200-800	Beta/alpha bl.
clorimipramine	Anafranil	D, OCD, PD	100-300	Antidepr.
trazodone	Desyrel	D	150-400	Antidepr.
paroxetine	Paxil	D, OCD, PD	20-50	SSRI
fluoxetine	Prozac	D, OCD, PD	20-80	SSRI
sertraline	Zoloft	D, OCD, PD	50-200	SSRI

KEY:

PD = Panic disorder
GAD = Generalized anxiety disorder
OCD = Obsessive-compulsive disorder
SP = Social phobia
D = Depression
PA = Performance anxiety
HBP = High blood pressure

Tri. antidepr. = tricyclic antidepressant
Antidepr. = antidepressant
Anti-anx. = anti-anxiety (tranquilizer)
Benzodiaz. = benzodiazepine
MAOI = monoamine oxidase inhibitor
SSRI = serotonin reuptake inhibitor
* Dosages are shown in milligrams per day
** Includes a sedative
*** 1 milligram per 2.2 pounds of body weight

19

Anxiety and Relationships

Intimate relationships can be both a source of anxiety—for those who have been hurt or disappointed in the past—as well as the most powerful opportunity for anxiety recovery and emotional healing.

Paul Foxman

Throughout this book, anxiety is discussed as a condition affecting individuals, and all anxiety sufferers would agree that anxiety is a very personal kind of terror. Indeed, before treatment many anxiety sufferers feel unique and alone, as if others would not understand what it is like to live with severe anxiety. Unfortunately, this is true in many cases where a spouse or significant other person shows impatience and frustration with the anxiety sufferer's condition. The sense of isolation is further reinforced when effective professional help is sought but not found, or when feelings of unreality are part of the condition. And yet most anxiety sufferers are involved in multiple relationships: with parents, spouse, children, boyfriend or girlfriend, peers and friends, or people at work. Anxiety invariably exists in a social context, being affected by others, and, in turn, affecting others. Even treatment for anxiety is an interpersonal process, not only in terms of the therapeutic relationship between therapist and patient but also in terms of how change in the recovering person affects the lives of others involved with that person. In this chapter, we will explore the interaction between anxiety and relationships. We will discover, among other things, that relationships can produce anxiety but they can also help heal anxiety. In addition, we will see how anxiety treatment can be a learning and growth opportunity not just for the afflicted person but for his or her relationships as well.

Every relationship is a *system*. Like the self-regulating mechanisms in a person's body, a relationship is a self-regulating system that seeks to survive stresses and strains and maintain stability. In a relationship system, behavior and feelings in one person affect the "fields" of others, who are thereby moved to compensate or adjust. This is sometimes called a *mutual reaction process,* implying simply that in any relationship the behavior of each party affects the behavior of the other.

The systems view of relationships is the foundation of most approaches to family therapy. While strategies vary within family therapy approaches, one principle unites them all, namely that symptoms often serve an equilibrium-maintaining function within a family. Often, a symptom-bearer—one person who carries the symptom—is the stress release valve in a family. In an alcoholic family, for example, one child may develop a behavior problem that diverts attention away from an impaired parent who may be in denial about his or her addiction and dysfunction. Another child, often the oldest, may become a high-achieving "hero" whose accomplishments serve to mask the family's dysfunction and "prove" that nothing is wrong.

When family stress is high, one member may develop an anxiety disorder. Anxiety usually occurs in the person whose personality fits the profile described in Chapter 4. While the anxious person may absorb the family stress, the anxiety disorder puts pressure on other members to provide support and reassurance. If the anxiety is incapacitating, other family members may then be required to fill in the gaps by providing transportation, doing extra household chores, and taking on other responsibilities. As roles shift additional stress is created and other family members, such as a spouse, may feel burdened or overwhelmed.

Sometimes the ego needs of a spouse or significant other may be fulfilled by the anxiety sufferer's dependency or incapacity, but in an unhealthy way. If a partner has strong needs for control, for example, the role of caretaker and "strong one" may be easily accepted, perhaps even welcomed, even if some resentment accompanies the role. This relationship pattern was evident in one of the few cases in which the CHAANGE anxiety treatment program was unsuccessful. The patient was an insecure and highly dependent woman whose husband called to make the initial appointment and brought her in for help. On the surface, the husband resented his wife's dependency, complaining that he had to drive her everywhere "like a taxi." He would also become angry if she left something off the grocery shopping list and needed to make a second trip to the supermarket within the same week. However, beneath his complaints and resentment, the husband felt more comfortable being dominant in the relationship. Although his participation in a number of therapy sessions seemed supportive, when the wife complained of his demanding and critical parenting style with their children, he agreed to talk about it, but only after she had overcome her anxiety disorder. About halfway through the program, when she was showing signs of greater risk-taking and independence, the woman called to cancel her next appointment and to indicate that she would not be continuing. When I telephoned her to discuss this decision, she told me that her husband did not think the program was helping and wanted her to stop. It was apparent, however, that her husband wanted her to stop because the program *was* working, which meant that the balance of power in the relationship would have to shift.

Normally, people who develop anxiety disorders have many strengths and competencies. Anxiety disorders tend to develop in people who are hard-working, dependable, perfectionistic, high-achieving, and eager to please. But the anxiety personality also has a strong need to be in control, as well as difficulty asking for help. Feeling out of control and dependent on others runs completely against the grain of the anxiety sufferer's personality. Usually, it is the person with this personality who keeps things going in relationships, but when this role is reversed the relationship may go into crisis.

Intimacy can be a special challenge for the person with these traits. The need to please others, fear of rejection, and extreme sensitivity to criticism will tend to make this type of person highly reactive to any kind of negative feedback. Even without unusual stresses or symptoms of anxiety, this type of person may react strongly to the slightest indication of displeasure, rejection, or criticism by others. In response, the anxiety-prone partner may try even harder to please, creating more stress and, eventually, an anxiety crisis. As discussed in Chapter 4, these are some of the liabilities in the anxiety personality. In an intimate relationship, such personality traits are almost guaranteed to trigger anxiety because conflict in relationships is inevitable.

A number of ideas from family therapy and systems theory can be helpful in understanding the impact of anxiety on relationships. One idea is that family or marital relationships must periodically reorganize in order to survive. Reorganization can be precipitated by a crisis, as discussed above, or as a result of one member undergoing change. An obvious example would be the impact of an adolescent maturing into an adult, asking for and capable of increased responsibility and freedom. If the family does not adapt to the changing needs of the adolescent, the adolescent may emotionally stop growing, act out, or reject the family in order to continue growing. Any relationship that is incapable of adapting to changes within itself or the surrounding world is unlikely to survive as a unit.

As an anxiety sufferer undergoes treatment and recovery, the key relationships of that person must adapt to make room for new patterns of behavior. As the recovering person becomes stronger, more assertive, or more independent, the spouse and other family members must accommodate these changes in order for them to become established as new patterns. Thus, therapy—and the changes it promotes—can introduce new information and skills into a social system to help it survive. Unfortunately, in the case described earlier in this chapter, the husband was unable to accommodate the positive changes in his wife as she developed new skills and showed signs of increasing strength and independence, and she, not wanting to jeopardize the security of her marriage, was unable to go forward and complete her anxiety treatment. In effect, the husband wanted his wife to overcome her anxiety without changing anything else within the marriage, and the wife wanted to change without rocking the boat.

In my work with couples, I find that there are four stages in the development of an intimate relationship. The first is *symbiosis,* a stage of mutual dependence which overshadows individuality. An undifferentiated togetherness is characteristic of this stage, and a couple speaks predominantly of "us" and "we." In symbiosis, the identity of each partner is based on being in the relationship. This is normal in the early stages of a relationship, when a couple first falls in love and wants to spend all their time together. The second stage is *rapprochement,* the French term for leaving and returning, in which the couple experiments tentatively with separation and individuation. In this stage, partners strive to find a balance between meeting their individual needs while preserving and protecting the relationship. A common issue in this stage is the extent to which each partner is permitted to have separate friends or spend time doing things that are not of interest to both. The third stage is *independence,* in which one partner may emotionally separate from the relationship, or even physically leave, in the process of "finding" himself or herself. Although necessary for the next and final stage of development, the drive for independence of one or both partners can be confused with incompatibility. The fourth and most mature stage is *mutual interdependence,* in which a couple can accommodate the independence of each partner, while allowing a reciprocal dependency on each other. In mutual interdependence each partner is acknowledged to be separate—that is no longer questioned—and mutual dependency can take place without symbiosis.

At any stage in a couple relationship, the potential for anxiety is high, especially for those with anxiety personality traits. During the symbiotic stage, for example, there is always the threat of the relationship not working out. Concerns about rejection or being alone if the relationship turns sour can make this stage anxiety arousing. During rapprochement, these concerns intensify, but if the relationship can accommodate each partner's individuality, anxiety can be minimized. However, as either partner becomes more independent, anxiety may develop in the other. If a relationship makes it to the fourth stage, mutual interdependence, there is usually sufficient security and trust to counteract anxiety.

In most cases of couples who present themselves for professional help, however, the two partners are not at the same stage at the same time. For example, while one partner may be experimenting with independence, the other partner may feel threatened and fearful about losing the relationship. In this case, the anxious partner will have difficulty letting go and supporting the growth of the other partner, a common problem in relationships. In turn, the partner seeking greater independence may experience anxiety about functioning more independently or relying more on himself or herself. In addition, self-confidence may waver, and fear of or guilt about hurting the other partner may stand in the way of growth. Sometimes, the solution—

not a good one—is to regress to an earlier stage, such as symbiotic dependence, with accompanying anxiety.

It is common for those with severe anxiety to feel insecure and become dependent on a support person. Typically, the support person is a spouse, family member, or close friend. Feeling weak, helpless, and out of control, the anxious person regresses in the relationship, but at the same time feels ashamed and disappointed in herself or himself for not being able to cope with the anxiety. Depending on the personality and sensitivity of the support person, such regression may be accepted with love and kindness as a temporary need or rejected impatiently. In the second, unfortunate alternative, the anxiety sufferer's shame and humiliation are intensified. There is also the issue of how long the period of regressed dependency lasts, since even the most patient spouse or significant other may become resentful of the increased responsibility. Appropriate anxiety treatment can, fortunately, reverse this process.

In a successful relationship, communication is *congruent,* as Satir (1976) points out. Satir, noted for her expertise in couples and family therapy, suggests that communication in successful relationships is straight, rather than disguised, and that there is congruence between what is said and how it is said, including voice tone and body language. Congruent communication is "face to face," as compared to "back to back," with eye contact between partners who acknowledge their real feelings and listen to each other. The "physics of relationships," as Satir calls it, determine not only the degree of congruence in communication but how much emotional contact is made.

In successful relationships people can share power, make decisions and plans, express feelings, and resolve conflict. The basis for these abilities is effective communication. Satir identifies five modes of communication, the most healthy being congruent communication, as described above. The other four modes—*blaming, placating, intellectual* (which Satir calls "super-reasonable"), and *irrelevant*—arise in response to stress, when trust or love in a relationship is threatened. These modes of communication are dysfunctional, and we can understand these modes by noting that in any interpersonal relationship there are three elements: the self, the other, and the relationship as a whole. Dysfunctional communication ignores the feelings or existence of at least one of these three elements. Blaming ("You never do anything right") disqualifies the other person. Placating ("I always do everything wrong") disqualifies the self. Intellectual communication ("One needs to accept the fact that nothing in life is perfect and people do make mistakes") ignores the feelings of both self and other. Irrelevant remarks—statements which direct attention away from feelings—ignore the emotional relationship altogether.

In contrast to these dysfunctional modes, congruent communication—"Yes, I am feeling angry right now," or "I can see that you are upset with me right now"—acknowledges the feelings of both partners. Congruent communication maintains emotional contact between partners and creates a safe place for feelings to be expressed and resolved.

Many people who develop anxiety have deficits in communication skills. The most common problem is with congruent communication. The anxiety personality has difficulty expressing feelings and emotional needs due to fears of rejection or criticism. Placating and blaming modes of communication, to use Satir's terms, are also characteristic. This is to be expected, since the family backgrounds of anxiety sufferers typically include problems with communication and expression of feelings. Anger, as we know from an earlier chapter, is the most difficult feeling to deal with, but other feelings, notably affection and hurt, can be a problem as well. In some cases, the anxiety sufferer may simply not be in touch with feelings, which makes it impossible to communicate effectively.

Recognizing these communication problems in anxiety sufferers, the CHAANGE program includes lessons in assertive communication and other interpersonal skills. This approach to anxiety treatment teaches that poor communication and interpersonal skills create stress and anxiety. Stress overload develops due to anxiety personality traits, such as a need to please others, difficulty setting reasonable limits, and fear of saying "no." In addition, anxiety is likely to develop when people fear conflict or the strong feelings that often arise in the course of relationships. Fortunately, new communication skills can be learned through practice, and they are included in the CHAANGE anxiety treatment program. In addition, group therapy offers an excellent opportunity to develop communication skills within a safe and supportive environment.

The very first relationship for each of us is with our mother. Mother, from *matrix,* the Latin word for womb, is the first source of security, energy, and life support. Matrix is also the Latin root of the words *matter* and *material,* and thus our relationship with mother is the beginning of our relationship with the physical world. In his explorations of child development, Pearce (1977) points out that development proceeds through a sequence of "matrix shifts," a series of relationships that begins with the mother. This developmental progression moves from a relationship with womb, to mother, to Earth, to self, and finally to a relationship with higher power, or God. The success of each of these relationships is built upon the bond established in the preceding matrix. Anxiety will develop when bonding fails in any given matrix—when we are deprived of security and confidence about moving forward to the next stage.

The womb, Pearce suggests, offers three things to a newly forming life: a source of possibility, a source of energy to explore that possibility, and a safe place within which that exploration can take place. Whenever these three needs are met, we have a matrix, a base for emotional growth. But while physical growth will take place under almost any circumstances, emotional growth requires more favorable conditions. For example, if the mother is anxious during pregnancy, producing the fight/flight response with activating steroids passing through the placenta, the infant will be surrounded by anxiety. In this case, stress rather than safety is offered, and the infant's anxiety will be carried forward into the next relationship and next stage of development. This can be repeated at any stage of development, jeopardizing emotional growth and transmitting anxiety into adulthood.

On the other hand, each matrix offers an opportunity to compensate for inadequate bonding in earlier stages; each relationship provides an opportunity to recover from anxiety created in earlier stages. From the safe place of a matrix, we can become more emotionally secure and make test flights into the unknown of the increasingly larger and more complex worlds ahead. But, paradoxically, in order to grow emotionally and overcome anxiety about the unknown, we must separate from the safe matrix and confidently explore the next stage. Security in relationship with the mother, for example, only translates into security within the world or with the self if the child can separate and move on successfully. This is the primary way we develop self-confidence and emotional independence.

Relationship skills seem to develop in a pattern that corresponds to these stages of biological development. The relationship to womb takes the nine or so months to develop from conception to birth, followed by a period of some seven years to complete the bonding process with the mother. During these seven years, rapprochement—exploratory forays into the larger world apart from mother—takes place within the safety and security of the mother matrix. When this process is successful, the child "graduates" to a new relationship with the world, the Earth matrix. This relationship develops between the ages of 7 and 11, roughly, followed by a shift to a new relationship with the self. Puberty is then marked by an emphasis on a relationship with the self. When all goes well, anxiety is minimized and self-confidence is maximized.

In many cases, however, the developmental process is marked by inadequate bonding and traumas that raise the potential for anxiety. As discussed elsewhere, anxiety disorders are more likely to develop when a particular personality type forms as a result of early family relationships. When self-confidence is damaged by criticism, secrecy, lack of safety, love contingent on performance or accomplishments, repression of feelings, and so on, the anxiety personality takes shape. Anxiety becomes a disorder waiting to erupt. All it takes is an overload of stress.

Pearce (1977) does not address adult relationships, since his work is focused on child development. However, his concept of relationships as the safety zone and energy source for emotional growth can certainly be applied to adult relationships. Emotional development is a lifelong process that does not end with adolescence, and relationships throughout the lifespan can provide the feedback necessary for emotional growth. Indeed, I believe that love relationships are the most helpful—and challenging—setting for emotional as well as spiritual growth.

Intimate love relationships provide the most useful feedback for emotional and spiritual growth because that is where we are most exposed. There are few places to hide in an intimate relationship, and our "hot buttons"—our emotionally sensitive spots—are more likely to be activated. This can actually be an advantage, if both partners recognize that an intimate relationship is a growth opportunity. In my opinion, the true purpose of a love relationship is to foster emotional and spiritual growth. A love relationship is a partnership designed to bring out the best in each partner, and to help both fulfill their individual goals and purpose in life. Briefly, my view of the purpose of life is to live a life with purpose. Purpose is not something to be determined intellectually, but rather something to be discovered and recognized by the heart. Purpose in life is a highly individual matter, and a love relationship can help both partners discover their unique purpose and achieve personal goals.

The way a love relationship fosters emotional growth is similar to Pearce's description of the bonding process. If bonding is adequate in an adult relationship, there is less likelihood of anxiety about emotional growth. Growth generally requires facing the new and unknown, and a love relationship can provide a safe base from which to do this. An intimate relationship can provide the support for learning, exploring, experimenting, and taking risks. By affirming the self-worth of each partner, a love relationship can enhance emotional growth and the journey of self-discovery.

But emotional growth often requires processing old business—issues brought to adult relationships from the past. Usually, unresolved issues go back to our families of origin, where key experiences affected our personality development. Incest, loss, divorce, or any number of significant experiences may have a lingering impact that can surface as anxiety in an intimate relationship. For example, based on a twenty-year follow-up study Wallerstein and Blakeslee (1989) document that the long-term impact of divorce on children includes problems with commitment in relationships when adulthood is reached. Sexual abuse is another example of a past experience that can surface in the form of anxiety in an intimate relationship, as discussed in Chapter 15. As Lerner (1989) points out in *The Dance of Intimacy,* even the anniversaries of past traumas can raise anxiety in an intimate relationship. Therefore, the process of solving problems in an intimate relationship may require dealing with much older or deeper issues. This may be painful, but it is the shortest path towards personal growth and healing.

A love relationship can be an opportunity for healing emotional damage that may have taken place in the family of origin. For example, where self-esteem has been damaged due to critical rearing or conditional love from parents, an adult love relationship can compensate by offering unconditional love. Where abuse of any kind may have occurred in childhood, an adult love relationship can offer acceptance, trust, love, respect, and sensitivity. And where an anxiety disorder may have already erupted in childhood or adolescence, an adult love relationship can provide a safe atmosphere for recovery.

Unfortunately, some people recreate their dysfunctional family relationships in their adult love relationships. They may marry a partner who has characteristics similar to a parent towards whom conflicting or negative feelings are harbored. In most relationships these recreated patterns are mutual—both partners are attracted to each other in a kind of unconscious drama to re-create old family patterns. Yet these recreated patterns provide opportunities for resolving unfinished business. In this sense, there is a higher purpose to relationships, an opportunity to grow emotionally through work within the relationship. Whether the relationship is healthy or unhealthy, or whether it survives or not, is often difficult to predict. Nevertheless, every love relationship is inherently an emotional and spiritual growth opportunity.

This view of love relationships is explored by Vissell and Vissell (1984) in *The Shared Heart*. A husband-and-wife therapy team, Vissell and Vissell tell us that the deeper we go with another person, the more we learn about ourselves. In other words, the less we hide, the more we grow. But a deep relationship involves many trials and tribulations, and can be like a hot fire that burns us in our places of vulnerability and imperfection. Our longings for love and security, however, combined with a commitment to growth, enable us to benefit from a love relationship. As Vissell and Vissell put it,

> The deeper the relationship, the more imperfection is brought to the surface. The deeper our longing for love, the more light floods our being, and the dark

> shadows of fear, doubt, pride, anger, jealousy, greed (and many others) emerge for their last stand. They are exposed by our desire for truth, and then transfigured by the light of love (p. 4).

Relationships, then, can be both a source of anxiety and an anxiety recovery opportunity. Relationships, particularly intimate relationships, require trust, commitment, openness, and love. Intimacy can raise anxiety for those who have been hurt, disappointed, or deprived in previous relationships. To protect ourselves, we may hold back, or keep some doors closed, although this will limit growth for both ourselves and our relationships. Or, as Lerner (1989) points out, anxiety may lead to pushing too hard for reassurance in a relationship. On the other hand, as Vissell and Vissell (1984) point out, our longing for love can motivate us to take some risks and, ultimately, to find healing in intimacy.

A love relationship can heal in several ways. First, unconditional love and acceptance can compensate for past emotional deprivation or betrayal. In fulfilling a deep human need, love affirms the self-worth of the loved person, even if self-worth has been damaged in past relationships. Within limits, humans are resilient and capable of changing their self-concepts as a result of positive feedback and love. Second, love provides the safe matrix, as Pearce (1977) points out, for interacting without anxiety in the larger world. In addition, love heals by opening the heart, which allows for positive feelings, along with the possibility of letting go of past emotional pain. Furthermore, love is the basis of forgiveness, which, in turn, is a way to let go of old hurt and anger.

A love relationship can help in anxiety recovery for just these reasons, since anxiety recovery involves learning new skills, replacing negativity, acquiring confidence in one's ability to handle new challenges, and so on. Facing feared situations, for example, is a challenge that requires self-confidence along with new skills. In the best of worlds, true love offers support for making the effort, knowing that "failure" will not jeopardize the relationship. With the right attitude, many of the opportunities for growth in intimate relationships can help with the anxiety recovery process. Love and trust in a relationship can counteract anxiety and other emotional problems caused by earlier life experiences.

Recognizing the important role of relationships in anxiety recovery, the CHAANGE program provides a letter to be given to a key person in the patient's life. The Dear Family Member letter, which is sent home early in treatment, discusses anxiety, and offers some dos and don'ts for those close to the anxiety sufferer. At the same time, the letter acknowledges that the anxious person's loved ones may have their own feelings about living with the condition, such as frustration, resentment, helplessness, depression, guilt, and fear. In asking the family to help enhance anxiety treatment, the letter advises a safe, low-pressure atmosphere, without impatience or checking on the recoverer's progress. It also sends a message that true anxiety recovery takes place when it is the responsibility of those going through it—when there is no doubt that recovery is accomplished by their own efforts. In keeping with this message, loved ones are urged to allow the anxiety recoverer to work the program on his or her own, but in an atmosphere of love and support.

Here is the CHAANGE program's letter to family members:

Dear Family Member:

As you may know, severe anxiety is extremely frustrating and incapacitating—not only for persons dealing with it directly, but also for those in their families. We know how difficult it must be for you and thought it might be helpful if we gave you some information about the condition and about things you might do that can be helpful and productive for the person close to you.

We view this condition as a physiological response that is brought on by an overload of stress in the life of a person who is typically intelligent, controlled, capable, sensitive, and perfectionistic. These heretofore unexplained bodily reactions are painful, misunderstood, and, therefore, frightening. The accompanying fears, worries, and anxieties are intense and consume an enormous amount of energy. Because it takes so much energy just to get through each day, those suffering are truly exhausted and emotionally wrung out by the day's end. During this exhausting period of their lives, people dealing with this condition have intense feelings of fear of being left alone in this state, and they are afraid that they would not be able to cope alone. They feel they cannot be separated from their family or close friends, on whom they must rely. The fear that they might be separated from, or rejected by, those close to them is overwhelming and stressful in itself. Therefore, it will be most helpful if you will try to do whatever you can to discourage this fear of separation through constant reassurance that you will "see it through" with him/her.

As your loved one is becoming used to new habits and patterns, she/he may have many ups and downs. The progress may be slow but steady over a period of several months. There may be frustrations for all of you, and much support and reassurance will be necessary. It has been our experience that those suffering from this condition are exceptionally bright, strong, strong-willed, sensitive people who are as resistant to change as are the rest of us! There may well be times when setbacks occur, but this is all a necessary part of the process of changing habits that have been established for years.

During the next weeks, when the focus will be on learning new and better ways of coping and regaining control, we suggest that you be as understanding and caring as possible. It has proven to be extremely helpful if you can give the feeling that you do, indeed, understand how hard this is, even if you don't understand the condition totally. Knowing that you really care will be encouraging and supportive in the arduous task of overcoming anxiety, and will help to shorten the recovery time. Because the nature of the condition is such that one is extremely sensitive to being judged, criticized, or rejected, it is counterproductive and will prolong the recovery time to insist that one "pick yourself up by your bootstraps" or that one is being ridiculous or silly.

We do not view this condition as a mental illness. It is behavior that is directly related to a physiological reaction to a constant state of fear in a strong, perfectionistic, controlled, and sensitive person. Since it is a learned response, it can be unlearned. This is what we will be doing—helping your affected family member unlearn unhealthy and nonproductive patterns and habits and replace them with more productive ones.

It is our hope and belief that it won't be long before all of you in your family regain control of your lives again and get on with the business of life, as well as have happier and more carefree times.

Many family members have asked us to spell out exactly how they can help while their loved one is going through our program. The following suggestions will be the most helpful things you can do during the next fifteen weeks:

1. Make a deliberate point not to talk about any symptoms—either yours or theirs or anyone else's. (People with anxiety are extremely suggestible and tend to take on symptoms.)

2. Let the program be their program, let the homework be their homework, and let the progress be their progress. (One of the things that has happened, due to the condition, is that most sufferers become more dependent than they want to be, and by letting this be their program it will begin to reinforce independence again.)

3. Try not to monitor their progress. Do not ask such questions as: "Are you all right?" "Are you sure you can do this?" "Do you feel up to going to such and such place?" (In other words, do not treat them as though they are sick—they certainly are not. Instead, they are dealing with a condition that will take a relearning process to deal with. It is not an illness, but a learned pattern.)

4. Try hard not to be critical or condescending. It is important that you be as positive and approving as possible, as well as accepting and nonjudgmental.

The more supportive you are of them, the more helpful you will be, and the more successful will be their recovery.

Living with someone who is severely anxious is stressful. Loved ones and family members may themselves need support and help. Family and friends may have a variety of reactions and feelings, which they may have difficulty keeping under control. Here are some of their common reactions and feelings:

Confusion: How can this possibly be just anxiety? I don't understand why everything is such a big ordeal.

Fear: What if she/he stays this way? What if the doctors missed something? Maybe she/he *is* going crazy or having a serious illness.

Depression: We don't have fun anymore. We're never happy.

Anger: This is not the person I married. What's wrong with her/him? I can't do it all by myself. Why can't she/he just get it together?

Guilt: Maybe it's my fault she/he is like this. Why can't I help better? What am I doing wrong? Is there something wrong with our marriage?

Loneliness: If I tell her/him what I'm feeling, that would be a burden. I can't tell other people what we're going through.

Resentment: What about my feelings and needs? She/he is trying to control me! She/he must be exaggerating. This is taking over—I have no freedom.

In addition to the suggestions in the CHAANGE program's Dear Family Member letter, there are some additional guidelines that can be helpful to a person going through anxiety recovery. To help a loved one succeed in anxiety recovery, here are some additional guidelines to remember:

Don't make assumptions about what she/he needs—ask!
Be consistent and predictable.
Let her/him set the pace for recovery.
Strive to find something positive in every effort.
Do not enable avoidance behavior. Negotiate steps in facing the fear.
Don't sacrifice your own life and build resentment.
It's okay to be anxious yourself and to say so.
Be patient and accepting, but don't fake it.
Setbacks are inevitable as people try new behaviors and challenges, but they do not mean going back to ground zero.
Some anxiety is necessary in the process of learning how to handle it.
New assertiveness may offend you or mix up the status quo. Seek counseling for yourself or for the relationship if needed.
Participate and support when asked. Don't get too involved unless wanted and requested.
Do not try to motivate with guilt ("We're wasting our money if you don't recover").
Read about anxiety to further your understanding.
Remember that your partner is the authority on what she/he feels.

Family members and loved ones can also help with appropriate comments. Here are some specific statements that would be helpful:

"Tell me what you need now."
"Go ahead and feel the anxiety—I'm here for you."
"Stay in the here and now. Don't anticipate the future."
"Don't what-if."
"Don't add the second fear."
"Face the fear and it will slowly disappear."
"It's not the place, it's the thought."
"Don't fight it. Float through it."
"Breathe slow and low."
"I'm proud of you. You're courageous."
"I love you no matter what."

One final idea from family therapy and systems theory is that a relationship is most receptive to change during a crisis, when the equilibrium of that system is out of balance. When the crisis is an anxiety disorder that leads to effective and successful treatment, everyone involved in the life of the anxiety sufferer can benefit. The skills learned in an anxiety treatment program, which lead to more independence and self-confidence, will usually cause a positive shift in relationship dynamics. In this sense, an anxiety disorder can be a disguised opportunity for growth and freedom, not only for the anxiety sufferer but for all who are touched by that special person.

20

Spirituality and Anxiety

> *A life of vain struggle can be relieved of pressure and anxiety and yet remain as vacuous and meaningless as before.*
>
> Adin Steinsaltz, *The Strife of the Spirit*

Is it possible that our lives have purpose, and that there are built-in feedback mechanisms to let us know when we are off track? Is it possible that anxiety is such a feedback mechanism—a signal system and a form of communication—whose function is to inform us that something is wrong or that we have lost our way? Is it possible that a crisis of severe anxiety is a disguised opportunity for change, improvement, and greater fulfillment? What would these possibilities mean for anxiety treatment and recovery? These are some of the questions to be explored in this chapter.

To begin viewing anxiety from a spiritual perspective, ask yourself, "What is the opposite of anxiety and fear?"

What comes to my mind are inner qualities such as peace, contentment, self-confidence, courage, safety, optimism, hope, and faith that things will work out. These are spiritual qualities, and they are the goals of anxiety recovery for most sufferers. Indeed, these life goals are desired by most people, although there is much confusion about how to achieve them. Anxiety inhibits these qualities, but in recovering from anxiety there is an opportunity to enrich our lives with these blessings. In seeking relief from anxiety and fear, we are more likely to be open to change in order to attain those elusive spiritual qualities.

No one would argue against the idea that anxiety is a form of suffering. Anyone with an anxiety disorder would attest to this. However, suffering is one of life's most powerful incentives for personal change and growth, and therefore it always has potential as a spiritual teacher. It is often a feedback mechanism, alerting us to a need for reevaluation and self-correction. By viewing anxiety spiritually, as an opportunity for redirection, it can become an opening to greater wholeness.

In this respect, effective anxiety treatment must include a spiritual dimension, and the therapist must be able to see the hidden potential and meaning in anxiety symptoms. Anxiety treatment must become more than a matter of symptom reduction or elimination, which is no simple accomplishment in itself. It must encompass the ideas of wholeness and spiritual development, whereby anxiety is understood as a call for acquiring skills for living more effectively, more completely, and more from the heart.

Roger and McWilliams (1991) offer a helpful distinction between what you *think* you want and what you *really* want. What you think you want falls into the category of concrete things, such as money, job or career, house, car, family, sex, educational degree, and travel. However, these things are actually *symbols* for what you really want or *methods* for obtaining it. What you really want are *inner experiences,* such as security, self-worth, freedom, satisfaction, self-respect, peace of mind, relationship with God, and love. These inner experiences are spiritual, in that they are deeper and nonmaterial, although they can be accessed through the material world. The symbols for what we really want quickly lose their luster, and they do not satisfy an inner longing for something more fulfilling, something more spiritual. There is nothing wrong with wanting the symbols, which are like flowers on the path of life. However, as we shall see, it is important to know that some things in life are essentially the means or methods for getting what you really want.

Confusion between what you think you want and what you really want contributes in several ways to anxiety. First, if you have the anxiety personality, you are likely to stress yourself out in the pursuit of your goals, or what you think are your goals. Second, if you do not recognize the distinction between external symbols and inner fulfillment, you are at risk for disappointment and frustration, and therefore more stress. Imagine having everything you thought you wanted. Surrounded by everything you wanted, consider how disappointing it would be if material things did not satisfy your deeper needs for security, love, purpose, and meaning. The happiness and excitement resulting from possessions, accomplishments, and symbols of success can only be temporary without inner fulfillment. Furthermore, if you mistake inner fulfillment for the pleasure associated with a possession or external symbol, you may become too identified with it and therefore fearful of losing it.

On the other hand, if you are aware that you want some things because you really want them, and that you want other things because you think they will help you have what you really want, you are more likely to experience personal fulfillment. You will make better judgments and fewer mistakes because you will be able to distinguish between the deeper qualities you seek and the methods for attaining them. In terms of anxiety recovery, if you want peace of mind, you could learn to calm your mind and let go of thoughts and worries. If you want contentment, the answer might be to learn how to want or appreciate what you already have. Knowing the distinction between what you really want and methods for attaining it will help clarify what is important to you and help increase your chances of fulfillment. In addition, knowing this distinction gives you the option of redefining your goals and focusing on what is really important to you.

What is the purpose of life, and how does it relate to anxiety and fear? Essentially, the purpose of life is to live a life with purpose. A life with purpose is one with a sense of direction, guided by the heart. You know you are serving your life's purpose by the feelings—the inner experiences—that affirm you are on the right path, like clues in a game of treasure hunt. You know you are off your purpose by symptoms, including anxiety, that signal you are going in the wrong direction. These signals may be difficult to decode, although they are often felt as physical sensations, such as weakness, mild nausea, and holding the breath. The heart feels full when you are with purpose and empty when you are without purpose.

One of the great mysteries of life is the question of purpose, and it is mysterious in part because each person's purpose in life is unique. You must discover your own personal life purpose. It is not something you decide about or achieve, but rather something you discover, accept, and honor. It is already within you, and it has already guided you to some extent. Your purpose is not really of your own making, although once it is discovered you must work to fulfill it. Your unique purpose awaits you, as if it were wisely assigned to you.

I experience my purpose as a beckoning or calling forth, as almost a magnetic pull in a particular direction, although I cannot make out the details of the landscape ahead. I have moments of awareness about the degree to which I am on course, about the extent to which I am fulfilling my purpose. When I am aligned with my purpose, I have energy, passion for life, and a sense of direction. I also feel a subtle gracefulness, even when I am suffering. On the other hand, when I deviate from my purpose, I become anxious, defensive, and tense. These are signals that help me realize that when I lose my way it is not the way that is lost, but rather that I have lost touch with myself. And yet fear sometimes arises as I face a phobic situation or new challenge and head in the right direction. For me, then, fear and anxiety play a significant role in keeping me on track.

Fear and anxiety can also be understood as resulting from a lack of faith or trust. Faith can be in yourself, based on sensing that you have the skills and resources to handle whatever may happen, or faith can be in a higher power to whom you can turn for guidance and direction. With faith, there is security and safety in life and a reassuring awareness that things will work out as they are supposed to. With faith, you can trust that whatever happens was meant to be. From the viewpoint of faith, there is only one basic fear, and all anxiety symptoms stem from it. Lack of faith is the root of anxiety and fear.

My spirituality developed without any religious training as a child. My father, who did not believe in God, related to his Judaism as an ethnic rather than a spiritual identity. My mother, referring to herself as an agnostic, celebrated Christian holidays such as Christmas and Easter as secular rather than religious events. The family never went to synagogue or church, although we observed some Jewish and Christian holidays such as Passover, Christmas, Chanukah, and Easter. Ours was an interfaith family, with no religious grounding. However, there were moral and ethical values in my family, with an emphasis on the difference between right and wrong conduct, similar to the fundamentals of any religion. No formal name was put on these values, and they were never considered spiritual or religious. Nevertheless, an interesting incident occurred at the age of 22, when I was a college student at Yale. As the war in Vietnam intensified, the Selective Service System ended the student deferment, and I applied for a military service exemption as a conscientious objector. Such status required a religious affiliation, but following an application and draft board interview, I was granted the conscientious objector classification. Apparently, the draft board considered my ethics to be equivalent to a religion.

As an adult I became a spiritual seeker, searching for answers to the existential questions of life and exploring many wisdom traditions. In the early years of this search, I could not comfortably use the name God, and I preferred to speak of spiritual energy and higher power. At that point, my spirituality had not yet integrated in a personal relationship with God. I studied Buddhism, Hinduism, Christianity, and Judaism, reading widely in classical and esoteric texts. As a result, I developed an eclectic spirituality. I became, as a friend joked, a "HindJew," or a "Judhist," and my religion was a synthesis of overlapping truths from many wisdom traditions. In addition, I traveled to a number of spiritual centers and communities, such as the Lama Foundation (New Mexico), Kripalu Center (Pennsylvania at the time), The Farm (Tennessee), Himalayan Institute (Chicago), Sivananda Yoga Center (Bahamas), as well as other spiritual places such as Rome, the Navaho and Hopi Indian lands in Arizona, and the Mayan ruins in Mexico. Had I more money, I would have traveled in India and the Orient at a time when I had a burning desire to experience the cultures of Hinduism and Buddhism.

My spiritual journey was part of my anxiety recovery process. As I began to answer the fundamental questions of life and death for myself, the ground became more solid and my insecurity, fears, and anxiety diminished. The fruits of my spiritual work came in many forms, including a sense of purpose, less fear and anxiety, more faith and trust in the future, a greater capacity for love, more personal power, a soulmate, and a personal relationship with God.

One of my questions was about the meaning of death. Death, of course, evokes tremendous fear and anxiety in many people. Why is death feared, and how does the fear of death affect our living? Although death cannot be separated from life, it is often treated as an unrelated event. Death represents the unknown, the ultimate loss of control, and separation from your physical identity. Considering the profile of the anxiety personality, particularly the need to be in control, discomfort with uncertainty, black-and-white thinking, and preference for structure and predictability, it is no surprise that for many of us death is cause for fear. As long as we fear death, we live with anxiety about many aspects of life, such as illness or symptoms that might be life-threatening, as well as uncertainty, unpredictability, and the unknown in general.

Death is a mystery because no one knows for sure what happens during and after death. Who has the credibility to tell us what death, or beyond, is like? Some clues are provided by individuals, such as Eadie (1993), who survived and reported their near-death experiences. The consensus of such reports is that death, or at least the moments immediately after death, can be safe and uplifting. Although reassuring, these reports are limited to the experience of dying, and do not answer the question of what happens beyond that. However, if we are willing to accept the possibility that some people are capable of communicating reliably with the dead, there is further reassurance. Rodegast (in Rodegast and Stanton 1985), who "channels" the teachings of Emmanuel, a deceased spiritual teacher, is one example. I spent a week with Rodegast at the Omega Institute in 1989, observing her communicate with Emmanuel, whose basic message about death is that it is absolutely safe—"like taking off a tight shoe." Here are some of Emmanuel's responses to questions about death:

> What does it actually feel like while we're dying?
>
> *Dying is akin to having been in a rather stuffy room*
> *where too many people are talking and smoking*
> *and suddenly you see a door that allows you to exit*
> *into fresh air and sunlight.*
> *Truly it is much like that.*

Matter becomes less dense.
Consciousness becomes less restricted.
Colors become more pleasant.
All the senses, finally released from the heavy cloak of the physical body
take flight with song.

What do we experience immediately after death?

There are as many individual ways
to leave a body
as there are to live in one.
Why is it supposed
that one's creative ability ceases
at the moment consciousness leaves the physical?

Other comments from Emmanuel on death:

If, in a lifetime, you find within your heart
the wisdom to forgive yourself
for your human imperfections,
there is a great possibility
that your death will be instantaneous
and extremely comfortable.

Death is nothing to be apprehensive about.
It is just part of a process
that you have been involved in for centuries.
You are not at the edge of an abyss.
You are merely taking another step
in your eternal existence.
Souls need ways to get out of bodies when ready.
My dears, why do you tremble so?
Death is a swinging door [pp. 175–181].

Emmanuel's messages about the safety and significance of death are consistent with teachings found elsewhere. For example, in the spiritual teachings of Meher Baba, as reported by Stevens (1957), we are told, "Death is like throwing away clothes which have become useless through wear and tear." Commenting on the fear of death, Meher Baba explains further,

> Some people are particularly afraid of the exact moment of death because they anticipate unbearable pain at that instant. In reality, all physical suffering experienced during illness or just before death terminates at the moment of death. The process of the actual dropping of the body is quite painless, contrary to the superstition that a person experiences indescribable agonies in death.

Meher Baba adds, "If death has any value, it is to teach the individual the true art of life" (p. 104). Likewise, Allione (1981), having researched the lives of "women of wisdom," tells us, "When you die the mind comes out of your body, like a piece of hair from butter" (p. 126).

The issue of death is at the core of most, if not all, religious and wisdom teachings. In some traditions, such as Hinduism and Christianity, there is an emphasis on the relationship between an afterlife and how you live before your death. Hinduism sees this relationship in terms of reincarnation. The essence of reincarnation is that your conduct determines the life circumstance assigned to you in future incarnations. In this spiritual system of cause and effect, your life circumstances are affected by your prior behavior. Thus, in Hinduism, you control your own destiny to a great extent, and since life goes round and round in an endless cycle, you have countless opportunities to improve your condition. Similarly, the essence of Christian teachings about death is that the quality of your life is judged after death, and your fate in the afterlife is based on how you conduct yourself in this life. Heaven or hell is where you go, determined by your choices and behavior on Earth. However, there is always an opportunity to counteract the consequences of wrongful conduct. Repentance, or recognition of your errors and taking responsibility for changing your ways, can lead to forgiveness and redemption. This is a hopeful teaching that puts you in control of your own fate.

The teachings of Judaism are similar, but differ in an interesting way as far as heaven and hell are concerned. Judaism is less preoccupied with the afterlife and more concerned with the consequences of your conduct in this life. Judaism takes life one year at a time, and you are rewritten into the book of life each year, based on the conduct of your life during the preceding year. In fact, there is a one-week window, between the high holidays of Rosh Hashanah and Yom Kippur, when you have an opportunity to make amends or correct any wrongful behavior, in hopes of affecting your fate for the coming year. In this tradition, heaven and hell are more immediate and accessible and, as in the other great wisdom traditions, you have some control over your fate and destiny. The common expressions "heaven on Earth" and "living hell" suggest that these conditions can be experienced in this life, not in the hereafter. Speaking personally, I have vividly experienced both states in my life, and I am convinced that these poignant experiences can be traced to my own behavior.

Anxiety recovery can be enhanced through a spiritual understanding of death. The world's great wisdom traditions all seem to agree that you have the power to determine your future, whether it is in this incarnation or the next. There is also an emphasis, in all spiritual teachings, on death as a passageway or step in the process of life. Death is not the end point, and does not need to be feared. We are not passive observers of our own life and death, and we can take an active, positive role in determining our future. We have choices, and, as we become more comfortable with the issue of death, we can let go of much fear and anxiety. Later in this chapter, I offer an exercise—Death Rehearsal—for working with our feelings about dying to enhance our living.

The anxiety personality has perfectionism, high standards, a need to please others, fear of rejection, and sensitivity to criticism as some of its most driving traits. If you have these traits, you are probably hard on yourself. You probably have difficulty forgiving yourself when you fail to live up to your unreasonably high standards. However, you can accelerate your anxiety recovery through greater compassion, love, and sensitivity towards yourself. Treat yourself as God would, with sensitivity, compassion, and forgiveness for your human imperfections. Or, to leave God out of it, treat yourself the way you would treat a friend who was down on himself or herself for a failure, mistake, or imperfection. What would you say to a friend in such a state? Would you not offer gentleness and love, and provide perspective by emphasizing your friend's good qualities and accomplishments?

As indicated earlier, no one would argue against the idea that anxiety and fear are forms of human suffering. As such, you can draw on spirituality to help overcome the suffering involved in fear and anxiety. I have personally found the teachings of Buddhism, Christianity, Judaism, and other spiritual traditions to be essential to my anxiety recovery. The wisdom of Buddhism has been helpful in its simplicity and practicality. It is said that after meditating for two years under a bodhi tree, Buddha pronounced his understanding of life, known as the Four Noble Truths. The first noble truth is that life is suffering, meaning that suffering is inherent in living. The second noble truth is that suffering is caused by attachment, craving, or desire. This includes attachment to our own thoughts and separate identities, an issue of special relevance for anxiety and anxiety recovery. The third noble truth is that freedom can be attained through nonattachment, or learning how to go beyond craving, addiction, attachment, and separateness. Finally, the fourth noble truth is that the way to nonattachment is through meditation, moral conduct, and wisdom.

Buddha's fourth noble truth is at the heart of anxiety recovery. Through meditation, we can transcend our obsessive thoughts, our need to control, our cravings, and our sense of separateness. Meditation also leads to peace of mind, the opposite of fear and anxiety. Living morally, another Buddhist recommendation and the essence of virtually all spiritual teachings, serves to prevent regrettable behavior, stress, and guilt, which are sources of anxious suffering. Finally, attaining wisdom is helpful because it is the basis for knowing that fear and anxiety are not life-threatening, and that it is never too late to overcome them.

There are a number of striking parallels between spiritual teachings, such as those of Buddhism, and effective anxiety treatment, such as the CHAANGE program. Both are therapeutic programs to help alleviate human suffering. Both involve learning to relax, let go, and attain peace of mind. Both involve cognitive change, or changing the way we think and react to our own thoughts. Both involve learning, although I would distinguish between education and wisdom. And, finally, both are experiential and advocate daily practice and development of life skills.

In the final analysis, it does not seem possible to be totally free from fear and anxiety without a spiritual viewpoint. Without a sense of a higher power, you are left with only psychology and pharmacology for facing fear and anxiety. And while these sciences are certainly powerful, they are limited compared to the force behind all life processes. Understandably, God is not a believable reality for some people, and for many years this was true for me. However, through advances in technology even the most rational, hard sciences now acknowledge the existence of an intelligent energy behind all life processes. In subatomic physics, for example, where matter can be viewed through magnification of more than a half-million power, the interchangeability between matter and energy is visible, and appears as a dance, having "charm," "wit," and "humor." In other words, the paths of science and spirituality are converging, and there is a new recognition of an intelligent power in the universe.

In medicine, an intriguing link has been established between health and spirituality. In an analysis of more than 250 health studies, Levin (1994) found a positive relationship between religious observance (prayer, church attendance, and declaration of belief in higher power) and physical and mental health. The overwhelmingly positive relationship between religious observance and health appears among men and women, different races, and among people with different geographical, educational, and medical histories. As a treatment provider, Koenig (cited in Isaacs 1994) affirms that spirituality can help with fear and anxiety. Koenig states, "Instead of struggling with the problem, focusing on it, obsessing over it, they [people with religious faith] are somehow able to give this problem up to God. They take the problem and place it outside themselves. They obtain control by giving it up" (p. 17).

Paradoxically, I find that some anxiety patients who were raised with religion have difficulty attaining spirituality and coming to terms with God. It appears that some religious background experiences, such as harsh discipline in religious school, boring church services, empty religious rituals, and moral teachings based on fear and threat, are traumatic for children. These experiences turn children off to spirituality or lead to a black-and-white attitude towards God. As a result, spiritual awakening in adulthood can be hindered, and some people may require healing from religious trauma before a spiritual attitude or personal relationship with God is possible.

In one case, a woman raised in a strict Catholic environment experienced abuse that interfered with her spiritual and emotional development. Paula, an attractive but quiet and passive woman, described a number of instances in which she was disciplined abusively by a nun in Catholic school. In one instance, she was smacked with a ruler on her hands in front of her class. In another instance, she was given a spanking over the nun's knee, again in the presence of her peers. What was most astounding, however, was that Paula's parents condoned the school's discipline methods, and she felt that they showed little concern for her feelings. Paula also reported that in her community, it was common practice for the Catholic priests to enter freely into the homes of parishioners, without knocking or prior notice. Combined with an abusive father and a passive mother, Paula's experience of religion was a mixture of fear, shame, and guilt. She was fearful of abandonment as well as punishment by authority figures. God apparently existed, but He was violent, unkind, and unprotective. As a result of her background, Paula had much to overcome before she could see God as benevolent, as a source of strength and reassurance in her anxiety recovery.

One of the most distorted ideas about God, as it relates to anxiety disorders, is that God is to be feared. In Christianity, a "God-fearing" person is one who believes in God and lives according to the commandments based on fear of God's wrath. Damnation, purgatory, and hell are the consequences of unholy living. In Judaism, it is advised that you should fulfill the *mitzvah* (good deed) of fearing God. Although these teachings are designed to encourage moral conduct and spiritual life, they are based on fear of God himself. In my view, it is not so much that God punishes us but that we create our own suffering by the choices we make. God's role may be more a matter of arranging for the consequences when we violate spiritual law, as well as providing opportunities for redemption, spiritual growth, and self-improvement. While God's interventions include negative consequences for wrongful behavior, they also include rewards for virtuous behavior. Grace, joy, strength, a sense of security, and inner peace accrue from living spiritually, and these blessings would be appreciated by all anxiety sufferers.

Without God or higher power, what is the basis for hope and dreams coming true? Without a source of inspiration, how could you hope to overcome anxiety, especially if you have suffered for a long time or feel that no one understands? First, and perhaps foremost, overcoming fear and anxiety requires belief in the possibility of change. You will only commit to anxiety treatment and the work required to change nonproductive habits if you have reason to believe change is possible. At the heart of all spiritual systems is the belief that it is never too late for renewal or change. This is the essence of hope: no matter how bad things become, it is always possible to turn things around. For anxiety sufferers, it is essential to know that change is possible, no matter how disabling the condition has become.

Overcoming anxiety means more than acquiring new skills. It also means developing personal power, faith in oneself, and trust in the universe. These are spiritual qualities, and a higher power, or God, is the wellspring from which these essential powers are drawn. As an anxiety treatment specialist, I can create a proper environment and provide the map for recovery, but there is something more to the process. Your commitment, my guidance, and a higher power are the alchemy for recovery.

With regard to anxiety and fear, one of the most unsettling aspects of the anxiety personality is the need for control. You feel most comfortable when you are in control, and most vulnerable and threatened when you are not in control. In your need to be in control, you seek routine, structure, and predictability, and you may even try to control other people in order to feel safe and secure. As a result, you may spend considerable time and energy anticipating the future, scrutinizing other people, and anxiously monitoring the environment, as well as your own body, so as to be prepared for whatever may happen. This approach is frequently at odds with life, which involves far too many variables beyond your influence to predict what will happen, let alone control it. As a more effective alternative, consider the idea that you are not in control but that you are nevertheless safe and secure. Who or what could provide such reassurance, other than a higher power?

Also consider the idea that your worrying and anticipating has little effect on what actually happens, and that to a great extent whatever happens was meant to be. This could only be possible by virtue of a higher power. You can gain control by giving up control, by putting it in the hands of a higher power. This does not mean you become passive, but that you do your best and leave room for life to unfold according to larger plans. Nor does this mean you should blindly trust or passively accept whatever happens. As a Sufi saying warns, "Trust God, but tie your camel."

As for who or what is in control, there are only two possibilities. One is that the universe is random, chaotic, and unregulated, and that you must exert control in order to feel safe. The other possibility is that the universe is lawful, ordered, and intelligently structured, in which case you do not need to be in control. We each choose and live by one of these two beliefs, although we may vacillate with uncertainty between them. For me, the universe is lawful, ordered, and intelligently structured. But even though God is in control, I must still do my part and work in collaboration with God. This point is delightfully illustrated by the story of a man who prayed every night to God to help him win the lottery. Every night, he would appeal to God to make it possible for him to win the Megabucks Lottery: "Dear God, I promise to do only good with the money. Just give me a chance to win, and prove myself." Night after night he prayed, but there was no response, until one night he heard a voice say, "Would you at least meet me half-way, and purchase a lottery ticket!"

In what language does God or a higher power speak? This is another one of life's big questions, one that has caused immense confusion and even led to war. I raise the question not as a matter of politics, but in terms of how to understand the meaning of fear and anxiety and how to use higher power in anxiety recovery. God seems to speak in a variety of formats, including symbols, dreams, images, synchronicities, and, for some attuned listeners, spoken words. Spiritual messages are often received in code, and may require deciphering or interpretation. God also speaks in the form of anxiety. Anxiety symptoms serve as warnings about stress overload, poor nutrition, insufficient rest, and other forms of inattention to the body's needs. Some may say that this is a matter of biology, not spirituality. But what about anxiety that arises when we are about to do something wrong, use bad judgment, or make poor choices? Perhaps God is speaking through such anxiety, providing us with a built-in moral smoke detector.

It is said that God's voice can be heard most clearly in stillness and silence. This is what is meant by the biblical passage, "Be still and know that I am God." In quiet moments, when you are relaxed and still, you are more open to receiving spiritual messages. Caddy (1977), co-founder of Findhorn, a spiritual community in Scotland, shares a personal experience that illustrates this kind of communication:

> I was aware of a great noise all around and then the noise died down and there was great stillness. In the stillness I could hear what seemed to be the faint ticking of a clock. As I listened very intently, the sound became louder and clearer.

> Then I heard the words: "I am always here but unless you become consciously aware of Me and of My divine Presence, you cannot hear My voice. Therefore, still that which is without so that you can hear that which is within." [p. 24].

In my own life, a number of similar experiences stand out as illustrations of God speaking to me. The experiences all took place in quiet moments—during the night or early in the morning—while I was relaxed, open, and turned toward God. One instance was a dream, occurring at a time of personal change and high anxiety, which seemed to come in response to my asking God for guidance. In the dream, I saw a room with a floor, three walls and no ceiling. It looked like a psychologist's office, decorated simply with the symbols of my profession, floating in space. In the dream I asked for guidance and heard an answer in what sounded like my own voice, but with words that seemed to come from a profound, other source. The words were, "Paul, follow your heart and everything will work out." Considering that I was about to leave a secure position to relocate across the country, the floating psychologist's office might have symbolized the upcoming relocation of my work, offering reassurance that I would be able to resume my practice elsewhere. As I reflected on the dream, I realized that God spoke to me in my own voice, and in my own persona. I experienced what Muktandanda (1974) meant when he frequently instructed:

> *Kneel to your own Self.*
> *Honour and worship your own Inner Being.*
> *Chant the mantra that is always going on within you.*
> *God dwells within you as you.* [p. 68]

In another memorable encounter, I experienced a lucid conversation with God. The occurrence took place, again, at a time of personal turmoil and high anxiety, when I turned to God for guidance. The dialogue is etched in my memory, and continues to reassure me. This is the exact exchange of words:

Me: Dear God, will you be there for me?
God: Yes, I am there every step and every minute.
Me: Will I be O.K.?
God: Yes, everything will be O.K.
Me: What will happen?
God: Whatever happens, everything will be O.K.
Me: Can you tell me what will happen?
God: There are many forces, currents, and crosswinds operating, which will affect the details. Look beyond, and know that everything will be O.K.
Me: I see the sun rising, and I feel that things will be better for me. Can I trust that?
God: The rising sun represents hope and dreams coming true. Everything will be O.K.

Notice the universal yet personal quality of God's responses to my questions. God is speaking to me, but with a kind of broadly applicable truth that feels valid, profound in its simplicity, and reassuring.

Spirituality, or soul, takes form in the human body, and we must understand this to fully understand anxiety. The idea that the physical body is a temple, a dwelling place for spirit, has a long history. Many biblical references to the body as a temple for God can be found, such as: "Do you not know that you are the temple of God, and that the Spirit of

God dwells in you?" (I Corinthians 4:16) and, "Or do you not know that your body is the temple of the Holy Spirit who is in you, whom you have from God, and you are not your own?" (I Corinthians 7:19). Another example, presented almost as a warning, is the passage, "If anyone defiles the temple of God, God will destroy him. For the temple of God is holy, which temple is you" (I Corinthians 4:17).

Steinsaltz (1988) indicates that "the soul of man functions through its instrument or vessel, which is the body." Addressing the relationship between soul and body, he explains,

> Just as the union of body and soul gives life to the body, so does it wrap the soul in material substance, providing it with the powers of the physical body. This is not a one-way process. The soul not only gives something to the body, vital force and life, it also gets something from the body, from the body's connection with matter and form, its physical capacities, its channels of perception, and its various links with both material and the immaterial worlds (p. 57). The contact and mutual attraction between body and soul creates a contingency, a unique situation, generating the human self, which is neither body nor soul but a merging of the two (p. 62)

If the body is a dwelling place for soul, or spirituality, what is the effect of fear on this relationship? In writing about the spirituality of the body, Lowen (1990) says, "Fear has a paralyzing effect on the spirit. It freezes the body, contracting the muscles. When this state persists, the body becomes numb, and the individual no longer feels his fear. This is the state in which most people come to therapy" (p.

79). Fear diminishes spirituality by contracting the body, as though squeezing spirit out of its dwelling place. Frequent anxiety causes the body to develop a protective pattern of muscular tension—body armor—which closes the door to feelings and spiritual energy. Thereafter, any strong feelings, including anger, sadness, and joy, but especially fear, are threatening and can produce panic attacks or other forms of severe anxiety. Lowen's work indicates that it is possible to increase spirituality through muscle relaxation and breath work, which open the body to inflow of spiritual energy. This was, indeed, the basic idea behind the work of Reich (1961), who used the term *orgone* in reference to spiritual energy. In addition, it is possible to release fear through an infusion of spiritual energy. This may help explain why spiritual study and certain spiritual practices, such as meditation, prayer, yoga, and cultivation of a personal relationship with God or higher power, seem to enhance anxiety recovery.

How can you increase spiritual awareness and cultivate a personal relationship with God? Like any meaningful goal, it is necessary to work toward it and give it time, attention, and energy. The result can be what Pearce (1981) calls the "bond of power." As an anxiety sufferer, you are already a sensitive person and have a disposition towards spirituality. Here are some suggestions for how to further develop your spirituality:

EXERCISES FOR SPIRITUALLY VITALIZING YOUR LIFE

Meditation: Meditation is the most essential spiritual practice, and should be practiced daily. In the quiet stillness of meditation, it is easier to attune to higher vibrations and the inner voice of God. Instructions for meditation practice are found in Chapter 8.

Spend time with nature: Spending time with nature brings you in contact with higher energies, and the world as it is. Nature helps you come out of yourself and increases your awareness of forces larger than yourself. This was known to naturalists such as Henry Thoreau, John Muir, Ansel Adams, and others, and it is the basis for the preservation of nature in our national parks system. In addition, fresh air invigorates the spirit by increasing intake of prana—spiritual energy.

Spiritual reading and study: You can cultivate spirituality through reading and study. The possibilities for spiritually inspiring reading are unlimited. They include biographies of great spiritual figures, such as Gandhi, Martin Luther King, Sri Aurobindo, Buddha, and Christ, books about spirituality, and spiritual text itself. A page or two a day can feed your growing spirituality.

Practice relaxation: You will be more open to spirituality when your body is relaxed and free of tension. The flow of life forces is greatest in a loose and receptive state. Stretch your muscles and exercise regularly. Check your breathing frequently to ensure that it is deep and full.

Develop physical strength and health: Health, energy, and strength are necessary for overcoming anxiety, as well as for joyful living. Health, energy, and strength increase personal power and enable you to do the work of anxiety recovery. Proper nutrition, adequate rest, and exercise are ways of building and maintaining these capacities. Hatha yoga, strength training, and the martial arts are also effective approaches.

Social support group/spiritual family: Spiritual energy and God often work through and between people. This is expressed in the biblical passage, "Wherever two or more are gathered in my name, there shall I be." It would be helpful to participate in a support group, preferably one with spiritual inclinations. Book discussion groups, therapy groups, self-help groups, and church/temple activity groups are all possibilities.

Volunteer service: Some professions, such as psychology, call for a percentage of "gratis work," service that is offered free of charge to those in need. When you volunteer your time and energy without material gain, or even perform a simple act to help another, you profit spiritually. In Judaism, performing an act to help another is called a *mitzvah,* a spiritual deed for which you are blessed by God. Volunteer work in your community, such as coaching an athletic team, chaperoning a school event, participating in a "green-up" day, providing meals-on-wheels, all bring you closer to God.

Tithing and giving: Giving to a spiritual cause is another way to increase your spirituality. This can include charitable donations of money or goods to organizations that represent your spiritual values, including church or temple or secular organizations, such as environmental efforts, public radio and television, and community service organizations. Taxes are enacted by congressional law, but spiritual giving comes from the heart and therefore enlarges your spiritual dimension.

Travel: An excellent way to transcend your ego and gain perspective is to travel, where you can see how other people live and deal with life. Travel expands your awareness, and usually your appreciation for what you have. If you can afford to travel, you are likely to notice that the majority of other people are less fortunate. This will help open your heart. However, you do not have to go to exotic places to expand your awareness. Visit any major American city for a course in life. On the other hand, seeing the awesome beauty of places around the world can also draw you closer to God.

Feelings: Getting out of your head and into your feelings and intuition can help develop your spirituality. Learn how to identify, experience, and express your feelings as a path to spiritual openness. Some techniques are offered in Chapter 13.

Practice love: Love is at the heart of all religions, and it is the primary vehicle through which spirituality is expressed. Practicing a loving attitude towards others, as well as towards yourself, is a powerful way to cultivate your spirituality. Remember that you usually get what you give.

Interact with God or higher power: It can be helpful to actively communicate with God by asking questions and listening for answers. I have a running dialogue with God, in which I ask for guidance with virtually every decision in terms of its compatibility with my higher purpose. You can consciously dedicate every act to enhancing your spirituality. It can also be helpful to place symbols of your relationship with God in locations you encounter daily, such as doorways, refrigerator, desk, computer, car, bathroom mirror, and so on. The symbol can be a flower, a cross, a Star of David, a holy name, or whatever. Each time you notice the symbol, take a second to remember God or affirm your spirituality.

EXERCISE: DEATH REHEARSAL

Relax, breathe deeply, and close your eyes. Imagine, in whatever form it comes, that you are at the end of your life. Perhaps you are lying on your bed. Your physical incarnation is ending and you must say goodbye to what you have known. You are poised to go through the doorway into the next stage of existence.

What do you feel at this moment? How do you feel about the life you have lived so far? Was it the life you hoped for? Did you do what was important to you? If not, what was missing? Have you left anything unfinished? What would you have done differently? Is there anyone you need to talk to, and if so, what do you need to say? Reflect quietly on these questions for a while, and take note of your answers.

Now, inexplicably, a miracle has occurred. You are being offered more time, another chance. You are not at the end. You may re-enter your body and social roles on the stage of life.

Will you go on living as usual, or will your visit to the threshold of death help you live differently? Will you still avoid or hold back due to anxiety?

EXERCISE: WISE FRIEND

Relax, breathe deeply, and close your eyes. Imagine the wisest and most benevolent being possible. Perhaps this being has a physical form, or perhaps it is more of a presence without visible form. Feel or picture the qualities of wisdom, compassion, kindness, fairness, and love that radiate from this special being. This being is your Wise Friend.

Locate the "vectors" or whereabouts of your Wise Friend. Is your Wise Friend within you, above you, behind you, over your shoulder, or all around you? Use all of your senses to experience the presence of your Wise Friend. Practice making contact with this being through repeated visits, and cultivate a relationship by spending time together.

From time to time, you may have a deep question, and need an answer or sense of direction. Bring it to your Wise Friend, and quietly listen for an answer.

Your Wise Friend may communicate in "sign language." Listen and look for signs, in the form of feelings, dreams, images, or even words, that seem to come to you from another source.

21

Successful Recovery Stories

> *I now have a positive outlook on my life. I feel I am heading in the right direction for the first time in years. I believe that if I continue to use the skills and tools I have learned, with time and experience I can improve my life far beyond what I thought possible.*
>
> John, age 35, ten weeks into the CHAANGE program

More than fourteen thousand individuals have achieved lasting recoveries from severe anxiety through the CHAANGE program. This chapter contains some of their recovery stories. In all cases reported, the improvements described occurred within approximately sixteen weeks, the time period required to complete the program.

To appreciate the remarkable progress made by graduates of the program, let's begin with a brief look at the procedure used to measure progress. The success stories included in this chapter are based on the information provided by program participants on self-evaluation forms, at the beginning and end of the program. The evaluation forms ask for the following information:

- Times per week feeling panicky or severely anxious
- Hours per day troubled by anxiety
- Medications
- Degree of disturbance by phobic symptoms
- Degree of control over own life
- Degree of depression
- Situations avoided due to anxiety
- Frequency of avoidant behavior
- Comfort level in phobic situations

The complete self-evaluation form is reproduced in Appendix A.

DANIEL

The first recovery story is that of a young man who, like many anxiety sufferers beginning the CHAANGE program, had undergone previous therapy that was not particularly successful. As a man, Daniel was reluctant to admit a problem with fear or ask for help. However, Daniel, who was a shy 32-year-old married man with two children, felt dependent on his wife in order to do anything in a public situation. His anxiety disorder included panic attacks and avoidance of shopping, meetings, parties, church, movies and any type of gathering of people. His condition intensified to the point where he was unable to take his children to their sports events or scout meetings. He could not go grocery or household shopping, and he was unable to drive on an interstate highway.

Daniel was embarrassed and humiliated by his anxiety disorder. Besides his wife, the only other person aware of his problem was his supervisor, who recognized the anxiety condition and agreed to give him time off for therapy appointments. In addition, his employer offered to pay for the CHAANGE program.

Daniel described his condition on the pre-program evaluation as follows:

> Currently, everywhere I go and everything I do, I need to think about how it (the anxiety) can or will affect me during the activity. Fear has almost total control over my life and I feel that it has enveloped me and is smothering me. I don't want to spend the rest of my life with this fear.
>
> For two years I went to therapy. They diagnosed the condition as panic disorder, put me on imipramine and lorazepam, and I was instructed in proper diet, exercise, etc. Most of the therapy was desensitization techniques. It seemed to help toward the end but as soon as I finished therapy, the panic attacks started all over again."

Approximately 16 weeks later, upon completion of the CHAANGE program, Daniel described his progress in the following way:

> On a day-to-day basis, I feel very calm and comfortable with myself. The situations where I used to be slightly to moderately anxious, I now feel totally relaxed. I'm still working on the two biggest avoidances—shopping malls and church. I'm still scaring myself some and

need to work on that. Everything else seemed to come easy as I learned to relax. I'm confident that as I develop the technique for confronting the last two, everything will fall in place. I'm looking forward to getting on with my life and I see the light at the end of the tunnel.

A summary of Daniel's recovery, showing progress measured by the evaluation forms, is displayed in Table 21–1.

TABLE 21–1: DANIEL'S RECOVERY PROGRESS

Anxiety Factors	Pre-CHAANGE	Post-CHAANGE
Times per week feeling panicky	5	1
Hours per day troubled by anxiety	8	.5
Medications	None	None
Phobic symptoms disturbance (1–8 scale)	7	3
How much control over my life (1–8 scale)	3	6
How depressed I feel (1–8 scale)	7	1
Phobic situations: avoidance		
Shopping malls	Always	Sometimes
Church	Always	Often
Grocery stores	Sometimes	Never
Being in crowds	Often	Sometimes
Phobic situations: comfort level		
Shopping malls	Panicky	Uncomfortable
Church	Panicky	Very uncomfortable
Grocery stores	Very uncomfortable	Comfortable
Being in crowds	Very uncomfortable	Slightly uncomfort.

In a follow-up appointment one year after completion of the CHAANGE program, I learned that Daniel was actually coaching his son's Little League baseball team! Daniel's recovery from anxiety also allowed him to socialize with people during the children's school and community activities, as well as go to church, shop, and enjoy life.

HARRIET

Let's now look at the recovery achieved by Harriet, the 37-year-old woman who was unable to come by herself to the first few appointments due to her fear of driving. Harriet was introduced earlier in the book. A married school teacher with three children, Harriet was referred by her physician after revealing a severe anxiety condition. Initially, Harriet was tearful and depressed about her inability to control her fear. The condition became so intense that she required her husband to accompany her to any new situation, including her initial appointments with me. To get to work she would offer to pick up a colleague who lived on the way to school, in order to avoid being alone in the car. During the work day, Harriet would become anxious just thinking about the drive home. Like many sufferers who have panic disorder with agoraphobia, Harriet spent considerable energy anticipating and worrying about every trip out of the house.

At the outset of treatment, Harriet described her condition on the pre-program evaluation as follows:

> Presently, this condition is making it difficult to focus on daily activities. I'm nervous about driving nearly all the time so I am often uncomfortable and scared I'm

> going crazy. In addition, I feel depressed, which triggers its own set of anxieties.

Approximately sixteen weeks later, Harriet described her progress on the post-program evaluation form as follows:

> At present, I feel 85–90 percent recovered. I am driving everywhere I need to drive without panic and I am beginning to drive other places a little at a time. I am finding myself using the relaxation techniques when I start to feel anxious. Deep breathing seems second nature now. I am without doubt more comfortable in my work environment. I can sit through meetings and lunch with co-workers and practically relax!"

The details of Harriet's progress are summarized in Table 21–2. Notice that Harriet was able to discontinue her medication, and her depression completely lifted. In addition, the amount of time spent worrying was reduced to "maybe 5 minutes" per day.

LISA

Lisa's recovery story is interesting because it illustrates so clearly the role of stress in the onset of anxiety symptoms. Lisa was referred to me by her physician shortly after she developed food poisoning from a meal at a restaurant. At the time, there had been an outbreak of salmonellosis traced to the eggs served at several restaurants in the area. The newspapers featured articles on the severity of the disease, including cases of fatal illness.

TABLE 21–2: HARRIET'S RECOVERY PROGRESS

Anxiety Factors	Pre-CHAANGE	Post-CHAANGE
Times per week feeling panicky	15–20	1–2
Hours per day troubled by anxiety	4–5	"maybe 5 min."
Medications	Xanax 25 mg/day	None
Phobic symptoms disturbance (1–8 scale)	7	1
How much control over my life (1–8 scale)	1	7
How depressed I feel (1–8 scale)	5.5	0 ("Yeah!")
Phobic situations: avoidance		
Driving	Sometimes	Seldom
Going alone far from home	Always	Never
Phobic situations: comfort level		
Driving	Panicky	Slightly uncomfort.
Going alone far from home	Panicky	(Unrated)

Lisa was 34 years old and had no history of panic attacks or severe anxiety. However, Lisa had a mild but generalized feeling of discomfort and anxiety in many situations, which were sometimes avoided. She was predisposed to developing a severe anxiety condition due to the personality and sensitivity factors that were discussed earlier in the book. In Lisa's case it was the food poisoning that triggered her fears of losing control and dying. Although she was put on Xanax medication by her physician, the early detection of severe anxiety and appropriate referral by Lisa's physician was important in her rapid recovery. Effective psychological treatment at such an early stage of Lisa's anxiety prevented years of suffering that might otherwise have developed. I am certain that without proper help Lisa would have developed a fear and avoidance of restaurants, as well as a phobia about certain foods.

On the initial self-evaluation form, Lisa described her condition as follows:

> I experience some anxiety attacks from time to time, but I feel I have more generalized anxiety. I tend to worry a lot about the future and people closest to me. Since experiencing anxiety symptoms, I'm often frightened about them happening again. I would like to learn to control my anxiety in order to be able to enjoy my life more fully. I also would like to live my life with less of the "shoulds." I feel a need to be more in touch with my wants and needs. I would hope to learn to channel my energies into positive things instead of worrying and the resulting stress it causes. I do not feel I have a problem with depression, although sometimes the anxiety symptoms make me somewhat discouraged at my current inability to fully control them.

Just before the end of the sixteen-week CHAANGE program, Lisa discontinued her anxiety medication. She felt much more control over herself and was no longer troubled by anxiety. Like many CHAANGE graduates, Lisa still needed to practice doing the things that were previously avoided or anxiety-producing. With some situations, such as doctor or dentist appointments, the opportunities for practice were infrequent and would require more time. In her own words, this was Lisa's post-program status:

> At present, I feel that I am progressing well in dealing with my anxiety. I am continuing to practice the skills I have acquired throughout the CHAANGE program . I am doing more of the things I once avoided and I am

> experiencing less discomfort. I have stopped taking the Xanax medication as of a week or so ago. I feel good about being free of the medication. It seems nice to practice being unafraid without the influence of the Xanax.
>
> I fully intend to continue using the things I have learned in the past sixteen weeks. I now realize that to feel good, I must take care of myself both physically and emotionally. I also understand that normal anxiety is a natural feeling in certain situations and nothing to be frightened by.
>
> I am also beginning to feel more comfortable with other feelings (sadness, excitement, etc.) and bodily reactions (aches, pains, fatigue). I believe that I am becoming more accepting of myself and also of others.

A detailed summary of Lisa's progress on the anxiety factors is displayed in Table 21–3.

JENNIFER

Jennifer's recovery story illustrates, once again, the role of stress in severe anxiety. Jennifer's symptoms indicate how difficult it is for some people to identify the source of their stress. In her case, Jennifer would wake up in the morning shaking and trembling all over for no apparent reason. When people cannot understand the reason for such a reaction, their fear intensifies and more body reactions are triggered. A cycle of panic anxiety develops as the increase in body reactions leads to more fear, as discussed in Chapter 2.

Jennifer had a history of health problems but she did not recognize the relationship between stress and her

TABLE 21–3: LISA'S RECOVERY PROGRESS

Anxiety Factors	Pre-CHAANGE	Post-CHAANGE
Times per week feeling panicky	2–3	0
Hours per day troubled by anxiety	10–12	0–1
Medications	Xanax 1.5 mg/day	None
Phobic symptoms disturbance (1–8 scale)	4	2
How much control over my life (1–8 scale)	4	7
How depressed I feel (1–8 scale)	2	0
Phobic situations: avoidance		
Shopping malls	Often	Never
Grocery stores	Sometimes	Never
Being in crowds	Sometimes	Sometimes
Going into crowded shops or stores	Often	Sometimes
Going alone far from home	Seldom	Seldom
Phobic situations: comfort		
Shopping malls	Uncomfortable	Comfortable
Grocery stores	Uncomfortable	Comfortable
Being in crowds	Uncomfortable	Slightly uncomfort.
Going into crowded shops or stores	Very uncomfortable	Slightly uncomfort.
Going alone far from home	Uncomfortable	Slightly uncomfort.

health. She developed a phobic fear of physical symptoms, along with fears of losing control and dying.

In addition, Jennifer's story shows the pattern of avoidant behavior that develops as people try to protect themselves from anxiety. She often avoided crowded shops and stores because of fear that she would become anxious and lose control of herself. A fear of being noticed by others if she were to lose control in public added to Jennifer's anxiety.

Jennifer was 36 years old, married, and had two children. Although she did not work outside the home, she transported her children a considerable distance to a private school on a daily basis, did community volunteer work, and maintained a large home that she and her husband had built themselves over a period of many years. The family also had a home business in addition to her husband's salaried job. It was apparent to me that Jennifer's stress level was high, but from her point of view the problem was that she was "not good enough" to handle it.

On her initial self-evaluation form, Jennifer described her condition as follows:

> Every morning I wake up with my legs shaky and my entire body in a nervous state. Sometimes something as simple as talking on the phone and trying to hold on to a conversation will send my body into an uncontrollable tremble from head to foot, and I find it very difficult to continue on my daily chores. Because of this shaky condition I avoid situations where I need to converse with other people because the trembling makes it difficult at times to even talk straight.
>
> Over the past ten years I have had numerous health problems due to stress. Just recently with the start of my body trembling as severe as it is I was referred by my physician to seek help from a professional dealing with stress and anxiety. I was directed to Dr. Paul Foxman, who introduced me to the CHAANGE program.

Sixteen weeks after beginning the program, Jennifer completed the post-program form. You will notice in her progress summary that like many others who participate in CHAANGE, Jennifer was able to discontinue her anxiety medication. She progressed from daily anxiety episodes to one per week. Her morning body tremors discontinued completely, not only because she was able to relax herself but also because she was no longer afraid they would occur. She had developed the self-confidence that she could handle anxiety if it were to occur. Jennifer's comfort level improved, particularly in her most feared situation—being in crowds and public places. In her own words, this was Jennifer's status at the end of the program:

> I've been feeling pretty good lately. The holidays were extremely busy and I had a harder time making quiet time for myself. I still have a couple of health problems which tend to bring me down a little sometimes, but I don't think that's unusual of anyone. I have no more body tremors because I know the relaxing techniques I've learned through CHAANGE will help. I can't say that I feel totally cured of the agoraphobia, but considering the state I was in several months ago, I'm doing real good.

Jennifer's anxiety recovery progress is summarized in more detail in Table 21–4.

RACHEL

Rachel's recovery story is another example of stress-induced anxiety, as well as of ability to discontinue medication after a relatively brief treatment. Rachel was introduced previously in Chapter 15, in the discussion of

TABLE 21–4: JENNIFER'S RECOVERY PROGRESS

Anxiety Factors	Pre-CHAANGE	Post-CHAANGE
Times per week feeling panicky	7	1
Hours per day troubled by anxiety	5	0–1
Medications	Lorazepam .5 mg/day	None
Phobic symptoms disturbance (1–8 scale)	4	2
How much control over my life (1–8 scale)	4	7
How depressed I feel (1–8 scale)	4	1
Phobic situations: avoidance		
Standing in lines	Often	Seldom
Driving	Sometimes	Never
Shopping malls	Sometimes	Seldom
Crowded stores	Often	Sometimes
Being in crowds	Often	Sometimes
Phobic situations: comfort level		
Standing in lines	Very uncomfortable	Slightly uncomfort.
Driving	Slightly uncomfort.	Comfortable
Shopping malls	Uncomfortable	Slightly uncomfort.
Crowded stores	Very uncomfortable	Slightly uncomfort.
Being in crowds	Panicky	Slightly uncomfort.

sexual abuse and anxiety. When she started anxiety treatment, her stress included the recent deaths of both her parents. Rachel worked as a nurse on a medical-surgical unit at a hospital, another high stress factor. In addition, Rachel and her husband had moved several times in the process of relocating, selling a home, and building a new house, all with three children. Her style of approaching all activities was perfectionistic and compulsive.

The most interesting aspect of Rachel's story was that her recovery from anxiety allowed her to face an issue that was affecting her deeply. She had always been uncomfortable and anxious around "a certain kind of person." People perceived by Rachel as controlling, powerful, or dominating made her feel frightened and helpless. Rachel would become either passive and compliant or resistant and stubborn when she was around such people. This pattern led to difficulties at work with colleagues, particularly supervisors and other authority figures. As it turned out, Rachel was sexually abused by an older brother on several occasions at the ages of about 11 and 14. As an adult, Rachel had absolutely no memory about the abuse until after she overcame her panic disorder through the CHAANGE program. In fact, Rachel returned to therapy several months after completing CHAANGE in order to deal with some dreams she was having about being sexually abused, even though she was free of previous anxiety symptoms.

At the outset of anxiety treatment, this is how Rachel described her condition:

> I view my condition as a struggle to find a balance, to find more confidence. Some days I feel very good but other days I feel overwhelmed. At work I have extreme anxiety and panic ½ to ¾ of the time. In social groups I have extreme anxiety all the time. Church ranges from uncomfortable to panic.
>
> I am feeling good ½ of the time. The panic anxiety tends to discourage me and lowers my self-esteem. Especially in situations where I have had panic before, my anxiety level is high just thinking about going into that situation.

Notice the compulsive style reflected in Rachel's use of language. Her perfectionism, need for control, and difficulty with feelings—key aspects of the anxiety personality—are reflected in her language.

Rachel's recovery was remarkable in the amount of progress made in sixteen weeks, especially with respect to the feared situations. Note that in her pre-program evaluation Rachel offers an excellent explanation of how fear becomes linked to specific situations: "Especially in situations where I have had panic before, my anxiety level is high just thinking about going into that situation." Within sixteen weeks she was able to unlink this connection and control her anxiety. She was able to resume normal functioning in the many previously avoided and feared situations. In her own words, this was Rachel's progress as she completed the program:

> I have not had a panic attack in about a month, maybe longer. My worst phobic situation, in-law family gatherings, is more comfortable. I have had no panic attacks in those situations. If I avoid those gatherings now it is because of a choice to do other activities and I am overtired and have been under a lot of stress.
>
> I am much better about setting limits and taking care of myself. When I am under more stress because of work, I let things go at home. If my children are demanding a lot of my time during summer vacation, I let things go around the house that I would try to do while they were in school. I have a new pattern of exercise which includes walking and running 5 times/week. I am reviewing the CHAANGE tapes for the second time. I enjoy doing relaxation in the mornings and at night as a treat to myself, but it is automatic in anxiety or anger situations.

Rachel's anxiety condition before and after the CHAANGE program is summarized in Table 21–5.

TABLE 21–5: RACHEL'S RECOVERY PROGRESS

Anxiety Factors	Pre-CHAANGE	Post-CHAANGE
Times per week feeling panicky	5	0
Hours per day troubled by anxiety	4–5	0*
Medications	Prozac 20 mg/day	None
Phobic symptoms disturbance (1–8 scale)	6	1
How much control over my life (1–8 scale)	4	8
How depressed I feel (1–8 scale)	4	0
Phobic situations: avoidance		
Shopping malls	Sometimes	Never
Church	Sometimes	Never
Grocery stores	Sometimes	Never
Being in crowds	Often	Seldom
Walking on busy streets	Often	Seldom
Crowded stores	Always	Seldom
Going alone far from home	Always	(Unrated)
Social groups	Often	Seldom
Phobic situations: comfort level		
Shopping malls	Slightly uncomfort.	Comfortable
Church	Panicky	Comfortable
Grocery stores	Panicky	Comfortable
Being in crowds	Panicky	Slightly uncomfort.
Crowded stores	Panicky	Comfortable
Going alone far from home	Panicky	Comfortable
Social groups	Panicky	Slightly uncomfort.

* "1–2 times/week but I accept anxiety better and relax before it goes to panic."

JOHN

John's case of panic disorder with agoraphobia demonstrates the interaction of a medical problem and anxiety. A competent and perfectionistic computer engineer, John's first anxiety experience occurred in his early twenties, when he went through an extremely painful attack of kidney stones. Several subsequent kidney stone episodes, combined with a series of other gastrointestinal problems, left John with an ongoing fear of another medical trauma. He overreacted to every abnormal physical sensation or symptom, fearing that pain or a panic attack was near. John's marriage suffered as a result of his anxiety disorder, and he was referred to me by a psychologist working with the couple. A prior therapy experience approximately six years earlier resulted in no significant improvement in John's anxiety.

John described his anxiety condition as he began the CHAANGE program as follows:

> I feel my condition was brought on and is sustained by health problems. These health problems are not life-threatening but they make normal social interaction very difficult. I have a chronic hyper-acidic stomach causing gas, cramping, diarrhea, and constipation. This condition occurs at all times and does not appear to be caused by anxiety, although anxiety greatly worsens it. This problem is kept under control for the most part by medication (Pepcid).
>
> I have had four kidney stones, two in 1976, one in 1979, and one in 1991. They caused an *extremely* painful attack lasting several hours each, brought under control only through heavy pain medication (morphine, Demerol). Kidney stone attacks leave a person totally helpless and dependent on medical care. The attacks are unpredictable and can happen at any time. I also suffer from constant sinus attacks involving moderate–severe pain, dizziness, and weakness.

> These health problems create anxiety when I have to travel or have social or family obligations.

It is apparent even in John's initial description of his anxiety that loss of control is a key issue, as it is for most anxiety sufferers. He also uses the word "attack" frequently, suggesting that he feels like a victim of his health problems. John's case illustrates how physical pain can be a basis for anxiety, but also how anxiety exaggerates the pain. Fear of fear is also evident in John's case.

What is remarkable about John's recovery story is how quickly he gained control, and how much progress he made in a short time, in spite of suffering for fifteen years starting with the first kidney "attack" until he started the CHAANGE program. Here is John's evaluation of his own progress at only ten weeks, just over halfway through the program.

> I feel I have made significant progress. While I do not consider myself "cured," I have much more confidence now than before. I am now aware that anxiety in general is quite common, even among those who are not considered agoraphobic. It only becomes problematic when a person lacks the tools, skills, and confidence to properly cope with anxieties.
>
> I have also learned that certain elements of my personality can cause unnecessary anxiety. I have a tendency to be a perfectionist and sometimes expect too much of myself. I am too critical of myself and have to learn to develop a more positive outlook. This will take time. I cannot change my personality entirely, but I understand that I can modify it with guidance and persistence.
>
> I no longer try to avoid situations that make me feel uncomfortable. I have had significant success at fac-

ing these situations and I am developing the confidence I need to overcome more difficult obstacles. I realize that life can sometimes be difficult but I am building the confidence I need to cope with these situations.

I still suffer from relatively minor but annoying health problems that sometimes cause my difficulties. I have had success at reducing and sometimes eliminating the anxiety that used to accompany these problems causing varying degrees of debilitation. This has helped significantly. With the anxiety out of the way, I plan to improve my health through proper diet and exercise.

I now have a positive outlook on my life. I feel I am heading in the right direction for the first time in years. I believe that if I continue to use the skills and tools I have learned, with time and experience I can improve my life far beyond what I thought possible.

A summary of other aspects of John's progress is displayed in Table 21–6.

These inspiring recovery stories offer hope and demonstrate that with effective treatment severe anxiety can be overcome. Sadly, only 25 percent of those who are suffering do reach out for help, and many of them receive inappropriate and unsuccessful care. Most anxiety sufferers who seek help begin with a physician or hospital emergency room, but typically they are not referred to an anxiety treatment specialist. In cases where a mental health referral is made, the therapist may not have training in severe anxiety treatment or offer a structured approach to anxiety recovery.

Anyone who has an anxiety disorder can contact the CHAANGE headquarters or other national organizations listed in Appendix B, and ask for a list of anxiety treatment specialists. When contacting the specialists in your area to

TABLE 21–6: JOHN'S RECOVERY PROGRESS

Anxiety Factors	Pre-CHAANGE	Post-CHAANGE
Times per week feeling panicky	4–5	"significantly less"
Hours per day troubled by anxiety	2	"less than 1"
Medications	Pepcid 40 mg/day	Pepcid 40 mg/day
Phobic symptoms disturbance (1–8 scale)	5	3
How much control over my life (1–8 scale)	2	5
How depressed I feel (1–8 scale)	6	2
Phobic situations: avoidance		
Church	Often	Often
Being in crowds	Sometimes	Sometimes
Going alone far from home	Often	Often
Planning future events	Often	Sometimes
Scheduling future events	Often	Sometimes
Flying	Often	Often
Phobic situations: comfort level		
Church	Slightly uncomfort.	Slightly uncomfort.
Being in crowds	Slightly uncomfort.	Slightly uncomfort.
Going alone far from home	Uncomfortable	Uncomfortable
Flying	Uncomfortable	Slightly uncomfort.

inquire about their programs, request a brochure or other printed material on their approach, credentials, and experience. Review and evaluate the information for its compatibility with your needs and preferences. Once you have selected a therapist, make an appointment or talk on the telephone and be satisfied that you have found the right person to help you recover from anxiety.

May you overcome anxiety and live fearlessly.

22

Questions and Answers

Asking is the beginning of understanding.
Paul Foxman

As a specialist in treating anxiety disorders, I have worked with hundreds of anxiety sufferers over a period of many years. During this time, numerous questions have been asked by patients during their therapy and recovery process. This chapter presents some of the most frequently asked questions and my responses. I have selected questions that represent common concerns about severe anxiety and the recovery process. In addition, a few unusual but interesting questions are included.

Will I get over my anxiety disorder completely, or will I have it on and off for the rest of my life?

Many people do recover completely from their anxiety disorders, and thereafter experience only "normal" fear and anxiety. You can realistically expect to overcome your fear of fear and any avoidant behavior patterns you have developed to protect yourself from anxiety.

Anxiety recovery can be defined as having the skills and confidence to know that you can handle anxiety, whenever and wherever it might occur. Paradoxically, when you trust that you can handle anxiety, it is much less likely to occur. Even if you experience no anxiety for months or years, you are *recovered* only when you no longer fear it. At that point in anxiety recovery, you will no longer worry or remain in a state of anxious anticipation.

Overcoming anxiety is largely a matter of relearning and developing new skills and thinking patterns. The primary ingredient in successful recovery is motivation and commitment to the change process. Most anxiety sufferers are highly motivated for recovery because of the intensity of their emotional pain and because of the life restriction they endure. If you are motivated and receive appropriate help, you are likely to succeed in long-term recovery.

As you begin to feel better and experience relief from anxiety symptoms, your motivation may *decrease*. You may be tempted to discontinue your practices before you replace anxiety-creating habits with new patterns. In order to maintain your recovery, you must continue to implement what you have learned. In some areas, such as exercise, proper diet, and stress management, you will need to take care of yourself on an ongoing basis.

Anxiety recovery will not change your personality, although it will involve some modifications to the way you think, handle feelings, and behave. Furthermore, anxiety treatment will not alter your basic biological sensitivity. Therefore, you will always be somewhat at risk for stress symptoms and strong reactions to many stimuli. However, with proper help and a successful initial recovery, you will no longer fear your own reactions.

I'm concerned that I've had this anxiety condition for so long. How long will it take to recover?

Recovery from long-term anxiety usually requires professional help. However, the good news is that the success of proper anxiety treatment is not directly related to the length of time you have suffered. Many people who have suffered profoundly for twenty-five or thirty years are able to recover successfully. On the other hand, long-term anxiety usually reflects strong maladaptive thinking and behavior habits. Such habits are powerful and will yield to change only with sustained effort. Therefore, a strong commitment to change and a willingness to stay with it in spite of inevitable relapses are necessary for recovery. If you are willing to do the work and you have proper guidance, you can recover successfully.

Naturally, the success of treatment depends on the qualifications of the professional you choose. It is important to work with a therapist who believes from direct experience that anxiety recovery is possible for virtually everyone who is willing to do the work. A structured anxiety recovery program, administered by a skilled and experienced professional, is advised. The CHAANGE program is an excellent example of a structured anxiety treatment process. A state-by-state listing of CHAANGE-affiliated therapists is available from the national office at CHAANGE (see Appendix B).

As you may know from my own anxiety story, I personally suffered with severe anxiety for many years, beginning in childhood. Although I am free from fear, I do not take my recovery for granted. I continue to practice what I teach, and I am susceptible to relapses of anxiety when I am under high stress or fail to keep balance in my life. However, even when anxiety does occur, I recognize what it is and I do not fear it.

As for how long it takes to recover, it is important to distinguish between the time period for acquiring the necessary skills and the time required for complete recovery. The CHAANGE program, for example, takes approximately sixteen weeks to complete. This is a learning period, within which you acquire information and practical skills. At the end of the program, you will have acquired all the information and skills needed for successful recovery. Most participants in the program report significant improvement by the end of the sixteen weeks, evidenced by discontinuing anxiety medications, having less anxiety and worry, feeling more relaxed and in control, and beginning to engage in previously avoided activities and situations. However, it is necessary to continue practicing until the new skills become automatic habits. Complete recovery can take from four to eighteen months, depending on a number of issues. These include motivation level, learning style, stress level during the treatment period, and coexisting issues such as relationship difficulties or health problems.

I have had other therapy that didn't help. Can I still recover?

Yes, you can still overcome your anxiety, despite your unsuccessful prior therapy experiences. To understand why your past therapy was ineffective, I would need to know much more about it. Was it a structured anxiety treatment program or an insight-oriented psychotherapy? Was the therapist trained in anxiety treatment? Was your presenting problem one of anxiety, or did you present other issues as your primary concerns? What was the diagnosis used by the therapist during the treatment?

The National Institute of Mental Health reports that only 25 percent of anxiety sufferers seek help, and of that percent most receive inappropriate or ineffective care. A startling 98 percent of those who seek help for severe anxiety are treated with tranquilizers for up to fifteen years, with no significant improvement. It is likely that you fall into the category of those who did not receive appropriate or effective treatment.

Naturally, you are skeptical about anxiety recovery, based on your disappointment with past efforts. You are probably hesitant to commit to another treatment effort, in spite of your dream of freedom from fear and anxiety. Here are some things to consider, to help you develop a more optimistic attitude:

1. With appropriate and effective treatment, you will know within approximately eight weeks if your anxiety condition is improving. In the CHAANGE program, for example, you would complete a progress evaluation at approximately eight weeks, and compare it to your initial self-evaluation. You do not have to spend months in therapy before you know if it is working. If it is not working, you have the option to discuss your lack of progress, or to discontinue the treatment.

2. It would be helpful to talk with some other people who have overcome their anxiety disorders. You can ask your therapist to put you in touch with others who suffered from a similar form of anxiety and who recovered successfully. For example, I have a list of names of former patients who have offered to talk with anyone who is considering the CHAANGE program. Another option is to participate in group therapy or a self-help group, where you can meet other people who are in the recovery process. It can be reassuring to know that others like yourself have recovered or are making progress towards recovery.
3. Keep in mind that severe anxiety is a treatable condition, in spite of the fact that so many people receive inappropriate and ineffective help. For example, the National Institute of Mental Health reports that when properly treated, there is a 70 to 90 percent recovery rate for panic disorder. The success rate for the CHAANGE program is in this range, and this method has helped approximately fourteen thousand people who suffered from panic disorder, agoraphobia, generalized anxiety disorder, post-traumatic stress disorder, and other forms of severe anxiety.

Can low blood sugar cause panic attacks?

Blood sugar level does play an important role in anxiety, although it does not directly cause panic attacks. Blood sugar is the fuel for energy and most body functions, and it is influenced largely by the intervals between meals, as well as the quality and sugar content of the foods you eat. Sharp *rises* in blood sugar, resulting from intake of sugared foods and refined carbohydrates, are associated with increases in adrenaline. Adrenaline, as you know, is the activating hormone in anxiety symptoms and fear. *Low* blood sugar, resulting from poor eating habits and poor diet, produces symptoms such as fatigue, irritability, blurred vision, mental confusion, and weak or "strung out" feelings. These symptoms are also commonly associated with fear and anxiety. As a biologically sensitive person, you may react emotionally to your body's symptoms and believe something is wrong. When changes in blood sugar level are sudden, such as the sharp rises and drops caused by intake of sugared foods and the neutralizing action of insulin produced by the body to control it, you may react with panic anxiety or fear.

The first step in counteracting this pattern is to understand the circumstances that affect blood sugar level, so that you do not fear your own body changes, reactions, and symptoms. The next step is to adjust your diet and eating habits to maintain steady blood sugar level.

Fluctuations in blood sugar are typically caused by the types of food you eat and your eating schedule. For example, both high and low blood sugar levels can be caused by a diet that is high in sugar and refined carbohydrates. Such foods overwork organs such as the adrenal glands and pancreas, interfering with their ability to control blood sugar level. An overworked pancreas, for example, is unable to properly produce insulin, a blood sugar regulator. Without proper insulin production, your blood sugar fluctuates uncontrollably, causing physical, emotional, and mental symptoms. Therefore, a diet emphasizing complex carbohydrates that provide consistent energy release is advised. Low blood sugar level can also result from too long an interval between meals. It is important to eat regularly, and perhaps more frequently in smaller amounts, to maintain consistent blood sugar level. In addition, keep in mind that your nutritional needs vary from day to day based on activities, season, and stress level. Tune in to your body's needs and respond accordingly.

I was having sexual relations and as I became aroused and my breathing became erratic, I had a panic attack. Why did it happen when I didn't want it to?

Sexual arousal has many qualities that are similar to anxiety. Sexual arousal involves activation of the cardiovascular, respiratory, glandular, and other organ systems, and such activation is virtually identical to the mechanisms in anxiety. Normally, sexual arousal is pleasurable. However, if you are fearful of arousal, as is common among those with severe anxiety, you might react to some aspect of sexual arousal as a signal of impending panic anxiety. Your erratic breathing appears to have triggered the panic, perhaps because it reminded you of hyperventilating during past anxiety reactions. Your fear probably intensified as your arousal increased, and you spiraled into panic anxiety.

As an anxious person, you probably have a high need to be in control, and you probably spend considerable time watching for signs of impending anxiety. You may be on guard, uptight, and tense. In order to feel comfortable with sexuality, you must relax and let go. Sexual orgasm, in fact, is a letting-go experience, and orgasmic release is only possible when you give up control. Therefore, another issue to explore is your ability to relax and give up control for the sake of sexual pleasure.

Another question is whether you have any feelings towards your mate, such as anger or resentment, that might interfere with intimacy. You may need to resolve any conflicts or negative feelings before you can enter comfortably into sexual intimacy. Also consider the effect of stress, or other negative concerns, on your ability to relax and let go sexually.

Does guilt have something to do with my anxiety?

In some cases, guilt does play a significant role in anxiety. For example, I have worked with a number of people whose anxiety was a form of self-punishment. These individuals were unconsciously punishing themselves for past behavior about which they felt guilty. In one case, a woman felt she deserved to suffer for an extramarital affair she had prior to the death of her husband. In another case, a death cause by an automobile accident left a survivor with tremendous guilt. Those who feel they deserve to suffer have a high risk of developing an anxiety disorder. The probability of anxiety increases even further in people who fit the anxiety personality profile.

Guilt is a method used in some families to control behavior. If you were raised with guilt as a method of control, you may be accustomed to feeling guilty about your thoughts or behavior. You may also tend to take too much responsibility for the behavior of others, as if you were the cause of their problems.

If you are a religious person, who believes in punishment by God for wrongful behavior, anxiety may arise as a result of something you feel guilty about. In this case, your belief system will determine the degree of guilt, and associated anxiety, that you may experience.

My biggest problem is waking up in the morning trembling all over. I can't think of anything that would cause the trembling. Can you explain it?

It certainly is confusing and frightening to wake up trembling for no apparent reason. However, there are several explanations to consider. One likely reason for the trembling is that in the morning your mind may begin to focus on all the things you expect to accomplish during the day. You may be overwhelming yourself with plans and expectations, in which case your body will react as if it is actually being stressed. A related possibility is that there may be some unpleasant aspect of your life to be faced during the day ahead.

Another possibility is that relaxation may be anxiety-arousing for you, and you are probably the most relaxed in the morning after sleeping. Relaxation may be frightening if you have a high need for control or if you are generally on the lookout for danger or threat. In addition, lying in bed is the most vulnerable body position, and this may challenge your sense of control.

Also consider the possibility that your blood sugar is low in the morning, since you have not eaten for many hours. Your trembling could be a sign of weakness from low blood sugar and a signal that you need to refuel early in the day. Try breaking fast immediately upon rising in the morning, with diluted fruit juice or fresh fruit.

One further possibility is that mornings are a "phobic" time of day for you, due to having had previous anxiety episodes in the morning. If this is the case, your body may "remember" morning anxiety and may anticipate a reoccurrence. As you know, when you anticipate having an anxiety episode, your body becomes activated in defensive preparation for it, and the likelihood of panic or severe anxiety rises sharply.

The best way to handle the trembling is to practice your relaxation skills in the morning and to change your dialogue about what the morning trembling means. Reassure yourself that anxiety is not life-threatening, that you can handle it with your new skills. Replace any "what-if?" thoughts with "so-what's." In addition, morning may be the best time for you to exercise and energize yourself for the day ahead. Finally, make sure you have a healthy carbohydrate morning meal, after breaking fast early in the day with diluted fruit juice or fresh fruit.

What is the relationship between anxiety and depression? Do I have two conditions, or is one caused by the other?

Depression almost always accompanies an anxiety disorder as a secondary reaction to the inability to control anxiety symptoms. Considering the personality profile of people who develop severe anxiety, which includes a high need for control, the feeling of losing control is discouraging and depressing, especially when it is prolonged.

Several other issues add to the secondary depression. Anxiety sufferers frequently feel dependent on others, such as a spouse, for security. For example, you might develop an emotional dependency on another person if you cannot face certain situations alone. Such dependency makes you feel like a child, especially if you experience separation anxiety in the absence of a security figure. One example was a man who experienced panic anxiety whenever his wife went out of town on business. His anxiety would also emerge whenever his wife was late coming home from work or meetings. The fear of separation made this individual feel dependent and unable to handle even a few hours on his own, which contributed to feelings of shame and depression.

Another factor is the exhaustion and fatigue that typically occur in chronic anxiety. It takes energy to worry and to always be on guard against anxiety. Inevitably, this wears you down, leaving you tired and drained. This condition overlaps with one of the most common symptoms of depression, namely lack of energy. Chronic fatigue leads to a loss of interest in activities that once were pleasurable, another common symptom of depression.

Other symptoms of depression are likely to develop along with severe anxiety. They include hopelessness, social withdrawal, life restriction, and even suicidal thoughts or feelings. Hopelessness is likely to develop if you believe that you cannot overcome the anxiety condition. The hopelessness is intensified if you project this belief into the future and assume that you must suffer with anxiety for the rest of your life. I have noticed that hopelessness also makes it difficult for anxiety sufferers to have faith. If you believe in God, you may feel abandoned if your wish to overcome anxiety does not seem to be answered. If you do not believe in God, it will be difficult to acquire a spiritual attitude as long as you are suffering with anxiety.

If your phobic situation involves crowds or interacting with other people, you may develop a pattern of social withdrawal. Social withdrawal and isolation are life-restricting and add to the secondary depression. Life restriction is inevitable if you begin to avoid activities such as travel, shopping, socializing, or exercising.

Anxiety can damage your self-esteem and lead to depression. Virtually all of the secondary consequences of anxiety, including fear of losing control, hopeless feelings, fatigue, life restriction, pessimism about the future, and emotional dependency, affect your feelings about yourself. You simply cannot feel good about yourself when you are experiencing these depressive aspects of anxiety.

It is obviously important to have a proper diagnosis for your anxiety disorder. Unfortunately, because depression is commonly associated with anxiety, some sufferers are misdiagnosed as having a primary depressive disorder. Counseling and medication for depression differ from the treatment for an anxiety disorder and therefore it is essential to identify the primary condition.

Fortunately, I can say with complete confidence that the secondary depression in anxiety disorders usually clears up with anxiety recovery. I have personally witnessed hundreds of cases that bear this out. Furthermore, in the CHAANGE program, participants are asked to rate how depressed they feel at the beginning and end of the treatment. The results indicate that the degree of depression invariably decreases as progress is made in anxiety recovery.

Can a person have a panic attack in the middle of the night while sleeping? I sometimes used to wake up with panic anxiety in the middle of the night.

Some people do, indeed, wake up with panic anxiety in the middle of the night, several hours after falling asleep. This is, of course, a terrifying experience because you have no warning signal, and you feel out of control and vulnerable.

Panic anxiety in the middle of the night can be triggered by several causes. First, the mind is active even during sleep, and can generate anxiety-provoking thoughts that are powerful enough to interrupt sleep. Such thoughts, and the resulting anxiety, are no different from what can occur during the day. However, because you are sleeping, you are less likely to be aware of the anxiety-arousing thoughts.

Another factor is the lowering of defense mechanisms during sleep. In order to fall asleep, you must reach a degree of relaxation and letting go. When you are tired, this comes more easily. However, as you relax, you also let down your guard, and you become more vulnerable to your own thoughts. You are actually more vulnerable to influence by your own thoughts during sleep than when you are awake. Anxiety may result from thoughts concerning stress, worry, fear, or memories of painful or upsetting events.

Once an episode of panic or severe anxiety occurs during the night, you may begin to anticipate a repeat performance. Your anxious anticipation of another panic attack creates anxiety associated with sleeping, and you may then begin to produce the experience you dread.

It would be helpful to calm your mind before going to sleep. Practice your relaxation skills, or try meditating at night before bed. Dim lighting and peaceful music may also help to prepare for peaceful sleep. If you wake up in the middle of the night with anxiety, use your anxiety reduction skills, such as floating through, changing your inner dialogue, and using appropriate distraction. Sometimes, getting up to go to the bathroom, having a drink of water, and returning to bed will be sufficient to break the cycle and resume sleeping. Also keep in mind that this problem is likely to disappear as you progress in your anxiety recovery.

I know that learning to relax is necessary to recover from anxiety. But as soon as I start to relax, I get uptight and scared. How can I learn how to relax?

One aspect of the anxiety personality is difficulty relaxing, in spite of a desire to be calm. There are several reasons why relaxing is difficult for your type of personality. First, you like to be in control as a way of feeling protected and safe. Being in control means maintaining an alert, watchful, guarded, tense state of being. You are, in effect, in continuous fight/flight arousal. To relax requires that you let down your guard, trust, and open to the universe. This may be threatening to your sense of control and self-protection.

In addition, your body adapts to your emotional attitude. When you are habitually anxious or fearful, your body develops a self-protective rigidity or muscular armor. Like the hard shell of some animals, your body adapts physically to a state of self-protection in the form of chronic muscular tension. Such tension becomes your normal body experience. As you begin to relax, you may feel threatened and vulnerable, and as your fight/flight reaction is activated, tension returns.

You cannot be relaxed and activated at the same time. As result, your survival instinct must choose between the two states and, as a conservative defense mechanism, it will choose activation for self-protection. If you have tense body armor and a strong need for control, you will have to train your body to enjoy the safety of relaxation.

Another obstacle is the activity of your mind. Remember that your body responds in some way to virtually every thought. If you are unable to control your thoughts, your body is repeatedly activated. Thus, while you may be practicing your relaxation techniques, their effect may be canceled by the stimulation and stress caused by your thoughts. Learning to relax, therefore, may require that you learn to shut off or disengage from your thoughts.

One other issue may affect your ability to relax. If you mistake relaxation for laziness or nonproductivity, you may resist relaxation. It is important to realize that relaxation actually improves productivity because it restores energy and enhances efficiency.

Learning how to relax is similar to developing any new skill. It requires proper instructions combined with a will to learn, including devoting time and energy to practicing on a regular basis. Take several breaks each day when you can devote ten to twenty minutes to practicing relaxation. Using a cassette tape with relaxation instructions is advised. Play it several times a day during relaxation breaks. Several more times each day, think about relaxing while you are doing other activities that do not require intense concentration, such as washing dishes, folding laundry, or straightening up your office or home. In addition, consider learning how to meditate as a way of slowing down your mind. Be patient with these practices, and remember that you are replacing old, well-established habits and patterns. Also, remind yourself that slowing down and relaxation are safe, good, and necessary for survival and health.

I sometimes feel so different and alone because of my anxiety. How many people have this condition?

You are not alone as an anxiety sufferer. According to the National Institute of Mental Health (NIMH), approximately twenty-five million adult Americans suffer from an anxiety disorder severe enough to warrant professional help. The number may be even higher because many anxiety sufferers are diagnosed with other conditions, such as depression and substance abuse. An additional three million children experience anxiety severe enough to affect their school attendance, sleep, and learning ability.

Unfortunately, only about 25 percent of severe anxiety sufferers seek help. What is more discouraging is that most anxiety sufferers who do seek help receive inappropriate or ineffective care. Thus, most anxiety sufferers feel isolated because they do not make contact with others who might understand and offer help. The minority who do reach out for help may also feel isolated because they usually do not receive a proper diagnosis or referral and, as a result, continue to suffer.

One of the most reassuring steps you can take is to talk with others who have recovered from the same type of anxiety disorder as yours. Seek a professional with expertise in severe anxiety treatment, and request an opportunity to make such contact. Participation in group therapy with others who are successfully recovering is also an excellent way to receive reassurance and support. An alternative would be a self-help group, if there is one in your community. However, with self-help groups make sure you find others who are, indeed, overcoming their condition, so as to avoid reinforcing your anxiety or negative thinking.

Although you feel different and alone, it is important to realize there is hope and help. You do not need to live with fear and anxiety. Like most anxiety sufferers, you were probably relieved to learn that there is a name for your condition, and that there are many others like you. Knowing that many others have had the same feelings, and that they have overcome their anxiety, should be an inspiration. Again, do not despair or give up hope. I speak from personal and professional experience when I say there is an answer. There is life beyond irrational fear.

I'm afraid I'll pass out if my anxiety gets really bad. Has anyone ever passed out from anxiety?

You are not the first person to fear passing out from severe anxiety, but be assured that it is an irrational fear. In twenty-five years of counseling practice, I have never encountered a case in which someone passed out from anxiety, and I have not heard of any such cases.

The fear of passing out is, essentially, the fear of fainting or losing consciousness, and it is usually triggered by difficulty breathing. Breathing aberrations, such as rapid breathing and hyperventilating, are associated with severe anxiety episodes, and they are caused by adrenaline acting on the respiratory system. These breathing changes are the same as those associated with vigorous exercise, except that with anxiety they are triggered by fear or stress. The fear of smothering, choking, or not being able to breathe intensifies the initial breathing abnormality, which feeds back into more fear, including the fear of passing out.

Fear of losing control is part of the problem. Passing out or fainting would be a form of losing control of your conscious mind. This is certainly a frightening thought, but it is an unlikely possibility. In cases where other patients feared passing out, it never actually occurred, and the individuals recognized that the chances of it happening were extremely low. Those individuals realized, upon deeper reflection, that there were a number of options they could exercise before passing out, such as leaving the anxiety-arousing situation, distracting themselves, or simply waiting until the feeling passed.

As in any severe anxiety episode, the first thing to do is tell yourself that it is *not* a life-threatening situation and that you will be all right. Trust that it will pass, and apply your relaxation skills. Use distraction, if necessary, and remind yourself that in most instances you have the option of leaving the situation. If you obtain proper treatment, you will learn the necessary skills for handling anxiety, and you will develop confidence that you can handle it. When you no longer fear anxiety, your concern about passing out will diminish.

How can I know the difference between heart palpitations caused by anxiety and a serious heart problem like a heart attack?

There are three core fears for anxiety sufferers, and your question raises one of them, namely the fear of having a heart attack or fatal illness. The other two common fears are of going mentally insane and of losing control in public.

If you have had a physical examination verifying that your heart is not at risk, it is unlikely that your heart palpitations are dangerous or life-threatening. Anxiety symptoms occur within every organ system, including the heart, due to the stimulating effect of adrenaline and other activating hormones. Some common cardiovascular symptoms are rapid heart beat, heart arrhythmias, chest tightness or pain, high blood pressure, and vascular headaches. Naturally, these can be frightening, especially when you do not understand the arousal mechanisms involved in anxiety. If you do not have a history of heart problems, and you have been medically cleared of a heart condition, be assured that your heart can take a lot of stimulation without damage.

The best response to an anxiety symptom such as heart palpitations is to relax. This is difficult to do because it goes against your survival instinct, which produces arousal when you perceive danger. Nevertheless, it is important to train yourself to relax whenever you become aware of anxiety symptoms. An anxiety treatment program will teach you how to do this. Tell yourself that even if your heart palpitations mean that something is wrong with your heart, the best response would be to relax and not go into panic mode.

I feel like I'm losing my mind and that I might go crazy from not being able to control my anxiety. Can a person actually go crazy this way?

Your fear of going crazy is one of the three core fears in anxiety disorders, and it is directly related to your fear of losing control of yourself. Your fear of going crazy is a secondary reaction to feeling out of control, and serves no purpose other than to scare yourself and intensify your anxiety.

"Going crazy," "losing your mind," "becoming mental," "going insane," and "losing touch with reality" are all phrases used to describe a psychotic state of mind. It would be most helpful to remember that anxiety is not a mental illness, and that you will not become psychotic from anxiety. The background factors leading to psychotic states are different from those producing your type of personality and anxiety. You will not have a psychotic break from reality if you are not predisposed to that form of disorder.

In some cases, fear of going crazy is reinforced by knowledge of someone who has lost touch with reality or become psychotic. News about suicides and homicides may also represent out-of-control behavior and serve to reinforce your fear of going crazy. Any weird or "crazy" thoughts you might have would also scare you into fearing that you could lose your mind.

Another aspect of anxiety that reinforces fear of going crazy is racing thoughts and not being able to turn off your mind. Your personality type keeps your mind in a continuously active state. You probably have many shoulds, what-ifs, and stressful lists of things to do. As a sensitive person, you react strongly to these thoughts. When you cannot turn off your mind or control your thoughts, you remain mentally activated and inevitably develop body reactions. Because your mind is the source of such stressful activation, it is logical for you to conclude that you might lose your mind or go crazy.

In anxiety treatment, the very first step is learning that you do not have a mental illness. I spend several sessions at the outset of treatment on education about anxiety, to ensure that my patients are confident about this. Your anxiety will begin to diminish when you stop scaring yourself about what may happen to your mind. Learning to relax and developing control over your thoughts are the next steps that will help counteract your fear of going crazy. Meditation, practiced within an anxiety treatment program, is also helpful in developing a more relaxed and detached attitude towards your thoughts.

I think I have an obsessive-compulsive disorder. Is this a form of anxiety, and can I overcome it?

Obsessive-compulsive disorder *is* a form of anxiety, and it is classified as a severe anxiety disorder. Your condition is probably characterized by repeated but unwanted thoughts, or irresistible urges to perform certain behaviors or rituals. The obsessive thoughts and compulsive behaviors are ways you attempt to prevent anxiety from taking control of you. You may fear that if you do not give in to them, you will be flooded with anxiety over which you will have no control.

Naturally, your feeling of being controlled by your thoughts and compulsions is frightening and may lead you to fear you are going crazy or insane. Furthermore, you may be ashamed of the obsessive-compulsive pattern and hide these traits from others, which isolates you socially.

Obsessive-compulsive disorder is not a mental illness and you are not going crazy or insane. The condition is treatable and you can learn to overcome it. Medication is not necessary in the long run, although it may be helpful in the early phases of treatment while you are learning new thought and behavior patterns.

Keep in mind several considerations. First, you are afraid of anxiety, and your obsessive-compulsive condition is essentially a defensive pattern used to keep yourself from feeling anxious. You have learned to use obsessive-compulsive mechanisms to cope with anxiety and, although they seem to protect you, the solution is actually controlling you. In order to overcome the condition, it will ultimately be necessary for you to learn to experience anxiety and develop confidence that you can handle it. You can do this by acquiring new skills for floating through anxiety and changing your inner dialogue. The obsessive-compulsive condition is primarily a learned pattern, and you can relearn healthier patterns.

What do you think of using meditation instead of relaxation training?

As you may know from my own story, meditation played a significant role in my recovery from anxiety. Before I learned and practiced meditation, my thoughts and personality controlled me, and I had difficulty relaxing and sitting still. Meditation practice was, and still is, essential to my slowing down, transcending my thoughts, and experiencing inner peace. Meditation provided many other benefits, such as improving my concentration and focus, improving my sleep, and opening my heart to spiritual reality.

There are many parallels between relaxation training and meditation practice, and I believe that you can successfully use meditation instead of relaxation training. A change to meditation may be advisable if you find yourself tiring of a particular relaxation technique or if you are interested in the spiritual benefits of meditation. The basic approach to both is the same. Take some quiet time on a regular basis to practice the techniques and deepen the benefits. Keep in mind that patience is necessary with both relaxation and meditation techniques because you are learning to change old habits and patterns.

Just as there are different forms of relaxation, such as progressive muscle relaxation, visualization, and breathing techniques, there are also different forms of meditation. The two forms I have practiced most are *vipassana*, also known as insight meditation, and *transcendental* meditation. Although you may experiment with these techniques, my recommendation for meditation is that you work in depth with only one method for a period of time to obtain the maximum benefit. One of the most rewarding aspects of meditation is that the more you practice, the more you will benefit.

I don't like the idea of taking medication. Is medication necessary to overcome anxiety?

The role of medication in anxiety treatment is controversial, and I offer you my opinion on the subject. From a strictly biological viewpoint, it is claimed that anxiety results from chemical imbalances that require medication to control. On the other extreme, the behavioral viewpoint would claim that anxiety results from learning that can be reversed without medication. My position is that drugs can have an important, but very limited, role in anxiety recovery, and that they are most effective when used temporarily during specialized anxiety treatment.

There are both advantages and disadvantages to the use of medication. The advantages are that medication can block some anxiety symptoms, which may improve concentration and energy for learning new skills. Some medications, such as the beta-blockers, suppress adrenaline, which can reduce rapid heart beats and other symptoms. This might be advantageous for coping with infrequent phobias, such as flying.

However, I believe the disadvantages far outweigh the advantages of using medication. As you say, you do not like the idea of taking medication, and this is a common feeling among anxiety sufferers. The sensitivity, need to be in control, and other personality traits usually make medication an unattractive option. Many anxiety sufferers simply do not like the idea of being controlled by or dependent on drugs. From a practical viewpoint, medication often requires several trials to find the right dosages, and the side effects can be troublesome for sensitive people who react strongly to drug instead of body reactions. Any new symptoms that develop during the body's adjustment to drugs may add to the anxiety sufferer's fears.

My strongest objection to medications is that they do not teach any new skills, such as how to relax, how to control your thoughts, how to reduce stress, or how to express your feelings and needs assertively. These are all necessary skills for preventing anxiety and maintaining your anxiety recovery. In addition, medications do not educate you about the causes and other factors involved in anxiety, or about other anxiety recovery information, such as the important role of exercise and proper nutrition.

Finally, there is the issue of discontinuing medication once a person's body has adapted to a drug. Withdrawal should be medically supervised to prevent rebound effects or other complications. Some patients with long-term dependence on drugs may fear discontinuation. Another problem is that the effectiveness of some drugs decreases with long-term use, which leads to more drugs and perpetuation of the disadvantages.

Another significant problem with medications is that they are often prescribed as the only answer to anxiety disorders. The first step taken by virtually all anxiety sufferers is to visit a doctor or hospital emergency room. When medication is prescribed with no further services or referral to an anxiety treatment program, drugs may become the last step, despite the probability of no lasting relief or recovery.

23

Dancing Without Fear

We learn by practice. Whether it means to learn to dance by practicing dancing or to learn to live by practicing living, the principles are the same.

Martha Graham

Is it possible to overcome anxiety altogether—to live and dance without fear? What does it take to successfully recover from an anxiety disorder? Can anxiety recovery be permanent, or do we have to adjust to having periods of severe anxiety for the rest of our lives? How and why do some people change while others do not? What are the obstacles and pitfalls to effective treatment for anxiety recovery? This chapter will explore anxiety recovery in terms of these and related questions.

The very first issue in anxiety recovery is *commitment.* To overcome an anxiety disorder requires a commitment to face the condition, seek help, and do the work. It is not enough to hope or pray for anxiety recovery. It is essential to recognize that a commitment must be made to learn the skills necessary for dancing without fear.

Some anxiety sufferers hesitate to commit to a therapy program due to fear of failing. This fear is understandable, especially for those who sought help in the past and who were unsuccessful in gaining control of anxiety. For others, failing might mean that they are "hopeless cases" and that recovery is not possible. Held back by these concerns, people often feel some ambivalence about seeking help or making a commitment to treatment. Fortunately, these fears and concerns are usually dispelled within a few weeks of treatment, as people begin to understand their condition and experience some improvement.

Still others, particularly those with low self-esteem, may hesitate to commit because they do not believe they deserve to succeed, live without suffering, or enjoy life. Fortunately, self-esteem is recognized in the CHAANGE program as a personality issue that plays a part in anxiety. Therefore, CHAANGE addresses the self-esteem of program participants by including exercises and activities prescribed specifically for this purpose. These include training in positive thinking, assertive communication, reevaluating family history, and recognizing personal rights. In addition, self-esteem grows as a result of learning new skills and making progress in facing and overcoming fear. Once a decision is made to go forward with treatment, therefore, a person's self-esteem is likely to be enhanced.

For some, there is a fear of *too much* change. Some anxiety sufferers fear that treatment will result in an unrecognizable change in personality or other unfamiliar outcome. This activates anxiety about the unknown, as compared to predictable patterns of behavior.

Before a commitment to treatment can be made, most people need to be reassured that living without fear is possible. One of the most helpful ways to receive such reassurance is to hear it from others who have been successful in anxiety recovery. In some cases, I may offer my own story or put new patients in contact with former patients who want to share their success with others. These personal stories about anxiety recovery are among the most credible sources of inspiration, hope, and reassurance to the new anxiety patient. Group therapy is another opportunity for new patients to learn firsthand about the progress made by others with the same condition. Books that chronicle the successful recovery of other anxiety sufferers, such as *Free From Fears* (Seagrave and Covington 1984) and *Triumph Over Fear* (Ross 1994), can also be helpful. Reassurance and hope are the usual starting points for anxiety recovery.

Although offering reassurance and hope is an essential early intervention, I emphasize that successful recovery is a collaborative effort, in which the patient must play a key role. I dispel the myth that therapy works by magic or osmosis, and point out that the patient must do the work leading to recovery. This is another aspect of the commitment issue, since the most important ingredient in anxiety treatment is a person's motivation to change. Success depends largely on the patient's willingness to work actively between therapy sessions on the necessary skills and learning process.

Commitment to anxiety recovery means determination and a willingness to follow through, even when things do not go smoothly or predictably. Commitment to the process is important because progress is often inconsistent, involving steps forward and backward. In addition, results are not always immediate, which may be discouraging to those who start treatment with skepticism, impatience, or fear of failure. Since behavior patterns and thinking habits, as well as personality style, are key to anxiety, recovery cannot take place quickly, although progress can begin immediately. Furthermore, ongoing practice of new skills—between therapy sessions and after therapy ends—is necessary for recovery.

In my work with anxious patients, I begin with a diagnostic interview, to make sure that we are dealing with an anxiety disorder. As discussed earlier in the book, most anxiety sufferers have already been medically evaluated before coming for psychological help and have been cleared of an organic or physical basis for their anxiety condition. This is an important step in helping to dispel unrealistic fears about having a life-threatening disease or illness. Once the anxiety condition is diagnosed, my next intervention is to reassure people that severe anxiety is a treatable condition, and that people can and do recover. I use my own case as an example, if appropriate, or describe other examples of successful recovery. The initial interview is also important for establishing trust and rapport, as a good working relationship is essential when dealing with anxiety.

As a collaborative effort, the patient and therapist both have responsibilities for the success of anxiety treatment. The therapist's responsibility begins with conducting a proper assessment, making an accurate diagnosis, and developing an appropriate treatment plan. If the primary problem is severe anxiety and the therapist is not skilled in anxiety treatment, he or she is responsible for referring the patient to an anxiety treatment specialist.

Unfortunately, this does not happen as often as it should, which contributes to the high percentage of anxiety sufferers who receive inappropriate or ineffective care. A number of organizations have formed to correct this, including the National Institute of Mental Health's Panic Disorder Education Program, the Anxiety Disorders Association of America, the Obsessive-Compulsive Foundation, Freedom From Fear, the National Anxiety Council, and others. The mission of these organizations includes public and professional education about anxiety disorders and effective treatment, with the hope of increasing the number of anxiety sufferers who receive appropriate care. Some of these organizations maintain lists of anxiety treatment specialists, although they do not set any practice standards. Appendix B contains a list of these organizations.

The anxiety specialist's next responsibility is to provide a treatment program involving the tools and skills known to be effective for overcoming anxiety. It is known, for example, that effective treatment involves several phases or components, such as education about the nature of anxiety, relaxation training, stress management skills, cognitive change, and desensitization. In my opinion, some additional components are also necessary for anxiety recovery in most cases. These include learning how to deal with feelings, regular exercise, good nutrition and eating habits, recreation and play, and effective communication skills.

As I emphasize throughout this book, the ideal anxiety treatment program provides all these components in a structured process. The CHAANGE program meets these criteria, and I use it as the treatment base for many types of anxiety. I like the fact that a patient's progress is monitored by self-evaluations at the beginning, middle, and end of the process. The CHAANGE program also offers the advantage of providing learning materials to be used by patients at home, between therapy sessions, to ensure daily effort towards recovery. In addition, the materials are presented in a personal style by other patients who were successful in their own recoveries. This format provides hope, inspiration, and an opportunity for new patients to identify with success cases.

With a structured therapy program in place, the patient's role is to make a commitment to the recovery process and stay with it even when progress seems slow or inconsistent. The patient is also responsible for daily practice of the prescribed skills and exercises. Some of my patients demonstrate responsibility by recording questions and comments from their homework and personal experiences and bringing them to therapy sessions for discussion. Some keep a diary of their progress, and some make cue cards with inspiring affirmations and instructions to themselves, to be carried in a pocket or purse as daily reminders. As a patient, you must recognize that progress takes place as a result of effort that only you can make. No one can do it for you.

What can people realistically expect to achieve in anxiety recovery? Anxiety recovery can be defined as having the confidence to know that you can handle anxiety if and when it occurs. This confidence comes from acquiring and practicing the skills necessary for dancing gracefully through fear and by successfully facing fear with those skills. Anxiety recovery also means a new understanding of the mind–body relationship.

It is possible to dance without fear, but it is not possible to live without periodic anxiety. To a certain extent, anxiety is inherent in life and cannot be eliminated completely. We are all subject to decay, illness, imperfection, death, disappointment, and loss, and we are not in total control of our destinies. Therefore, we live with constant vulnerability. Epstein (1995), who describes psychotherapy from a Buddhist perspective in *Thoughts Without a Thinker,* calls this vulnerability an "inescapable humiliation." Epstein points out that no matter what we do, we cannot sustain the illusion of control and invulnerability. As he puts it, "We are all engaged in a futile struggle to maintain ourselves in our own image. The crises in our lives inevitably reveal how impossible our attempts to control our destinies really are" (p. 44). On the other hand, despite our lack of control an optimistic attitude is possible. For those who understand this, and who acquire the skills for accepting and dancing without fear, there can be joy and inner peace in daily living. Furthermore, we can learn to be in control of ourselves and our reactions to those aspects of life that we cannot control.

The ever-present potential for anxiety is even higher in people who have the personality traits discussed in Chapter 4. To highlight the anxiety personality briefly, the profile includes biological and emotional sensitivity, an active and creative mind, fear of rejection, sensitivity to criticism, a high need to please other people, need to feel in control, perfectionism, suggestibility, and a strong preference for certainty, structure, and predictability. When these traits control us, we are at risk for stress and anxiety. Our personality can not be remade entirely, but with appropriate help we can modify these traits so that we can be more in control of them and therefore of our stress and anxiety.

Stress is an inevitable part of life, adding to our potential for experiencing anxiety. The natural biological reaction to stress involves the same body arousal and "symptoms" as anxiety. However, anxiety recovery means no longer fearing the body's reactions to stress. This is accomplished by learning to trust that the body's reaction to stress is not life-threatening, as well as by learning to recognize the early warning signs of stress and intervening with skills that reduce stress and minimize its impact on the body. Stress itself is not the problem. The problem is that we typically do not have sufficient stress recovery, which leads to chronic stress and breakdown symptoms. Overcoming anxiety, then, includes learning how to identify, manage, and recover from stress. And since stress is a daily occurrence for most of us, we must practice relaxation and other stress recovery activities on a daily basis. As the world around us becomes more stressful, these skills are increasingly necessary for dancing without fear.

I believe that anxiety is both a necessary survival mechanism and a learned pattern of behavior. As a survival mechanism, anxiety is part of the fight/flight response to threat and stress. In this respect, anxiety is a warning signal and a mechanism of arousal necessary for defense against danger. Anxiety also serves survival by energizing the self when coping with stress. Therefore, we would not want to eliminate the survival function of anxiety, even if it were possible to do so. Instead, as part of overcoming anxiety we must learn to call this arousal mechanism by another name, such as "survival response" or "stress reaction," since anxiety is, essentially, a person's *fear* of the fight/flight mechanism.

As discussed throughout this book, the intensity of body reactions to stress and the intensity of fear triggered by those body reactions, are often traumatic, especially for sensitive people who tend to react strongly. Anxiety and fear become linked to the "trauma" of intense or uncontrollable physical reactions, as well as to the situations in which those reactions were triggered. In addition, thinking patterns play a major role in anxiety. Worry, negative thinking, memory of trauma experiences, what-ifs, black-and-white thinking, and so on, all add to the likelihood of repeated anxiety. Furthermore, the personality style of sensitive people in itself creates stress and more anxiety. In these ways, anxiety is a learned pattern of behavior that must be unlearned with proper help in order to dance without fear.

Success in the relearning process is influenced by several factors. The first, motivation, was touched on earlier in the discussion of commitment and responsibility. The higher the motivation, the more likely a person will do the work and stay with it. Combined with an effective treatment program, motivation is the most important ingredient in overcoming anxiety and dancing without fear.

The probability of successful recovery from anxiety is also influenced by the amount of concurrent stress in a person's life during the treatment program. Medical conditions, relationship problems, financial hardship, illness in the family, or recent death or loss of a loved one take up energy and can disrupt the attention and concentration required to absorb new information and learn new skills. Under such conditions, anxiety treatment may need to focus on other issues as part of the recovery process. However, since stress, loss, and misfortune are all part of life, these issues can be readily incorporated into the treatment program, where new learning and skills can be applied to them. At worst, length of treatment may need to be extended, but as long as the person is motivated to succeed, there is every reason to be optimistic about attaining recovery.

Length of treatment is also affected by the degree to which a person is impaired by anxiety. For example, if a person has developed a compulsive pattern of anxiety avoidance, or a pattern of withdrawal from other people, recovery may take longer. In such cases, coping patterns and defense mechanisms can become strong habits that are difficult to modify. Therefore, a longer period of relearning may be required in order to handle phobic situations without anxiety. On the other hand, I have often had the gratification of working with people who recovered within months, despite years of living with fear and anxiety. In fact, most adults with an anxiety disorder have a long history of anxiety symptoms, though they may not have recognized them earlier in life. Regardless of how long you have suffered, overcoming anxiety is a totally realistic goal if the other ingredients for successful recovery are present.

A number of obstacles and pitfalls can interfere with your anxiety recovery. One pitfall is the temptation to stop practicing new skills when you feel better or when your anxiety symptoms subside. This can happen towards the end of treatment, after you have made progress and feel "normal" once again. Naturally, for some people there is a tendency to become less consistent about taking care of themselves when things are going well. Motivation for managing stress, exercising, eating properly, thinking positively, and daily practice of relaxation or meditation may drop as suffering is relieved. This pitfall should be avoided since your basic sensitivity and other personality traits will not change, and your potential for reacting strongly remains high under new stress.

Another pitfall is to approach anxiety recovery with unrealistic expectations. It is unrealistic, for example, to expect to never experience anxiety again. As discussed in Chapter 20, anxiety is sometimes a signal that you are on the right track, as you face a change or challenge that is good for you, even though it may take you out of your comfort zone. In addition, since stress is inevitable, your body is likely to periodically react with arousal symptoms, as it was designed by nature to do. It is also important to remember that anxiety is normal for everyone under certain circumstances. Of course, sometimes anxiety is simply an irrational reaction, reflecting old behavior patterns and unproductive ways of thinking. Whatever the source, you are likely to experience anxiety from time to time. However, after receiving proper help, you will not fear anxiety or find yourself bewildered by it. You will recognize what it is, and you will know that it is not life-threatening. You will also see anxiety as an opportunity to practice many new skills and to develop a new way of thinking. You will be able to take it in stride, and see anxiety for what it really is: an adrenaline reaction in your body triggered by identifiable stress.

Another pitfall in learning to dance without fear is to become discouraged by anxiety setbacks. The CHAANGE program teaches that anxiety setbacks are inevitable during recovery, but that they are practice opportunities. As a practice opportunity, a resurgence of anxiety symptoms can provide the impetus for applying new skills, such as the relaxation response, changing inner dialogue, thinking positively, floating through, trusting yourself, keeping faith in the universe, and other components of living fearlessly. You must have some anxiety in order to overcome anxiety, to develop the skills and confidence to know that you can handle it. Remember that you will never be given more than you can handle, and that a program such as CHAANGE is a lifelong resource that you can turn to at any time for reinforcement and inspiration.

Your faith will grow as you develop confidence in your ability to handle anxiety. You will also learn to trust that whatever happens, you can find a way to deal with it. Having faith and confidence that everything will work out is the most liberating aspect of anxiety recovery. Faith allows you to live more fully in the present, knowing that you have the intelligence, skills, and resourcefulness to handle whatever may happen. With faith and self-confidence, you do not need to know what will happen in the future in order to feel safe or in control. Your life will be more joyful and spontaneous, because you will be less concerned about preparing for dreaded future possibilities. You can still plan for the future, but you will be more able to live in the present.

For many people, the strengthening of self-confidence and faith creates a more spiritual attitude towards life. This seems to come naturally to those who are sensitive and compassionate to begin with. As noted in Chapter 4, the anxiety personality has both assets and liabilities. A spiritual orientation seems to be part of the personality in many cases. Anxiety treatment can build on this foundation, and help apply what Benson (1984) calls the *faith factor* to the recovery process. For some, spirituality is expressed as trust in God or in the universe. For others, spirituality is expressed as a belief that whatever happens was meant to be. However it is expressed, a spiritual perspective can help tremendously in anxiety recovery if it is included in the treatment process. A spiritual attitude makes it easier to give up the need for control. Feelings of safety and security can also be increased with greater spirituality. Indeed, the goal of anxiety treatment for most people is to have more security, safety, peace of mind, contentment, optimism, positive thinking, courage, and hope. These are all spiritual qualities that can be developed as part of anxiety treatment.

The CHAANGE program recognizes that dancing without fear is a lifelong process that cannot be taken for granted, even when people appear to be free of anxiety symptoms. Therefore, at the end of the program, a checklist is provided for periodic use by CHAANGE graduates. The checklist consists of several dozen questions, grouped in the four main stages of anxiety treatment: understanding the condition, relaxation, changes in thinking and attitude, and behavior change. Here are some sample questions from the CHAANGE program checklist:

- Am I still ashamed of having had this condition or do I view it as a fantastic growth process for myself?
- Am I relaxing automatically when I feel tense or anxious?
- Do I listen to my early body signals which may be warning me to slow down?
- Have I stopped scaring myself about my feelings or thoughts?
- Do I continually reaffirm to myself that I am a human being with worth, dignity, and rights?
- Do I continually change my negative thoughts and statements to positive ones?

- When I am physically ill (with a cold, flu, etc.), do I still insist on doing everything I've always done, or do I allow myself to get more rest?
- Am I doing something good just for myself every day?
- Am I careful not to do too much, not because of anxiety, but because as a human I have human limitations?
- Do I review my homework and last tape at least once a month?

The checklist at the end of the CHAANGE program concludes with the following statement:

> We hope you will use this checklist to get yourself back on track if you feel yourself slipping into old behaviors. Remember, it is a relearning process. You may find yourself more vulnerable to slipping back when you are under more stress, when you are ill, or when you are tired. Be good to yourself and to your body. When it is tired or overused, remember to give it rest and maintenance. Relax yourself any time that you begin to feel anxious or tense. Say positive things to yourself all the time, and do the things that enhance your self-esteem.

If you answer "no" to any of the questions on the checklist, you will be directed back to the learning materials in the CHAANGE program that correspond to each question. You may need to brush up on certain skills, or be reminded of what you learned the first time through the program. In this way, progress in anxiety recovery can be maintained and even improved.

In addition to the CHAANGE program checklist, there are some other anxiety recovery boosters to consider. One is group therapy or a support group led by an anxiety specialist. This would be an opportunity to continue your recovery process, with the support of others who have similar goals. It is important to surround yourself with positive energy and people committed to furthering their own growth. A word of caution, however, is to stay away from groups that do not provide a positive focus and structure for overcoming anxiety. As a sensitive person, you can be affected by other people's lack of progress, anxiety symptoms, and frustrations. The best policy is to seek a group with a professional leader, or at least a support group with people who have been successful in their progress towards overcoming fear and anxiety.

Individual psychotherapy may be advisable from time to time, when stress reaches unusually high levels or during times of significant change. Taking this step can help prevent relapses, and provide support for the challenges you may face in life.

Another recovery booster is to make a set of cue cards containing reminders and inspiring affirmations. You can periodically review these cards or notes to keep your attention directed towards a healthy lifestyle, and on the daily activities and practices that will keep you dancing through life without fear. A list of such reminders—based on the ideas contained in this book—appears below. For quick reference, each reminder has a title that refers to an important aspect of anxiety recovery. As a special bonus for readers of this book, a starter set of *Dancing With Fear* Pocketcards is included at the end of this chapter. I created these cards for the purpose just described, and they are removable for convenient use.

As you continue to use the skills and knowledge gained during a program of anxiety treatment, new habits and patterns will form. You will think and behave differently, and this will reduce the stress in your life. In addition, you will be more relaxed and less concerned about what will happen in the future. You will know yourself more intimately, including when to take breaks, how to set reasonable limits, and how to care for yourself. You will also be more comfortable around other people, and you will develop the skills to communicate more effectively. Your attitude will be more optimistic, and you will be more able to pursue activities that bring you joy, pleasure, and satisfaction. You will no longer be controlled or restricted by fear, and your emotional life will become richer. Overcoming anxiety will help you become your true self and fulfill your purpose in life.

If this sounds like what you want, you can have it with proper help combined with a burning desire to dance without fear.

REMINDERS FOR ANXIETY RECOVERY

1. ***ANXIETY RECOVERY:*** Anxiety recovery comes from gaining confidence in your ability to handle anxious feelings. The major steps are insight, learning to relax, changing your thinking, facing your fears, and trusting that everything will be O.K.

2. ***BE HERE NOW:*** You may remember the past and plan for the future. But live in the present. Be here now—it's all you really have.

3. ***SIGNALS OR SYMPTOMS?:*** Anxiety symptoms result from stress overload in sensitive people. Identify and deal with early warning signals before they become symptoms.

4. ***ANXIETY PERSONALITY:*** Are you in control of your personality, or is your personality in control of you?

5. ***RELAXATION:*** Relaxation is like Chinese boxes—the deepest state of relaxation is hidden within many outer layers of tension and worry. Just let each layer melt away as you go deeper toward the center of relaxation.

6. ***WORRY:*** Worrying about the future has absolutely no effect on what will actually happen. Save your energy for more productive activities.

7. ***PACE YOURSELF:*** In every aspect of your life, stay within your limits and progress at your own pace. Do not compare yourself to others.

8. ***FEAR OF LOSING CONTROL:*** Let go of the fear of "losing control" or "going crazy." It will not happen. It's just not in you.

9. ***SHOULD YOU?:*** "Shoulds" create stress and stress produces anxiety symptoms. Remember to change every "I should . . . " to "I could choose . . . "

10. ***WHAT-IF?:*** Your survival instinct treats every "what-if" thought as an imminent reality. Remember to change your "what-ifs" to "so-whats."

11. ***ANGER:*** Anger is not bad or dangerous. Like any emotion, anger is part of being human. The only problem with anger is *how* it is expressed.

12. ***FLEXIBILITY:*** If you're loose and flexible you can bend with the stress of life instead of breaking. Stretch your body and mind every day. Stay loose.

13. ***RELAXATION:*** Relaxation is not something you *make* happen. It is a natural state you *allow* to happen. Let it happen. Don't try so hard.

14. ***RELAXATION:*** Allow yourself to relax by taking the time and practicing the skills of releasing tension and letting go of thoughts.

15. ***HEALTH:*** Your health is essential to anxiety recovery and dancing without fear. Maintain the basics of health: adequate rest, proper nutrition, exercise, and stress management.

16. ***PERFECTIONISM:*** Strive for excellence rather than perfectionism, and accept that you must often function under conditions that are less than ideal.

17. ***HANDLING ANXIETY:*** You need to experience anxiety in order to overcome your fear of it. Accept anxiety as an opportunity to practice your recovery skills.

18. ***FOOD:*** Everything you put in your body has an effect. Minimize or avoid sugar, caffeine, and chemicals in your diet.

19. ***STRESS:*** Stress can be compared to a violin string: if the string is too loose (not enough stress), it won't produce music. If the string is too tight (too much stress), it will break.

20. ***SETBACKS:*** Periodic setbacks will occur during the process of anxiety recovery. Learn from your setbacks . . . they are the feedback mechanisms for self-correction. Don't get down on yourself or compare yourself to others.

21. *BREATHE DEEPLY:* "Remember to breathe deeply." (Post copies of this reminder on your refrigerator, bathroom mirror, dashboard, calendar, computer, etc.)

22. *FEELINGS:* Learn to let feelings pass through you, like wind through the trees. Don't hold on to them. Sadness, anger, joy, fear . . . they are all like the wind.

23. *FEAR OF DEATH:* Death is feared most by those who have lived without satisfaction. Live fully—without fear—and enjoy the gift of life.

24. *ANGER:* Anger is more stressful for the person who harbors it than for the person toward whom it is directed.

25. *CONTROL:* Your need to be in control is a defense mechanism against your fear of losing control.

26. *FOOD:* A natural foods diet, emphasizing whole grains, fresh vegetables, and fruits, is necessary for health. Health is part of anxiety recovery.

27. *WORRY:* The future is like the weather: you can try to predict it, but you can't control it. Stop worrying about the future.

28. *CONTENTMENT:* Be more content with where you are and what you have now. Don't compare yourself to others.

29. *ANXIETY RECOVERY DIET:* Eat small meals often to keep your blood sugar level steady. Don't get strung out.

30. *NEGATIVE THINKING:* Stop concentrating on other people's faults. Choose to enjoy the good in people.

31. *COMPARING YOURSELF:* Each person's situation is different. Is it reasonable to compare yourself to others?

32. *PROCRASTINATION:* Procrastination is often perfection in disguise. Do you fear failure or less-than-perfect performance and then protect yourself by avoiding?

33. *REST DAY:* Once a week, take some time to heal yourself with rest and reflection. Even God rested on the seventh day.

34. *FOOD MEDITATION:* Close your eyes and imagine how your food becomes your energy. Decide what you will do with that energy.

35. *BLACK-AND-WHITE THINKING:* The world is in color. Therefore, black-and-white (all-or-nothing) thinking does not apply.

36. *HANDLING ANXIETY:* Recovery comes from gaining confidence in your ability to handle anxiety. Handle anxiety by facing it, accepting it, "floating" through it, and trusting that it will pass.

37. *MIND AND BODY:* Every thought has an effect, however subtle, on your body. Care for your body by choosing your thoughts.

38. *PANIC ANXIETY:* Regardless of how often—or how seldom—you have panic anxiety, you are recovered only when you no longer fear it.

39. *CHANGE:* To the caterpillar, change is death. To the butterfly, change is birth. Ask yourself, "How do I view change?"

40. *OVERBOOKED?:* When planning your schedule, leave room for life. Plan some unstructured time.

41. *FOOD MEDITATION:* Before you eat, close your eyes and visualize the journey of your food from the earth to your table.

42. *DEATH:* Death is like taking off a tight shoe. It is absolutely safe.

43. *SITTING STILL:* Sitting still with a quiet mind will counteract anxiety and recharge your battery.

44. *DANCING WITH FEAR:* There is a world of difference between dancing around fear (avoiding it) and dancing with fear (facing it).

Appendix A: CHAANGE Pre- and Post-Program Evaluations

CHAANGE®
128 Country Club Drive
Chula Vista, CA 91911
(800) 276-7800

PRE-PROGRAM EVALUATION
Please Answer Each Question
Please Include When Enrolling
Please print (in ink) or type

Date: ____________

Name: ____________ **Sex:** ______ **Age:** ______

Address: ____________

City: ____________ **State:** ______ **Zip:** ______

Marital Status ____________ **Daytime Phone:** ( ) ____________

• *Please include a street address when ordering so that we can send your first materials to you by UPS.*

Indicate below the situations / events with which you have difficulty due to your condition of agoraphobia or extreme anxiety. Indicate situations in which you experience only mild discomfort as well as those in which you feel more extreme discomfort. We have listed some which we see most often and which we track for research purposes. To the right of each situation / event, *please indicate how much you tend to avoid each and how much discomfort you experience in reaction to each.* List additional situations in the spaces provided and please respond to all items.

1. Situation / Event	Frequency or Avoidance of Situation					Level of Discomfort in Situation				
	Never avoid	Seldom Avoid	Sometimes avoid	Often avoid	Always avoid	Comfortable	Slightly uncomfortable	Uncomfortable	Very uncomfortable	Panicky
Example: Standing in Line										
Driving										
Shopping malls										
Church / Synagogue										
Grocery stores										
Being in crowds										
Flying										
Traveling alone by bus										
Walking alone on busy streets										
Going into crowded shops or stores										
Going alone far from home										
Large open spaces										
Add others below if appropriate:										

2. Approximately how many times per week do you feel panicky? _______________ times.

3. Indicate approximately the number of hours on a typical day you are actively troubled by anxiety (either thinking about it, worrying about it, frightened, etc.). It is important that you indicate a specific number, even if it is just an estimate. _______________ hours per day.

4. List below medications you are currently taking and the usual dosage per day:

Medications	Dosage	How often	Why prescribed

If you are currently taking medications for your anxiety condition, please indicate how helpful it (they) has (have) been in providing relief from your distress. (Circle a number).

0 1 2 3 4 5 6 7 8

No relief at all — Complete relief

5. How would you rate the present state of your phobic symptoms on the scale below? (Circle a number).*

0 1 2 3 4 5 6 7 8

No phobias present (0) • Slightly disturbing / not really disturbing (2) • Definitely disturbing / disabling (4) • Markedly disturbing / disabling (6) • Very severely disturbing / disabling (8)

6. Please indicate how much control of your life you feel now. (Please circle one number between 0 and 8).

(No control) 0 1 2 3 4 5 6 7 8 (Complete Control)

7. Circle the dot on the line below which best describes the overall level of happiness, everything considered, of your present marriage, or permanent relationship (If you are not currently married or in a relationship, just skip this question). The middle point, happy, represents the degree of happiness which most people get from marriage or a relationship, and the scale gradually ranges on one side to those few who are very unhappy, and on the other side, to those few who experience extreme joy or happiness in marriage, or in a permanent relationship.

0 2 7 15 20 25 35

Very unhappy (0) — Happy (15) — Perfectly happy (35)

8. In general, how satisfying do you find the way you're spending your life these days? Which of the following would you call it? (Circle one)

Not at all satisfying — Not very satisfying — Pretty satisfying — Completely satisfying

* Phobic Symptoms Scale courtesy of Mathews, Gelder & Johnson, from their book, *Agoraphobia: Nature & Treatment*.

9. Please indicate how depressed you feel at this time in your life (please circle one number between 0 and 8).

(Not at all depressed) 0 1 2 3 4 5 6 7 8 (Extremely depressed)

10. Please give us a brief descriptive paragraph on how you view your condition now, in the space provided below. If you are feeling depressed now, please discuss that in this space, as well.

11. What is the highest level of schooling you completed? ____________________

12. What is your occupation? ____________________

13. Do you have children living at home? ____ Yes ____ No

If yes, please list their ages: ____________________

____

____

14. We are interested in knowing how you heard of our program and how you came to the decision to enroll. Please tell us.

15. Have you ever seen a psychologist, psychiatrist or other professional or counselor for help for this or other anxiety conditions?

Yes__________ No __________

If you have sought help for this condition, please describe in the space below (when, from what type of source(s), for how long you went and how much it helped you with your distress).

If your answer to the previous question was yes, please include your therapist's name and complete address. Indicate below if, as a courtesy, we may send information about the CHAANGE program and that you have enrolled.

Therapist's name: ____________________

Address: ____________________ Zip: __________

______ You may send information to my therapist ______ You may not send information to my therapist

When did you last have a "thorough" physical examination? ____________________

What were the main findings of your most recent physical? ____________________

____

____

Please include your physician's name and complete address and indicate if we may send him / her information. (If you are not currently on medication, you may skip this question).

Physician's name: ____________________

Address: ____________________

____________________ Zip: ____________

_______ You may send information to my physician _______ You may *not* send information to my physician

REQUEST TO USE INFORMATION FOR RESEARCH PURPOSES / INFORMED CONSENT AGREEMENT

It is very helpful for us to be able to use certain information you provide to us for a variety of research and study purposes. The type of information we use are answers to questions such as your self-rating of your anxiety symptoms on the pre-, mid-, and post- program evaluations. In accordance with ethical standards, we are required to inform you of the following, and obtain your informed consent prior to using any of the information you supply us with.

WE WILL NEVER USE OR RELEASE YOUR NAME OR OTHER IDENTITY INFORMATION FOR ANY RESEARCH PURPOSE.

You are free to either participate or to decline to participate, or you may change your mind at any time by notifying us in writing. There is no foreseen effect of choosing either to participate or not to participate. There are no known risks or adverse effects if you choose to participate since the materials you will be filling out would be filled out in the normal course of your program participation. The benefits of participation would be to add your own experience to the knowledge base of anxiety research and treatment, information we can use to help others. If you have any questions at all concerning this matter, you are free to ask us for further information.

Please indicate your decision below.

_______ (Initials) I agree to allow information I supply to be used for research, statistical, and study purposes, *Excluding* information which would identify me.

_______ (Initials) I decline. Do not use any information I supply you with for research purposes.

128 Country Club Drive, Chula Vista, CA 91911 • (800) 276-7800

Date ______________________

CHAANGE Post-Program Evaluation

Name ______________________________

Address ______________________________

Please complete this form and return it to us. This will help us in understanding your particular areas of difficulty and will allow us to monitor your progress. As you fill it out, please refer to how you are doing now.

Indicate below the situations/events with which you have difficulty due to your condition of agoraphobia or extreme anxiety. Indicate situations in which you experience only mild discomfort as well as those in which you feel more extreme discomfort. We have listed some which we see most often and which we track for research purposes. To the right of each situation/event, please indicate how much you tend to avoid each, and how much discomfort you experience in reaction to each. List additional situations in the spaces provided and please respond to all items.

1. Situation/Event	Frequency of Avoidance of Situation					Level of Discomfort in Situation				
	never avoid	seldom avoid	sometimes avoid	often avoid	always avoid	comfortable	slightly uncomfortable	uncomfortable	very uncomfortable	panicky
Example: Standing in line				✓				✓		
Driving										
Shopping malls										
Church/Synagogue										
Grocery stores										
Being in crowds										
Flying										
Traveling alone by bus										
Walking alone on busy streets										
Going into crowded shops or stores										
Going alone far from home										
Large open spaces										
Staying alone										
Restaurants										
Add others below if appropriate:										

2. Approximately how many times per week do you feel panicky? ____________ times

3. Indicate approximately the number of hours on a typical day you are actively troubled by anxiety (either thinking about it, worrying about it, frightened, etc.) It is important that you indicate a specific number, even if it is just an estimate.

____________ hours per day

4. List below medications you are currently taking and the usual dosage per day:

Medications	Dosage	Why prescribed

If you are currently taking medication for your anxiety condition, please indicate how helpful it (they) has/have been in providing relief from your distress. (Circle a number.)

0 1 2 3 4 5 6 7 8

No relief at all — Complete relief

5. How would you rate the present state of your phobic symptoms on the scale below? (Circle a number)*

0	1	2	3	4	5	6	7	8
no phobias present		slightly disturbing/ not really disturbing		definitely disturbing/ disabling		markedly disturbing/ disabling		very severely disturbing/ disabling

6. Please indicate how much control of your life you feel now. (Please circle one number between 0 and 8)

(no control) 0 1 2 3 4 5 6 7 8 (complete control)

7. Circle the dot on the line below which best describes the overall level of happiness, everything considered, of your present marriage. (If you are not currently married, just skip this question.) The middle point, happy, represents the degree of happiness which most people get from marriage, and the scale gradually ranges on one side to those few who are very unhappy in marriage, and on the other side, to those few who experience extreme joy or happiness in marriage.

0	2	7	15	20	25	35
•	•	•	•	•	•	•
Very Unhappy			Happy			Perfectly Happy

8. In general, how satisfying do you find the way you're spending your life these days? Which of the following would you call it? (Circle one)

Not at all satisfying

Not very satisfying

Pretty satisfying

Completely satisfying

* Phobic Symptoms Scale courtesy of Mathews, Gelder & Johnson, from their book **Agoraphobia: Nature & Treatment.**

9. Please indicate how depressed you feel at this time in your life. (Please circle a number between 0 and 8)

(not at all depressed) 0 1 2 3 4 5 6 7 8 (extremely depressed)

10. Please give us a brief descriptive paragraph on how you view your condition now, in the space provided below. Pay special attention to your progress in doing things once avoided or difficult.

11. Are you currently seeing a therapist for this condition? ______ (yes) ______ (no)

Signature ____

Appendix B: National Organizations for Anxiety Education and Treatment

Anxiety Disorders Association of America (ADAA)
6000 Executive Boulevard
Rockville, MD 20852
(301) 231-9350, FAX (301) 231-7392

The ADAA is a nonprofit organization whose mission is to promote the prevention and cure of anxiety disorders and to improve the lives of all people who suffer from them. The organization disseminates information and facilitates access to treatment by providing a National Professional Membership Directory, including a state-by-state listing of mental health professionals who specialize in treatment of anxiety disorders.

The ADAA sponsors an annual conference open to both the public and professionals. A newsletter, *The Reporter*, is published quarterly.

CHAANGE
128 Country Club Drive
Chula Vista, CA 91911
(800) 276-7800, FAX (619) 691-7940

CHAANGE (Center for Help for Anxiety/Agoraphobia through New Growth Experiences) is a national organization dedicated to effective treatment of anxiety disorders. CHAANGE provides a state-by-state listing of professionals who specialize in anxiety treatment using the CHAANGE program, a step-by-step recovery process. Contact the organization for a free information kit, which includes the national list of affiliated therapists. A step-by-step children's anxiety recovery program, LifeSkills, is also available from CHAANGE. The organization also offers a catalogue of books and tapes related to anxiety recovery.

Dean Foundation
Obsessive Compulsive Information Center
8000 Excelsior Drive, Suite 302
Madison, WI 53717-1914
(608) 836-8070

Computer database of over 4,000 references updated daily. Computer searches done for a nominal fee. No charge for quick reference questions. Maintains physician referral and support group lists.

Freedom From Fear
308 Seaview Avenue
Staten Island, NY 10305
Tel (718) 351-1717, FAX (718) 667-8893

Freedom From Fear is "a nonprofit organization dedicated to helping those who suffer from fears, phobias, anxiety, and depression." Co-sponsor of National Anxiety Disorders Screening Day, an annual event offering public information and a free diagnostic clinic. The organization publishes *On Target*, a quarterly newsletter.

Journal of Anxiety Disorders
Pergamon Press, Inc.
Journal Division
660 White Plains Road
Tarrytown, NY 10591-5153
(914) 524-9200

This is an interdisciplinary research journal dealing with all aspects of anxiety disorders for all ages. Published quarterly, this journal is geared towards mental health professionals.

National Anxiety Foundation
3135 Custer Drive
Lexington, KY 40517-4001
(606) 272-7166

This organization is a "nonprofit public health education and research institution" that provides information on panic disorder and other anxiety conditions, as well as a list of anxiety treatment specialists in the United States. Panic disorder is referred to as a "medical illness," and the materials provided appear to emphasize a medication approach to treatment of anxiety disorders. For this service, send $10.00 to the address listed.

National Institute of Mental Health (NIMH)
Panic Disorder Education Program
Room 7C-02
5600 Fishers Lane
Rockville, MD 20857
1-800-64-PANIC

The NIMH Panic Disorder Education Program was launched to increase awareness about panic disorder and effective therapies for this emotional condition. The main goal of the program is to increase the number of people with panic disorder who are properly diagnosed and treated. The program offers a toll-free information line (1-800-64-PANIC) that provides callers with free printed materials.

Obsessive-Compulsive Foundation, Inc.
P.O. Box 70
Milford, CT 06460
(203) 878-5669, FAX (203) 874-2926

This nonprofit organization is devoted to research, treatment, and public information about the nature of obsessive-compulsive disorder (OCD), a form of severe anxiety. Publishes the *OCD Newsletter,* as well as *Kidscope,* a semi-annual newsletter by and for children with OCD.

The Council on Anxiety Disorders
P.O. Box 17011
Winston-Salem, NC 27116
(910) 722-7760

The Council on Anxiety Disorders is a nonprofit organization committed to making professionals and the public aware of anxiety disorders and developments in effective treatments. The Council provides assistance in locating treatment professionals specializing in anxiety disorders, educational seminars and workshops for professionals, and educational materials by mail. A newsletter, *Quest,* is published quarterly.

References

Allione, T. (1984). *Women of Wisdom.* Boston, MA: Routledge and Kegan Paul.

Arms, S. (1975). *Immaculate Deception: A New Look at Women and Childbirth in America.* Boston, MA: Houghton Mifflin.

Barefoot, J. C., Dahlstrom, W. G., and Williams, R. B. (1983). Hostility, CHD incidence, and total morbidity: a 25-year follow-up study of 255 physicians. *Psychosomatic Medicine.* 45:59–63.

Barlow, D. (1988). *Anxiety and Its Disorders.* New York: Guilford.

Bass, C. (1992). Chest pain and breathlessness: relationship to psychiatric illness. *American Journal of Medicine.* 92:12–19.

Benson, H. (1975). *The Relaxation Response.* New York: William Morrow.

——— (1984). *Beyond the Relaxation Response.* New York: Times Books.

Borysenko, J. (1987). *Minding the Body, Mending the Mind.* Reading, MA: Addison-Wesley.

Caddy, E. (1977). *The Living Word.* Forres, Scotland: Findhorn Foundation.

Canfield, J., and Hansen, V. (1994). *Dare to Win.* New York: Berkley.

Cousins, N. (1979). *Anatomy of an Illness.* New York: Norton.

——— (1983). *The Healing Heart.* New York: Norton.

Diagnostic and Statistical Manual of Mental Disorders (1994). 4th ed. Washington, DC: American Psychiatric Association.

Dossey, L. (1993). *Healing Words: The Power of Prayer.* New York: Harper.

Eadie, B. (1993). *Embraced by the Light.* New York: Bantam.

Elium, D., and Elium, J. (1992). *Raising a Son: Parents and the Making of a Healthy Man.* Hillsboro, OR: Beyond Words Publishing, Inc.

Elkind, D. (1981). *The Hurried Child: Growing Up Too Fast Too Soon.* Reading, MA: Addison-Wesley.

Ellis, A. (1994). *Reason and Emotion in Psychotherapy* (Revised ed.). New York: Carol Publishing Group.

Erikson, E. H. (1950). *Childhood and Society.* New York: Norton.

Epstein, M. ((1995). *Thoughts Without a Thinker.* New York: Basic Books.

Foxman, P. (1976). Self-actualization and tolerance for ambiguity. *Journal of Personality Assessment,* 40 (1):67–72.

——— (1980). Tolerance for ambiguity: implications for mental health. In *Encyclopedia of Clinical Assessment,* ed. R. Woody, pp. 455–462. San Francisco: Jossey-Bass.

Freud, S. (1911). Formulations regarding the two principles of mental functioning. *Standard Edition* 7.

——— (1933). New introductory lectures on psycho-analysis. *Standard Edition* 22:5–182.

Gardner, R. W., Holzman, P. S., Klein, G. S., et al. (1959). Cognitive control: a study of individual consistencies in cognitive behavior. *Psychological Issues,* 1 (4), Mono. 4.

Gawain, S. (1978). *Creative Visualization.* New York: Bantam.

Gendlin, E. (1978). *Focusing.* New York: Bantam.

Gittelman-Klein, R., and Klein, D. (1980). Separation anxiety in school refusal and its treatment with drugs. In *Out of School,* ed. L. Hersov and I. Berg, pp. 321–341. New York: Wiley.

Hay, L. (1987). *You Can Heal Your Life*. Santa Monica, CA: Hay House.

Holmes, T., and Masuda, M. (1967). The social readjustment rating scale. *Journal of Psychosomatic Research* 2: 213–218.

Isaacs, A. (1994). Studies: religion, health go hand in hand. *Vermont Maturity*, November, 1994, p. 17.

Janus, S., and Janus, C. (1993). *The Janus Report on Sexual Behavior*. New York: Wiley.

Kabat-Zinn, J. (1994a). *Full Catastrophe Living: Using the Wisdom of Your Body and Mind to Face Stress, Pain, and Illness*. New York: Delacorte.

——— (1994b). *Wherever You Go, There You Are: Mindfulness Meditation in Everyday Life*. New York: Hyperion.

Kaplan, H. (1974). *The New Sex Therapy*. New York: Brunner/Mazel.

Kornfield, J. (1993). *A Path With Heart: A Guide Through the Perils and Promises of Spiritual Life*. New York: Bantam.

Lappe, F. M. (1971). *Diet for a Small Planet*. New York: Ballantine.

Last, C. (1992). Anxiety disorders in childhood and adolescence. In *Internalizing Disorders in Children and Adolescents,* ed. W. Reynolds, pp. 61–106. New York: Wiley.

Lee, J. (1990). *Expressing Anger Appropriately* (Recorded workshop). Boulder, CO: Sounds True Recordings.

Lerner, H. (1989). *The Dance of Intimacy.* New York: Harper and Row.

Levin, J. (1994). Religion and health: Is there an association, is it valid, and is it causal? *Social and Scientific Medicine* 38 (11):1475–1482.

Levitt, J., Smith, L., and Warren, C. (1980). *Kripalu Kitchen: A Natural Foods Cookbook and Nutritional Guide.* Lenox, MA: Kripalu Publications.

Lidell, L. (1983). *The Sivananda Companion to Yoga.* New York: Simon and Schuster.

Lowen, A. (1975). *Bioenergetics.* New York: Penguin.

——— (1990). *The Spirituality of the Body.* New York: Macmillan.

Maddi, S., and Kobasa, S. (1984). *The Hardy Executive: Stress under Health.* Homewood, IL: Dow Jones-Irwin.

Mason, J. W., (1975). A historical view of the stress field. *Journal of Human Stress* 1:6–36.

Masters, W., and Johnson, V. (1966). *Human Sexual Response.* Boston, MA: Little, Brown.

——— (1970). *Human Sexual Inadequacy.* Boston, MA: Little, Brown.

Michael, R. (1995). *Sex in America: A Definitive Survey.* New York: Brunner/Mazel.

Mission Statement. (1994). Unpublished document. Williston Central School: Williston, VT.

Moyers, B. (1994). *Healing and the Mind.* New York: Doubleday.

Muggeridge, M. (1977). *Something Beautiful for God.* New York: Image/Harper and Row.

Muktananda, S. (1974). *American Tour 1970.* Piedmont, CA: Siddha Yoga Ashram.

Muller, W. (1992). *Legacy of the Heart: The Spiritual Advantages of a Painful Childhood.* New York: Simon and Schuster.

Munjack, D. (1988). *Medications in the Treatment of Panic Disorders and Panic Disorder with Agoraphobia: A Consumers Guide*. Rockville, MD: Anxiety Disorders Association of America.

Neill, A. S. (1960). *Summerhill: A Radical Approach to Child Rearing.* New York: Hart Publishing.

Ornstein, R., and Sobel, D. (1989). *Healthy Pleasures.* Reading, MA: Addison-Wesley.

Peale, N. V. (1952). *The Power of Positive Thinking.* New York: Prentice-Hall.

Pearce, J. C. (1977). *Magical Child: Rediscovering Nature's Plan for Our Children.* New York: Dutton.

——— (1981). *The Bond of Power.* New York: Dutton.

Pearl, B., and Moran, G. (1986). *Getting Stronger.* Bolinas, CA: Shelter Publications.

Peck, M. S. (1978). *The Road Less Traveled.* New York: Touchstone/Simon and Schuster.

Pelletier, K. (1977). *Mind as Healer, Mind as Slayer: A Holistic Approach to Preventing Stress Disorders.* New York: Delta.

Piaget, J. (1952). *The Origins of Intelligence in Children.* New York: Norton.

——— (1962). *Play, Dreams, and Imitation in Childhood.* New York: Norton.

Ponichtera, B. (1991). *Quick and Healthy Recipes and Ideas.* Dalles, OR: ScaleDown.

Ram Dass (1971). *Be Here Now.* New York: Crown Publishing.

Reich, W. (1961). *The Function of the Orgasm.* New York: Farrar, Straus, and Giroux.

——— (1972). *Character Analysis*. 3rd ed. New York: Farrar, Straus, and Giroux.

Reiter, S., Kutcher, S., and Gardner, D. (1992). Anxiety disorders in children and adolescents: clinical and related issues in pharmacological treatment. *Canadian Journal of Psychiatry* 37: 431–438.

Robertson, L., Flinders, C., and Godfrey, B. (1976). *Laurel's Kitchen: A Handbook for Vegetarian Cookery and Nutrition*. Berkeley, CA: Nilgiri Press.

Rodale, J. (1971). *The Complete Book of Food and Nutrition*. Emmaus, PA: Rodale.

Rodegast, P., and Stanton, J. (1985). *Emmanuel's Book: A Manual for Living Comfortably in the Cosmos*. New York: Bantam.

Roger, J., and McWilliams, P. (1991). *Life 101: Everything We Wish We had Learned About Life in School—But Didn't*. Los Angeles, CA: Prelude Press.

Ross, J. (1994). *Triumph Over Fear*. New York: Bantam.

Rubin, T. (1969). *The Angry Book*. New York: Collier.

Satchidananda, S. (1995). *Integral Yoga Hatha*. Buckingham, VA: Integral Yoga Publications.

Satir, V. (1976). *Making Contact*. Berkeley, CA: Celestial Arts.

Schafer, R. (1954). *Psychoanalytic Interpretation in Rorschach Testing*. New York: Grune and Stratton.

Seagrave, A., and Covington, F. (1987). *Free From Fears*. New York: Pocket Books.

Selye, H. (1956). *The Stress of Life*. New York: McGraw-Hill.

Shekelle, R. B., Gale, M., Ostfield, A. M., and Paul, O. (1983). Hostility, risk of CHD, and mortality. *Psychosomatic Medicine* 45:109–114.

Shurtleff, W., and Aoyagi, A. (1975). *The Book of Tofu: Food for Mankind*. Brookline, MA: Autumn Press.

Siegel, B. (1986). *Love, Medicine and Miracles.* New York: Harper and Row.

Silverstein, W. (1981). *A Light in the Attic.* New York: HarperCollins.

Sogyal, R. (1992). *The Tibetan Book of Living and Dying.* New York: HarperCollins.

St. James, E. (1994). *Simplify Your Life.* New York: Hyperion.

Steiner, R. (1947). *Knowledge of the Higher Worlds and Its Attainment.* 3rd ed. New York: Anthroposophic Press.

——— (1975). *Education of the Child in the Light of Anthroposophy,* ed. and trans. G. Adams and M. Adams. London: Rudolf Steiner Press.

Steinsaltz, A. (1988). *The Strife of the Spirit.* Northvale, NJ: Jason Aronson.

Stern, C. (1978). *Gates of Repentance.* New York: Central Conference of American Rabbis.

Stevens, D. E., ed. (1957). *Listen, Humanity—Meher Baba.* New York: Harper and Row.

Tavris, C. (1982). *Anger: The Misunderstood Emotion.* New York: Simon and Schuster.

Vissell, B., and Vissell, J. (1984). *The Shared Heart: Relationship Initiations and Celebrations.* Aptos, CA: Ramira Publishing.

Wallerstein, J., and Blakeslee, S. (1989). *Second Chances: Men, Women and Children a Decade after Divorce.* New York: Ticknor and Fields.

Watts, A. (1983a). Letting go: the art of playful living. *East West Journal,* April, pp. 30–36.

——— (1983b). *The Way of Liberation.* New York: Weatherhill.

Weekes, C. (1978). Simple, effective treatment of agoraphobia. *American Journal of Psychotherapy* 23(3): 357–369.

Wegscheider, S. (1981). *Another Chance—Hope and Health for the Alcoholic Family.* Palo Alto, CA: Science and Behavior Books.

Williams, R. B., Haney, T. L., Lee, K. I., et. al. (1980). Type A behavior, hostility, and coronary atherosclerosis. *Psychosomatic Medicine* 42:539–549.

Credits

The author gratefully acknowledges permission to reprint the following:

Chapter 11: "Whatif," *A Light in the Attic*, by Shel Silverstein, p. 90, © 1981 by Evil Eye Music, Inc. is reprinted by permission of HarperCollins Publishers.

Chapter 20: From *Emmanuel's Book* by Pat Rodegast and Judith Stanton. Copyright © 1985 by Pat Rodegast. Used by permission of Bantam Books, a division of Bantam Doubleday Dell Publishing Group, Inc.

Index